VOLUME 507   JANUARY 1990

THE ANNALS

of The American Academy *of* Political *and* Social Science

S0-ADX-560

RICHARD D. LAMBERT, *Editor*
ALAN W. HESTON, *Associate Editor*

PRIVATIZING AND MARKETIZING SOCIALISM

Special Editor of this Volume

JAN S. PRYBYLA

Pennsylvania State University
University Park

Ⓢ **SAGE** PUBLICATIONS   *NEWBURY PARK   LONDON   NEW DELHI*

#20925087

THE ANNALS

© 1990 *by* The American Academy *of* Political *and* Social Science

ERICA GINSBURG, *Assistant Editor*

Editorial Office: 3937 Chestnut Street, Philadelphia, PA 19104.

For information about membership* (individuals only) and subscriptions (institutions), address:

SAGE PUBLICATIONS, INC.
2111 West Hillcrest Drive
Newbury Park, CA 91320

From India and South Asia,
write to:
SAGE PUBLICATIONS INDIA Pvt. Ltd.
P.O. Box 4215
New Delhi 110 048
INDIA

From the UK, Europe, the Middle
East and Africa, write to:
SAGE PUBLICATIONS LTD
28 Banner Street
London EC1Y 8QE
ENGLAND

SAGE Production Editors: KITTY BEDNAR and LIANN LECH
*Please note that members of The Academy receive THE ANNALS with their membership.
Library of Congress Catalog Card Number 89-60679
International Standard Serial Number ISSN 0002-7162
International Standard Book Number ISBN 0-8039-3585-4 (Vol. 507, 1990 paper)
International Standard Book Number ISBN 0-8039-3584-6 (Vol. 507, 1990 cloth)
Manufactured in the United States of America. First printing, January 1990.

The articles appearing in THE ANNALS are indexed in *Book Review Index, Public Affairs Information Service Bulletin, Social Sciences Index, Current Contents, General Periodicals Index, Academic Index, Pro-Views,* and *Combined Retrospective Index Sets.* They are also abstracted and indexed in *ABC Pol Sci, Historical Abstracts, Human Resources Abstracts, Social Sciences Citation Index, United States Political Science Documents, Social Work Research & Abstracts, Sage Urban Studies Abstracts, International Political Science Abstracts, America: History and Life, Sociological Abstracts, Managing Abstracts, Social Planning/Policy & Development Abstracts, Automatic Subject Citation Alert, Book Review Digest,* and/or *Family Resources Database.*

Information about membership rates, institutional subscriptions, and back issue prices may be found on the facing page.

Advertising. Current rates and specifications may be obtained by writing to THE ANNALS Advertising and Promotion Manager at the Newbury Park office (address above).

Claims. Claims for undelivered copies must be made no later than three months following month of publication. The publisher will supply missing copies when losses have been sustained in transit and when the reserve stock will permit.

Change of Address. Six weeks' advance notice must be given when notifying of change of address to ensure proper identification. Please specify name of journal. Send change of address to: THE ANNALS, c/o Sage Publications, Inc., 2111 West Hillcrest Drive, Newbury Park, CA 91320.

The American Academy of Political and Social Science

3937 Chestnut Street   Philadelphia, Pennsylvania 19104

Origin and Purpose. The Academy was organized December 14, 1889, to promote the progress of political and social science, especially through publications and meetings. The Academy does not take sides in controverted questions, but seeks to gather and present reliable information to assist the public in forming an intelligent and accurate judgment.

Meetings. The Academy holds an annual meeting in the spring extending over two days.

Publications. THE ANNALS is the bimonthly publication of The Academy. Each issue contains articles on some prominent social or political problem, written at the invitation of the editors. Also, monographs are published from time to time, numbers of which are distributed to pertinent professional organizations. These volumes constitute important reference works on the topics with which they deal, and they are extensively cited by authorities throughout the United States and abroad. The papers presented at the meetings of The Academy are included in THE ANNALS.

Membership. Each member of The Academy receives THE ANNALS and may attend the meetings of The Academy. Membership is open only to individuals. Annual dues: $30.00 for the regular paperbound edition (clothbound, $45.00). Add $9.00 per year for membership outside the U.S.A. Members may also purchase single issues of THE ANNALS for $7.95 each (clothbound, $12.00).

Subscriptions. THE ANNALS (ISSN 0002-7162) is published six times annually — in January, March, May, July, September, and November. Institutions may subscribe to THE ANNALS at the annual rate: $66.00 (clothbound, $84.00). Add $9.00 per year for subscriptions outside the U.S.A. Institutional rates for single issues: $12.00 each (clothbound, $17.00).

Second class postage paid at Philadelphia, Pennsylvania, and at additional mailing offices.

Single issues of THE ANNALS may be obtained by individuals who are not members of The Academy for $8.95 each (clothbound, $17.00). Single issues of THE ANNALS have proven to be excellent supplementary texts for classroom use. Direct inquiries regarding adoptions to THE ANNALS c/o Sage Publications (address below).

All correspondence concerning membership in The Academy, dues renewals, inquiries about membership status, and/or purchase of single issues of THE ANNALS should be sent to THE ANNALS c/o Sage Publications, Inc., 2111 West Hillcrest Drive, Newbury Park, CA 91320. *Please note that orders under $25 must be prepaid.* Sage affiliates in London and India will assist institutional subscribers abroad with regard to orders, claims, and inquiries for both subscriptions and single issues.

THE ANNALS

of The American Academy *of* Political *and* Social Science

RICHARD D. LAMBERT, *Editor*
ALAN W. HESTON, *Associate Editor*

----------- FORTHCOMING -----------

See page 3 for information on Academy membership and
purchase of single volumes of **The Annals.**

CONTENTS

BOOK DEPARTMENT CONTENTS

INTERNATIONAL RELATIONS AND POLITICS

AFRICA, ASIA, AND LATIN AMERICA

EUROPE

UNITED STATES

SOCIOLOGY

ECONOMICS

PREFACE

"Socialism" in this volume means the centrally planned, administrative command economies that make up what is sometimes called the "Soviet-type" system. The emphasis is on the achievements of and the problems that beset central planning and on the remedies that are currently being tried, with varying degrees of determination and success, in parts of the socialist world. In this review the participation of economists from socialist countries has been secured. Their contributions are welcome not least because of their hands-on experience of the economies with which this volume is concerned but for broader glasnostic reasons as well.

This introduction serves as a sort of reader's guide to the articles contained in this volume and the many themes raised by the authors. As special editor, I have tried to summarize the authors' arguments accurately, to show where they logically link up and where they diverge. I hope that I have understood the various theses correctly, but the interpretation is mine alone and certainly does not bind the authors in any way.

In any cooperative project involving busy contributors from different parts of the country and different countries, for no financial reward, over many months, last-minute accidents are bound to happen. This undertaking has not escaped them. A promised essay from France on the ideological implications of socialist privatization and marketization failed to materialize at the last moment, creating a gap that, unfortunately, for scheduling reasons it was not possible to fill. But the damage, although annoying, is not lethal. The articles in this collection implicitly make the point — some do so quite explicitly — that an economic system consists of both a set of integrated institutional arrangements for resource allocation and a set of ideas that explain the workings of the institutions and provide ethical guidelines for the system. Any changes that go beyond surface adjustment and affect the foundations of the system require not only radical transformation of institutions but also new positive and normative theories that explain the laws governing the reformed system's operational mechanisms and moral code. In the context of a closed philosophical system, economic reform necessitates the removal of Marxist-Leninist dogma — and its Stalinist, neo-Stalinist, Maoist, latter-day Dengist, and other extensions and accretions — at both the level of economic theory and that of economic ethics. Consequently, systemic reform is a very arduous and usually painful undertaking, a wrenching institutional, intellectual, and moral experience, which few socialist power holders have so far been willing to carry through to its logical conclusion of their self-liquidation. China is the latest illustration of this thesis, but other less blood-splattered examples abound, some currently in the making.

SOCIALIST PRINCIPLES AND INSTITUTIONS
AND THE NEED FOR CHANGE

The principles and institutions of the centrally planned, administrative command system are discussed by Paul Gregory. He notes the intimate involvement of the Communist Party elite in economic decision making — the party's "leading role." This involvement represents a hefty hindrance to efficiency- and rationality-tending reforms not only by reason of the elite's often more than functional economic illiteracy but for other reasons — privileged stratum self-interest — as well, as pointed out by Polish economist Jan Winiecki. Near the end of his article, Gregory touches on some shortcomings of the centrally planned socialist economy, among them the principal-agent problem, which includes strange managerial incentives and opportunistic behavior.

These and other difficulties are further discussed by Marshall Goldman, who traces the progression of Soviet thinking on the causes of the growing troubles. With intellectual support from enlightened Soviet analysts such as Tatiana Zaslavskaya, the Communist Party leadership under Gorbachev gradually came to the conclusion — by no means, one might add, unanimously or enthusiastically — that "instead of being the solution, central planning had become the problem." The main causes of the economy's dysfunctions, in other words, seemed to reside in the system of central administrative command planning. "What the Soviet Union needed was to stimulate individual initiative and enthusiasm," not by yet another round of administrative reorganizations and personnel reassignments but through thorough economic decentralization. Economic decentralization is synonymous with market self-determination, which, in turn, necessitates privatization of property rights — discussed in this volume by Don Lavoie — and profound changes in thinking on subjects such as risk taking and the ethics-versus-efficiency conundrum of income leveling.

The need for a fundamental transformation of the centrally planned system's ideas and institutions and the inadequacy of past neoreformist syncretistics in the Soviet Union — Khrushchev's and Kosygin's rent-a-change experiments before Brezhnev's immobilism — a "saga of almost continuous efforts to reform the reforms," are discussed by Gertrude Schroeder. She examines Gorbachev's early and later — "radical" — reform record and the reaction of the authorities to problems encountered on the reformist path. This reaction is to reimpose administrative controls as the principal means of course correction, in part, as Goldman notes earlier, because of the continuing absence at this chrysalid stage of the reform of "institutions on which market economists depend to provide indirect controls," an observation that reappears in the article on China's Dengist course. Schroeder brings up the critical issue of price-system reform, "the key to the success of marketization." This is a dolorous subject in the context of chronic excess demand, wrapped up in subsidies and budgetary deficits. It is also political dynamite.

Another must of marketization, extensive privatization of property structures, has been absent so far from Gorbachev's applied agenda despite the sanctioning of all forms of property. The reform blueprint leaves state and collective property dominant. The failure of the Soviet economy to clamber out of depression, therefore, is due less to policy mistakes and other errors of work style than to an insufficiency of the reform blueprint, the inability or unwillingness or both to chop off the system's suppurating limbs. Even if in the face of political difficulties such deepening of reforms were to materialize, formidable obstacles to an effective implementation of the radical reform program would remain. These arise from ingrained attitudes of workers, consumers, politicians, managers, and bureaucrats adept at making their way through the reefs and shoals of central planning but who lack the "experience and the requisite skills for functioning in a competitive market economy." There has to be much more new thinking than once was thought to be enough.

This experience and these skills are, however, present in a twisted form in the underground neomarket, neo-private-property economy, the frightening dimensions and corrupting influence of which in the USSR are explored by Gregory Grossman. His analysis, it should be added, applies to other socialist economies, China being one clear instance. Sub-rosa privatization and marketization, from which the majority of the Soviet population draw "about half again as much income . . . as . . . from official sources," is very largely brought into being by the pervasive and chronic shortages of useful goods, the huge excess of useless money, the crazy pricing, quasi-total formal state ownership, miserable product quality, and other irrationalities of the officially misplanned economy. It has been said that the difference between the legitimate market system and the underground market economy is like that between a wife and a courtesan. Competitive transactions under the rule of law are replaced by theft, embezzlement, fraud, graft, tribute, bribes, kickbacks, outsize tips and gifts, extortion, blackmail, purposive violence, intimidation, patronage, and clientism. "Much of this criminal . . . activity is taken for granted by the public. . . . It is a crucible of moral values." It insinuates itself into every aspect of life at all social levels. On the other hand, it helps stay the total collapse of the centrally planned component of the overall mixed-up system. At least it puts sausage on the table.

WHY IS REFORM
SO DIFFICULT?

Barry Ickes and Jan Winiecki tackle the question of why it is so hard to reform the socialist economic system; in Gertrude Schroeder's word, why the seemingly interminable reform "treadmill"? Ickes looks at the question from the side of institutional choice, Winiecki from that of property rights.

Ickes argues that the insertion of markets — voluntary coalitions by economic actors to promote their self-interest — into an exogenous socialist system where the economic structure is imposed from above means that marketization is seen as a change independent of other changes in the economic system, especially price formation and the entry and exit process. In the absence of systemic changes of the price-entry-exit type, marketization will not produce the desired efficiency and other ameliorating results, the changes will be incomplete, and administrative retrenchment will follow: reforming the reforms, back on the old treadmill. The hybrid of markets, grafted from the endogenous market system where no central authority imposes a design from above, and a socialist, exogenously determined — that is, imposed from above — coordination mechanism lacking free entry, an automatic exit process such as bankruptcy, and a price system that would reflect opportunity costs will not come to grips with the problems that marketization is supposed to address and, it is hoped, solve. In fact, the combination might make things worse.

Winiecki's analysis of the failure of reforms to resolve socialism's efficiency and other quality problems focuses on the incentives that the ruling stratum of "Communist Party *apparatchiks,* bureaucracy, police, [and] the military" has to preserve the institutional status quo. These incentives arise from the current pattern of wealth distribution, which, in turn, depends on the existing structure of property rights favoring the ruling stratum, a state of affairs common to all traditional autocracies. Additionally, in the Soviet-type system, the rent accruing to party *apparatchiks* and the economic bureaucracy is maximized by "protracted interference in the process of wealth creation itself" through, first, the *nomenklatura* system of monopolized party appointments to all managerial positions and, second, gratuities (*vzyatka*), mostly nonpecuniary, received by the privilegentsia from enterprise managers. To thwart meaningful economic change, the ruling stratum's preferred — least costly — procedure is to abort all reforms that threaten the current property-rights structure in the state sector or significantly alter the institutions and procedures of central planning. The second-best procedure is to allow quasi reforms, that is, changes that are internally inconsistent and doomed to fail. Fundamental reform of the economic system, Winiecki concludes, could materialize if the consensus within the ruling stratum on preserving political power and the existing property-rights structure were to break down or if the Communist Party were to withdraw gradually — or perhaps not so gradually — from the scene "as the decline drags on." The probability of such — and other more daring — scenarios occurring in Soviet-type states will, Winiecki thinks, increase in the coming years.

THE FEASIBILITY OF
HALFWAY SOLUTIONS

The incompleteness of socialist economic reforms examined by Ickes and emphasized in the article on the Dengist course in China — a course that since the time of writing has gone pfut as predicted — poses the question of the viability of systemic half-loaf constructs sometimes referred to as "market socialism," the "socialist market," or the "labor-managed economy," about the merits of which there is much theoretical speculation but no conclusive practical evidence. On the theoretical plane, the feasibility, in terms of efficient resource allocation, of market socialism — that is, something between a market system with private property rights dominant and a centrally planned system with socialized property dominant — is denied by some; market socialism is seen by others as not only possible but superior to the market system.

Don Lavoie examines the feasibility of market socialism as an issue in the cognitive function that markets are expected to provide, cognition in this context being looked at in its three interpretations of computation, incentives, and discovery. The last two specifically involve questions of private and social ownership. Lavoie regards discovery as the basic and essential cognitive function of markets: "a creative process of interplay in which the knowledge that emerges exceeds that of any of the participants." In this dialogical learning experience, competition is seen as a "creative learning process among minds," profit as a "signal about where opportunities lie. The role of profits is not primarily to motivate people to do the right thing but to find out, through the process of interplay itself, what the right thing to do might be." Significantly, the discovery approach to the cognitive function of markets makes private ownership an indispensable part of the system in which "the process of competitive interplay between separate owners in a real estate market provides rental information about the value of alternative uses of the property. . . . replacing the dialogical process of interacting private owners with a single social owner would only eliminate the very give-and-take process that generates market information." Lavoie concludes that "the discovery approach suggests that socialism needs to accommodate itself not only to profits as abstract numbers [market cognition as computation] and to profits as psychological incentives for labor services [market cognition as concrete incentive to the provision of real services by decision makers] but also to profits as returns for separate, private owners of material resources."

From the USSR comes the resonant voice of Larissa Popkova-Pijasheva arguing the fundamental theoretical and institutional incompatibility of central command planning and the market system. She gives three reasons for the incompatibility. First is the difference in the process of valuation. Under central planning, all planned output is ipso facto valuable because the planners say so and regardless of whether or not it is of any use to anyone. This output is priced ex ante by the planners in calculated — non-opportunity-cost, funny — prices. The valuation process is closely associated with the system's ethics of full employment. In the market system the value of output is not determined until the product is sold to uncoerced consumers. If the planned system's socially useless output were properly handled, a lot of people would lose their jobs for there would be no takers for what they produce. But this would be in contravention of the full-employment constraint, which is one of the supporting pillars of the state's social compact under which surpluses and shortages are accepted by the citizens in exchange for guaranteed employment. Popkova-Pijasheva raises in this context a deeper issue that has been discussed back and forth on and off since the 1920s. Ex ante valuation is an illusion because "economic life cannot be planned in advance, as the very development of the human organism cannot be, nor can that of any process in nature itself." In other words, the economic problem of rational resource allocation cannot be solved under the regime of Marxist socialism, as "the experience of all socialist countries that have done their best to put into practice Marx's idea of a planned economy has corroborated only too well."

The second reason is that mandatory input and output norms are antithetical to the economic freedom needed by the market system philosophically and operationally. This is so whether directives take the form of commands from the planners, as in the old days, or of state purchase orders, as now. Commanding or ordering is made possible by monopolization of power by the state through the abolition of private property. There is no competition under central planning, whereas for the market system, competition is an absolute condition of existence.

The third reason is that if private capital — presupposing private ownership of assets — were to compete with state capital — the "common stock" — it would quite simply wipe state capital off the face of the earth, and "a number of people would have ... to ... leave their cushy jobs in the hierarchical system of administrative power."[1]

The attempt by socialist ideologues "to develop a model of a mixed economy" — a socialist market — is, if not a complete waste of time, pretty close to it. The socialist market is supposed to be a "market economy without capitalism ... with no private-property institutions ... without a democratic power system ... without the spirit of enterprise ... and without ... the entrepreneur ... without ... economic liberalism." In scientific parlance, that is a "blind alley."

---

1. Cf. Jan Winiecki, "Obstacles to Economic Reform of Socialism: A Property-Rights Approach," this issue of The Annals of the American Academy of Political and Social Science.

ECONOMIC AND
POLITICAL REFORM

The linkage between economic reform — privatization and marketization — of central administrative command planning and reform of the totalitarian socialist polity — pluralization, democratization — which has been dramatically put on the agenda by the events in Tiananmen Square of May-June 1989, is analyzed by Yu-Shan Wu. Wu argues that socialist political reforms — one-party pluralism and multiparty democracy — cannot be understood by considering merely the demand side, that is, political relaxation stemming from various kinds of social needs — economic viability, social integration, political stability, cultural assertion — or from expansion of private-property rights in a socialist economy, there being a high correlation between property-rights structures and political arrangements. What really matters when it comes to the institutionalization of political pluralism in a Leninist system is the supply side, that is to say, the ruling elite's strategic thinking on the need for and degree of political reform. The prime cause of such thinking is the need to improve economic efficiency for reasons of international competition — that is, so as not to fall behind in the worldwide productivity contest — and domestic legitimacy — the need to raise living standards to avoid nastiness at the population's threshold of tolerance. If at all possible, Leninist elites will opt for pure economic reform — a homogenized so-called perfecting of the planning system through administrative reorganization or through restructuring the system by some reassignment of property rights — without any political change. If neither works, and further economic reform requires the removal of political obstacles to its implementation, "the reformers may experiment with changes of the political system out of desperation." Such pluralizing changes may be launched to stifle conservative opponents in the regime who oppose economic reform and/or to conclude a social contract with the citizens in order to make economic reform acceptable to the people. When this happens, the elite — Winiecki's ruling stratum — will first go for a single-party, multicandidate political model, or one-party pluralism — on Hungarian and Polish evidence, an unstable equilibrium. Next, if the heat is really on — see Winiecki's scenarios — the rulers might have to back into some version of multiparty democracy. Wu's analysis concludes on a pessimistic note. "It is doubtful, to say the least," he writes, "that democratization, particularly its multiparty version, can solve a socialist country's economic problems" — witness chunks of South America and the Philippines. Given the Leninists' exclusively manipulative interest in democracy and the *apparatchiks'* retention of powerful control levers never dreamed of in Marcos's philosophy, reconsolidation of the elite's power vis-à-vis society after political reform is more than a theoretical possibility. So much for the alleged irreversibility of reforms once they reach a certain stage.

EMPIRICAL EXAMPLES

The conceptual scaffolding built in these studies is further developed and applied to the structures of four socialist economies: Hungary, China, Yugoslavia, and East Germany. At the time of writing, the grouping made good sense. The first three were tending toward the liberal reform mode, while East Germany manned one of the remaining bastions of traditional neo-Stalinist centralism.

Tamás Bauer traces the zigzag progression of Hungarian reforms away from Soviet-style central planning, first toward an " 'organic combination of planning and market,' " in 1968, a "technocratic or managerial version of market-oriented economic reform," without "any significant increase in the role of private initiative in the economy" and without competition — "without capitalism," as Larissa Popkova-Pijasheva would put it. "In the absence of market forces, very little of the expected positive changes did occur," but at least the economy did not fall apart: "the economy, free of mandatory planning and centralized resource allocation, operated without any serious disturbance."

Then, after a pause for détente, when reforms were replaced by hard-currency imports on credit, the "reform naiveté" of the organic combination type, "surviving up to now in the Soviet Union," was followed in the early 1980s by partial, half-hearted reforms — the "second round" — in a setting of Brezhnevian stagnation in the socialist bloc. The second round enlarged the sphere of private sector activity, introduced some significant although not substantial changes in the ownership structure, and altered — again, not fundamentally — the relationship between enterprise managements and their ministerial and other supervisory authorities. Whereas formerly the ministries commanded, now they "informed" the enterprises of their "wishes" and "expectations."[2] All this was accompanied by institutionalist innovations, including the introduction from above of enterprise councils.[3] In systemic terms this second reform round produced a neither-this-nor-that economy, a hybrid that was "neither plan nor market" or, in Antal's phrase, an "indirectly centralized" whatever.

The third round, begun in the late 1980s in the more relaxed bloc atmosphere of *perestroika* and live and let live, is aimed at moving beyond indirect centralization, perhaps even toward a "market economy without any attribute." "The belief in the supremacy of planning had disappeared, and the conviction that a genuine market is indispensable prevailed." Still, the history of reforms, not least in Hungary, most recently in China, cautions against putting too much store by people's capacity for economically rational decisions when it comes to moving beyond a market economy with an attribute such as a socialist market.

My analysis of China's now apparently fizzled-out reforms raises several issues. The need for reform came from the economy's chronic shortages, waste, unsatisfactory incentives, and technological retardation. By the late 1970s the systemic origin of these quality problems had been recognized. It had also been recognized that remedy had to be sought in economic decentralization, that is to say, in marketization and privatization. It was not recognized, however, that marketization and privatization must be system-wide — comprehensive, integrated — to work, not partial and selective. Chinese economic reforms therefore quickly ran into two big potholes, not unlike the systemic jalopies of other socialist contenders. The first was the unwillingness to go all the way to the market system, but instead to head for a variant of market socialism called "socialism with Chinese characteristics," whatever that means. The second was the continued absence of

2. Cf. discussion on commands versus state orders in Larissa Popkova-Pijasheva, "Why Is the Plan Incompatible with the Market?" this issue of *The Annals* of the American Academy of Political and Social Science.

3. Cf. comment on involuntary labor management in Svetozar Pejovich, "A Property-Rights Analysis of the Yugoslav Miracle," this issue of *The Annals* of the American Academy of Political and Social Science.

the rule of law, even though paper laws proliferated. While structural reforms went farther in agriculture than in industry, they stopped in both sectors far short of the conditions necessary for a market system to take hold and successfully remove the centrally planned system's problems of shortage, waste, apathy, and technological backwardness in the civilian realm. Predictably, China joined others on the treadmill of reforms, exhibiting by mid-1988 unmistakable symptoms of relapse into administrative command planning, most of its economic problems unsolved, some new ones added.

Pejovich argues that in Yugoslavia, another example of an in-between condition, the involuntary labor-managed — self-management — economy once hailed by many as the definitive answer to both the market system, or capitalism, and central administrative command planning, or real socialism, has produced a crisis of imposing dimensions. The crisis is inherent in the institutional structure of property rights specific to the involuntary labor-managed economy that creates some positive transaction costs — the costs of all the resources required to transfer property rights from one economic agent to another — and negative incentives that contribute to a contraction of the social opportunity set. "The conclusion," says Pejovich, "is that the labor-managed economy is not a viable institutional arrangement."

Pejovich sees economic reforms as a vehicle through which the ruling group modifies the terms of the contract — the institutional structure — between itself and the people. Such reforms "should best be ignored until they are actually implemented . . . [when they] carry a powerful message" — a sober reminder at a time of renewed Western emotional involvement in socialist reform projects. Because the Marxist theory of the historical inevitability and superiority of socialism is deceased, "the ruling elite . . . cannot continue to justify its political monopoly by claiming to be the 'torch' of history . . . [and must therefore] substitute some real results for a hazy vision of things to come. The accomplishments of capitalism then become the strongest case against socialism." It is not, to paraphrase Adam Smith, from the benevolence or greater enlightenment of a new-generation ruling group that people should expect reform but from the group's regard for its own interest: "the very survival of the ruling group depends on its willingness to identify trade-offs and to respond to them."[4] In the Yugoslav case, the current reform package tries to save the basic features of the labor-managed economy, so as to preserve the ruling group's political power, and tries to make institutional changes in the direction of private-property, free-market economy, so as to make the system work — a problematic combination.

East Germany, which has done next to nothing in the way of marketizing reform but has instead concentrated on the so-called perfecting of central planning, stands as a statistical exception to the poor record of central planning. The statistics, incidentally, raise serious questions of credibility. Phillip Bryson analyzes East Germany's performance. He notes, in passing, what certainly is an important clue to the solution of the puzzle: "the favorable access that the country enjoys to West German and European Community markets, as well as . . . . the sizable transfers of various sorts the GDR

4. Cf. Winiecki, "Obstacles to Economic Reform"; Yu-Shan Wu, "The Linkage between Economic and Political Reform in the Socialist Countries: A Supply-Side Explanation," this issue of *The Annals* of the American Academy of Political and Social Science.

[German Democratic Republic] receives from the Federal Republic of Germany." Bryson argues that "part of the credit [for the success] should go to the extensive efforts of the GDR in the early 1980s to refine [its] planning organization and techniques," that is, to intrasystemic adjustments. Whatever the reasons, East Germany's relative success — relative to other centrally planned performances — stands as an encouragement to those in the socialist ruling stratum who think that old-fashioned command planning is all right and that *perestroiniks* are people with ulterior motives. But if East Germany is to compete with the best rather than the worst and keep the 1.5 million of its citizens who currently intend to emigrate to the West,[5] it will very likely have to do more than readjust, even with all the West German payments propping up the central plan and its de facto associate membership in the European Community secured through intra-German trade with the Federal Republic.

The subject of the present volume is large and, as they say, fluid. There is always room for more. One fault, frankly acknowledged, is the absence of discussion about what the reaction of the market democracies should be to the privatization and marketization drives of the hitherto centrally planned economies. Some insightful suggestions in this regard are offered by Mark Palmer, the U.S. ambassador to Hungary, in a volume entitled *Central and Eastern Europe: The Opening Curtain?* edited by William E. Griffith (Westview Press, 1989). Unfortunately, like many other important topics on the periphery of privatization and marketization, it is just not possible here to give this topic the attention it deserves, or, in fact, any attention.

Certain themes, I think, recur. Central administrative command planning is not viable any more — if, indeed, it ever was — in an environment in which quality of economic performance increasingly matters. In-between solutions — between central planning and the market system — are of little use in solving the centrally planned system's quality problems. Socialist marketizing and privatizing reforms have so far lacked the resolve to push on to their logical systemic denouement. As a result, semi-reforms have by and large created more problems than there had been before. As the London *Economist* recently put it, the difference between today and earlier post-Stalin years is that whereas then the socialist ruling elites were seeking different roads to socialism, now, with spirited encouragement from their restless subjects, they are looking for different roads from socialism.

JAN S. PRYBYLA

---

5. Heinz Vielain, "BND: 1,5 Millionen DDR-Bürger wollen ausreisen," *Welt am Sonntag,* 13 Aug. 1989, p. 1.

The Stalinist Command Economy

By PAUL R. GREGORY

ABSTRACT: This article outlines the key features of the traditional administrative command model used by the centrally planned socialist economies to allocate resources. It is this model that contemporary reformers in the Soviet Union, Eastern Europe, and China are seeking to change. The administrative command model permits the party leadership to set priorities and monitor their fulfillment through the state economic bureaucracy and local party apparatus. The state bureaucracy — led by a state planning commission — is charged with implementing party directives through operational plans. Central planning organs construct plans for industrial ministries, which devise operational plans for enterprises and allocate scarce funded materials among ministry enterprises. Central planning organs substitute administrative allocation of materials — through material balances — for market allocation. Both ministries and enterprises are judged by their superiors largely on the basis of output performance and know that future plans will be based upon past plan performance. Ministries and enterprises are therefore motivated to act contrary to the interests of their superiors — to conceal capacity, overorder inputs, and avoid new technology.

Paul R. Gregory is a professor of economics at the University of Houston. He received his B.A. and M.A. degrees from the University of Oklahoma and his Ph.D. from Harvard University in 1969, specializing in Soviet economics and comparative economic systems. Professor Gregory has authored and coauthored a number of works on Soviet economics and comparative economic systems, including Soviet Economic Structure and Performance; Comparative Economic Systems; Russian National Income; *and* The Soviet Economic Bureaucracy.

T HE Soviet Union created the proto-type of the centrally planned econ-omy. The Soviet economic system came into being in the early 1930s, after the turmoil of the revolution, civil war, and economic experimentation of the 1920s. The Soviet command planning system—designated the Stalinist administrative command system by its contemporary So-viet detractors—was largely in place by the mid-1930s, and it was this system that oversaw the rapid industrial transformation of the 1930s and the war effort of the 1940s.[1] The Soviet command planning sys-tem was introduced into Eastern Europe by the Soviet occupation forces in the late 1940s and early 1950s. The victorious Chi-nese Communist regime introduced the basic features of the Soviet economic sys-tem into China in the early 1950s.

According to Soviet calculations of the 1970s, approximately one-third of the world's population lives in economies that share the basic features of the Soviet com-mand system. In fact, earlier Soviet claims to the superiority of the command system were based on the spread of the Soviet economic and political system throughout the globe.

MARXIST-LENINIST ORIGINS

The command planning system evolved in response to the practical economic prob-lems the Soviet Union faced in the 1920s and 1930s, but its fundamental outlines were shaped by its Marxist-Leninist ideo-logical heritage. Marx and Engels had sur-

prisingly little to say about what happens after the socialist revolution installs the first socialist state.[2] Marx felt that the new socialist society would go through two phases, later called socialism and commu-nism by V. I. Lenin. During the lengthy transitional phase, elements of the old cap-italist order would remain; the powers of the new socialist state—called the dictator-ship of the proletariat by Marx—would have to be directed against these capitalist forces. During the transitional phase, a strong state would be required to direct the class struggle against capitalist elements and to build up society's productive capac-ity. Scarcity would still be present, and labor would be rewarded according to its productivity. Marx's formula for distribu-tion during the transition phase was "to each according to his contribution."

Eventually, a stage of abundance would be reached. At this point, full communism would be established, the state would wither away, and there would be enough to go around for everyone. There would no longer be any class struggle because there would be only one class, the class of work-ers. Work would cease to be a chore, and distribution could now proceed according to the formula "from each according to his ability, to each according to his needs."

Although Marx had little to say about actual resource-allocation practices during the socialist transition period, it is clear that the means of production would be owned by society—private ownership of the means of production was the source of capitalist exploitation—and that adminis-trative allocation would replace market al-location. Marx viewed market forces as anarchic, causing overproduction, busi-

1. For accounts of the origins of the Soviet planned economy, see Alec Nove, *An Economic History of the USSR* (London: Penguin Press, 1969); Eugene Zaleski, *Stalinist Planning for Economic Growth, 1933-1952* (Chapel Hill: University of North Carolina Press, 1980); E. H. Carr and R. W. Davies, *Founda-tions of a Planned Economy 1926-1929* (London: Macmillan, 1969).

2. On the Marxist-Leninist origins of the planned socialist economies, see Paul R. Gregory and Robert Stuart, *Soviet Economic Structure and Performance*, 3d ed. (New York: Harper & Row, 1986), chap. 3.

ness cycles, and crises. Scientific planning should replace the anarchy of the market.

Soviet attempts to combine market and administrative resource allocation in the mid and late 1920s appeared to confirm Marx's distrust of market allocation. Market allocation caused people — especially those involved in private peasant agriculture — to act contrary to the interests of the state and introduced an unnecessary measure of uncertainty to economic outcomes.

THE LEADING ROLE OF THE PARTY

In a planned socialist economy, the Communist Party assumes a leading role in directing economic activities. It is the responsibility of the party — and the state — to decide what is to be produced, how it is to be produced, and for whom. The purpose of the 1917 revolution in Russia was to place the Communist Party in charge of resource allocation. It is argued that the party will know what is best for society; the market leads only to anarchy. Therefore, it is essential for the party, not the market, to resolve the economic problem.

The party begins the process of resource allocation by setting economic priorities.[3] Party priorities are handed down to government and industry officials in the form of general instructions, or "control figures." These instructions set general goals for major industries, announce major changes in economic policy, set targets for agriculture, and define the general features of the state budget.

The party's role in the command economic system does not end with the setting of economic priorities. The party has gen-eral oversight obligations that extend from its national offices to its regional and local offices. This oversight function gives it the authority to intervene and monitor. The oversight function is particularly important at the regional and local level where regional and local party officials are held responsible for the economic results of their territories.

THE ECONOMIC BUREAUCRACY

The party's directives and interventions are made primarily through the state economic bureaucracy.[4] At the apex of the state economic bureaucracy is a council of ministers that oversees the actions of subordinate bureaucratic units. The council of ministers issues the decrees and laws that govern economic activities jointly with the party. The council of ministers, as a general oversight body, uses a number of state committees to do the actual administrative planning for the economy. The state planning committee is the operational planning body; it prepares binding operational plans, generally of one year's duration, and nonbinding long-term plans, generally of five years' duration.

The council of ministers and the state planning committee are assisted by a number of functional committees — such as a price committee, a technology committee, a standards committee — and financial committees — such as the state bank, which regulates the money supply, and the ministry of finance, which collects taxes and monitors financial plan fulfillment. These state committees devise technical norms, financial rules, compensation arrangements, and the like, which determine the

---

3. For discussions of the role of the party in resource allocation, see Alec Nove, *The Soviet Economic System* (London: Allen & Unwin, 1977), chaps. 1-3.

4. For a discussion of the Soviet economic bureaucracy, see Paul Gregory, *Restructuring the Soviet Economic Bureaucracy* (New York: Cambridge University Press, 1990).

rules of the game under which production units operate.

The state planning commission does not prepare operational plans for enterprises. There are too many enterprises and too many products. A national planning body cannot handle so much detail. Instead, the state planning commission draws up plans for industrial ministries, which then draw up detailed operational plans for their own enterprises. Actual operational planning is a cooperative effort between the industrial ministries and the state planning commission. Moreover, the actual allocations of major industrial materials are carried out by the industrial ministries. The state planning commission allocates material limits to the ministries, and the ministries — as the economy's fund holders — use their material limits to make the actual material allocation to enterprises.

BALANCING SUPPLIES AND DEMANDS

In the 1920s, there was a lively debate between economists about the feasibility of planned socialism. The skeptics in this socialist controversy — Friedrich von Hayek and Ludwig von Mises — argued that a modern economy, comprising thousands of enterprises, millions of consumers, and millions more distinct products, could not conceivably be planned in a satisfactory manner.[5] The job of balancing supplies and demands would simply be too large even in a world of high-speed computers. But the planned socialist economy — despite the dire predictions of Hayek and Mises — has survived as a centrally planned economy for more than sixty years.

The planning method developed by the Soviets in the 1930s — and still used in virtually the same form today — is called material-balance planning. Material-balance planning is a system of resource allocation in which centralized planning is used to control the output and input levels of only the most important industrial commodities that the economy produces.[6] Less important commodities are controlled at lower levels in the planning hierarchy.

Commodities such as electricity, steel, concrete, coal, oil, motor vehicles, cotton textiles, industrial chemicals, and machine tools determine the direction of the economy and are, therefore, planned and allocated from the center. Other, less important commodities — such as services, garments, and toys — are planned, but they are managed at lower planning levels. The highest planning authorities determine which ministries receive supplies of basic industrial commodities. Less important commodities are planned by the ministries themselves or by regional or even local authorities. Some commodities are not planned at all; in rare cases commodities are even allocated by the market. The notion of dealing centrally with only the most important industrial commodities derives from practical necessity and from the theory that the party can control the economy by controlling its most important industrial commodities.

For each of the several thousand commodities that are planned at the center, the state planning commission — and the responsible ministry — must determine a material balance. For example, the state planning commission knows from its preliminary production targets that 500 million tons of coal are to be produced in the coming year. It also knows that there are existing con-

5. For a discussion of the socialist controversy, see Abram Bergson, "Market Socialism Revisited," *Journal of Political Economy*, 75:663-75 (Oct. 1967).

6. J. M. Montias, "Planning with Material Balances in Soviet-Type Economies," *American Economic Review*, 49:963-85 (Dec. 1959).

tracts to export 50 million tons of coal. A domestic supply of 450 million tons remains. On the demand side, the state planning commission knows, largely on the basis of past experience, the amount of coal that each industry needs to meet its scheduled production targets and also the coal requirements of the population. The state planning commission can therefore estimate the anticipated demand and supply of coal for the coming year.

The state planning commission and the ministries draw up material balances for each centrally balanced commodity — for steel, for cement, for sulfuric acid, for trucks, and so on. Once the state planning commission has listed all the anticipated supplies and demands, it must make sure that there is an overall balance. It may find, for example, that the demand for coal exceeds the supply. In capitalist economies, supply-demand imbalances are corrected by spontaneous changes in relative prices. Material-balance planning corrects imbalances by making administrative changes that are independent of relative prices. If there is an excess demand for coal, planners can either raise production targets for coal or reduce the planned allocations of coal.

In the planned socialist economies, there is rarely an excess supply of any critical commodity. The problem that planners typically must correct is excess demand — what the Soviets call dictatorship of the supplier. Responding to excess demand by raising production targets could disrupt other balances. The state planning commission, therefore, typically corrects imbalances by reducing planned allocations — by reducing demand — and not by increasing supply.

The state planning commission does not reduce material allocations in a haphazard manner. It does not, for example, say that every firm must take a 10 percent cut in

coal allocations if it is necessary to reduce the demand for coal. Instead, the state planning commission follows a priority principle — that the most important industries are the last to take cuts. Historically, light industry, which produces goods for the consumer, has been the low-priority industry. Therefore, when cuts have had to be made, they are absorbed by light industry and, ultimately, by the consumer.

There are two reasons for the priority principle. The first is that the leadership has consistently favored heavy industry over light industry because heavy industry provides military hardware and the base for the future communist society. Second, it is better to avoid plan shortfalls in heavy industry. If steel, oil, or coal targets are not met, these shortfalls disrupt the entire plan. If the plan for men's suits or children's shoes is not met, the overall impact on the plan will be limited.

In addition to balances of materials, the state planning commission draws up labor balances, machinery balances, and financial and money balances. The total cash in the hands of the population should balance the value of consumer goods placed on the market.

PLAN EXECUTION BY MANAGERS

After intense negotiation and tough bargaining — between the party, the state planning commission, the ministries, regional authorities, and enterprises — the planning hierarchy prepares an operational plan for the economy. After approval, the economic plan becomes the law of the land. It is then the responsibility of every citizen and every enterprise to fulfill the tasks set out in the national plan.

Each enterprise receives a detailed enterprise plan that tells it what commodities to produce, how many employees to have on the payroll, what materials to receive, what new machinery to install, what bank credits to draw on, and so on down to relatively fine details of enterprise operation. The enterprise director is responsible for fulfilling the enterprise plan. Enterprise plans are broken down into weekly, monthly, quarterly, and annual segments.

The national economic plan is only the first phase in the resource-allocation process. Plan targets are not fulfilled in their entirety. In the course of plan fulfillment, some targets are not met and promised supplies are not delivered. Administrative decisions about what parts of the plan will be fulfilled and what targets must be set aside are made according to the priority principle. Low-priority branches bear the burden when resources are juggled. Ambitious increases in consumer goods are typically called for in the initial plan, but when the plan is completed, the shortfalls are concentrated in the consumer-goods area.

In actual practice, operational plans are corrected many times. These corrections take place within the ministry as plan targets are redistributed among ministry enterprises and among ministries. Presumably, intraministerial plans are corrected more frequently than interministerial plans.

Official accounts often portray the manager of a centrally planned enterprise as an unimportant actor.[7] After all, the economic plan provides the manager with a detailed set of instructions. It would appear that all the manager has to do is to follow these administrative instructions. In fact, however, the manager is given so many instructions — many of which are contradictory — that he or she has considerable discretionary authority in the conduct of the enterprise's business. The fact that the enterprise manager decides which plan directives to follow — and which to ignore — makes the enterprise manager a key participant in the resource-allocation process.

In the planned socialist economy, enterprise success is measured by the manager's ability to fulfill plan targets that superiors regard as important. The relative importance of different plan targets changes over the years — one year cost-reduction targets are important; in another year the labor-productivity plan is more important. A stable feature of the command socialist system is the dominant position of output targets. Managerial success tends to be judged primarily on the basis of the manager's ability to fulfill output targets. Other targets are secondary in comparison to the output target. Enterprise managers, therefore, devote their efforts to making sure that they meet output targets.

THE PRINCIPAL-AGENT PROBLEM IN THE PLANNED SOCIALIST ECONOMY

A principal-agent problem exists when a principal and its agent have different goals and the cost of monitoring the agent is high. In the planned socialist economy, there are a number of complex principal-agent relationships. The industrial ministries are agents for the state and party. The enterprises are agents for their industrial ministries. Enterprises of national importance are often directly agents of the state planning commission.

The leadership wants the industrial ministries to meet their output targets, producing high-quality products at minimum cost

---

7. The classic studies of Soviet management are J. S. Berliner, *Factory and Manager in the USSR* (Cambridge, MA: Harvard University Press, 1957); David Granick, *Management of the Industrial Firm in the USSR* (New York: Columbia University Press, 1954).

and delivering them to designated receiving units, while introducing new technologies. The ministries, for their part, want to keep the state and party content with their performance. They know that the state planning commission cannot monitor them fully and, therefore, must judge ministerial performance on the basis of readily observable indicators — such as quantities of products produced. The ministry maximizes its well-being by taking the least risky path: ministries seek to meet quantity output targets and tend to sacrifice other goals if they stand in the way. In pursuing this strategy, the ministries know that their superiors cannot monitor them well enough to penalize them for their failure to meet other targets.

A similar principal-agent problem exists between the ministries and their agent-enterprises. The ministry would like its enterprises to achieve all the targets set out in the enterprise plan — output, inputs, new technology, productivity improvements, new products, and the like. Yet the costs of monitoring the multiple dimensions of enterprise-plan fulfillment are too high. The ministry, therefore, evaluates enterprise performance on the basis of easily observable indicators, such as output quantities.

The use of output targets as the criterion for judging managerial success leads to dysfunctional economic behavior on the part of the enterprise manager. Soviet managers are led by their own incentive system to engage in activities that reduce output and waste economic resources. From the manager's viewpoint, an ideal plan is one that gives the manager more resources than are necessary to produce an output well below the enterprise's capacity. When these circumstances are met, the manager knows that the plan targets can be met with little risk of failure. The manager wishes to avoid a plan that supplies too few resources

and calls for an output beyond the capacity of the enterprise.

The search for easy outputs and ample inputs gives the enterprise manager an incentive to provide false or misleading information to superiors — to overstate input requirements and to understate output capacities. During the Stalin years, Soviet managers who failed to meet output targets were branded as capitalist saboteurs. Although contemporary penalties for such failures are by no means so drastic, the search for easy output targets and ample inputs continues.

When the enterprise manager receives an ideal plan of ample resources and small output requirements, the enterprise manager is still reluctant to impress his or her superiors by overfulfilling output targets. On the contrary, the manager who overfulfills risks receiving a much more ambitious set of targets next year. Managers fear the so-called ratchet effect, whereby planners respond to plan overfulfillment by "ratcheting up" plan targets for the next year. To avoid the ratchet, managers avoid impressive plan overfulfillment, preferring to overfulfill the output plan by a modest margin.

The difficulty of exactly defining the desired mix of output encourages enterprise managers to engage in other kinds of opportunistic behavior. If the manager is told to produced R10 million worth of children's shoes, the manager produces all shoes of the same size and color and floods the market with unwanted goods. If the manager is told to produce a specific mix of sizes and colors, he or she may skimp on materials and produce defective shoes, technically fulfilling the output targets.

The manager resists innovation because the risks of trying new things are great and the perceived benefits are small. New production technologies disrupt existing supply channels; construction delays endanger fulfillment of the all-important output plan. Planners might not recognize that a better product is being made or that output is being produced more efficiently.

LABOR ALLOCATION

With some exceptions, citizens select their own occupations and places of employment in planned socialist economies. This was not always the case. During the early years of the Soviet regime (1918-21), workers were treated like military conscripts — this was the time of the Russian civil war — and the state told people where they were to work and whether or not they could quit their jobs. The same was true during World War II, when there were severe penalties for tardiness or changing jobs without permission. The relative freedom of choice of occupation is a result of the realization that people work less efficiently when they are administratively assigned to jobs. Efficiency is better served by relative freedom of choice than by administrative allocation.

There are exceptions to the rule of freedom of choice. College graduates are assigned their first job and must remain in these jobs for a prescribed period of time. Authorities also limit the number of people who are allowed to move to major urban centers. The most important jobs in the economy, such as those of minister and industrial manager, are filled from a list of party nominees.

Planning authorities determine the demand for labor in different occupations and in different industries. To ensure that these demands will be met, industrial wages are set to equate supply and demand. As a result, occupations in undesirable locations or dangerous, unpleasant, or dirty jobs are paid more than others. In fact, wage differentials in planned socialist economies appear to be much like those of capitalist countries.

WEAKNESSES

The traditional command socialist system has a number of apparent defects that economic reformers would like to correct. Of particular importance is the problem of managerial incentives and opportunistic behavior. The traditional system encourages managers to conceal capacity, resist innovation, produce improper output mixes, be oblivious to consumer demand, and waste inputs. Although it is difficult to pinpoint their causes, managerial-incentive problems have contributed to the deterioration of the economic performance of the planned socialist economies of the last twenty years.

The Soviet Economy and the Need for Reform

By MARSHALL I. GOLDMAN

ABSTRACT: Because he was interested in rapid growth, Stalin decided to do away with private forms of economic ownership and the freely formulated prices and markets of the traditional economic system and replace them with state ownership and central planning. This brought some initial growth but considerable distortion of the Soviet economy. There was an overemphasis on heavy industry. Gorbachev in particular came to recognize how misguided such an approach has been, but recognition is not the same as implementation. The essence of his reform is to increase the role of private and cooperative decision making while reducing the role of central planners in decision making and state-owned enterprises. There have been many false starts in this process, and so far the results have not been encouraging. If anything, the real standard of living in the Soviet Union has declined, and Gorbachev's reforms are being blamed for many of these problems.

Marshall I. Goldman is the Katherine W. Davis Professor of Soviet Economics at Wellesley College. He is also associate director of the Russian Research Center at Harvard University. He is the author of Gorbachev's Challenge: Economic Reform in the Age of High Technology *and* The U.S.S.R. in Crisis: The Failure of an Economic Model. *Other recent books are* The Enigma of Soviet Petroleum: Half Empty or Half Full? *and* Détente and Dollars: Doing Business with the Soviets.

F OR those of college age, it is probably impossible to understand how anyone could have had nice things to say about a centrally planned economic system like the Soviet Union's. Nor is that because Western Sovietologists have been denigrating Soviet economic accomplishments. Today it is hard to find anything positive written even in the Soviet Union about that economy. The Stalinist era and virtually everything done during the three decades or so of Stalin's influence are now blamed for almost all the Soviet Union's current economic difficulties. Concepts such as central planning, collectivization, a ban on private business and foreign investment, and the inconvertibility of the ruble, which were once praised as models of achievement worthy of duplication in the rest of the world, are now officially criticized or condemned. Now there are warnings that unless rapid reforms are introduced that are designed to reverse most of the heritage of the past, the Soviet Union will be unable to break out of what are called "the years of stagnation" associated with the Brezhnev era.

The preferred model for Soviet recovery owes more to the market system associated with capitalism or at least some variant of capitalism than it does to the economic institutions that have heretofore been encompassed by the Soviet economic establishment. Why has the Soviet economic system fallen on such hard times — some say the economic conditions today are even more serious than they were during the years of stagnation — and why, for those of us with long memories, did the Soviet economic system once seem to be so impressive?

QUESTIONS ABOUT THE
STALINIST ECONOMY

There is little doubt that under proper conditions, the Stalinist economic system with centrally administrative controls is capable of generating very impressive economic growth. Admittedly, the system developed serious distortions along the way. Moreover, in almost every case where such a system was adopted, it brought with it a draconian form of political control. Some argue about which came first, totalitarian government or the Stalinist economic model, or whether the model can exist in a more open democratic society. Those are important questions, and there is good reason to insist the model makes no sense unless it is also accompanied by an undemocratic government. The sacrifices imposed on the public by the model in order to produce results preclude the existence of a more democratic political entity. If given a free choice, it is most unlikely that the population would allow itself to be subjected to the rigors and deprivations necessitated by the model. For the model to work, therefore, the population must suffer in silence. Since the odds are that it will not do that voluntarily, there must be an all-powerful state capable of implementing a radical upending of existing institutions and of suppressing those unprepared to make the necessary sacrifices.

There are many disputes about exactly how fast and far-reaching Soviet economic growth was during the Stalinist period. The statistical procedures used were sometimes outright lies and distortions, and in other cases, the technical nature of measurement was such that even with precise and complete data, there would be disputes.[1] Moreover, many economists have insisted that Soviet growth would have been equally impressive and considerably more human-

1. Alexander Gerschenkron, *Economic Backwardness in Historical Perspective: A Book of Essays* (Cambridge, MA: Harvard University Press, Belknap Press, 1962), pp. 249-50.

itarian if central planning had not been introduced.[2] As they see it, the existing methods of the New Economic Policy implemented by Lenin in 1921 seemed to be generating impressive enough growth. Had Stalin stuck with the existing arrangements, overall growth rates might have been lower, but institutional growth would have probably been better balanced.

In any event, Stalin argued that the status quo was inadequate and that the odds were that the growth rate would soon begin to slow. Because of what he saw as the encirclement of the Soviet Union and a determination to bring about the collapse of the Soviet Union on the part of the outside capitalist world, Stalin decided he needed a forced-march style of economic expansion in order to build up the Soviet economy and its military might. Only in that way could he hope to hold off those who had declared their intention to force a change in the Soviet system. Stalin insisted that the traditional market approach to economic growth would not suffice. Waiting for members of the business community to decide to expand in order to take advantage of high prices and thus greater profit potential was too slow a process.

AMASSING CAPITAL

To achieve the speed and type of growth he sought, Stalin understood that he would need massive amounts of capital. But the Soviet Union was a poor country, and given the antagonisms of the capitalist world, there was no chance of obtaining the necessary funds from foreign lenders. Besides, Stalin had decided that reliance on foreign lenders and investors would open up the Soviet Union to foreign influence, manipulation, and even ownership. Out of

necessity, Stalin decided to turn to agriculture for his capital.

At first glance, that might seem like a strange choice. Agriculture was, after all, as poor as the urban sector of the economy and the peasants were even poorer. But partly because of ideological reasons — the Communists were supposed to be the vanguard of the proletariat — and partly because the peasants constituted 80-90 percent of the population, agriculture seemed to represent the only source of funds. Of course, it would not be easy to extract those funds. The peasants would have to be squeezed, and since there was not much wealth to begin with, squeezing would have to be exerted from the outside and it was likely to be a painful process.

Collectivization served that purpose. The peasants were forced to cede their farm land, animals, and equipment to the state, which then transformed rural villages and the surrounding fields into collective and state farms. No compensation was paid, and the prices collected for crops grown on these new farms usually ensured that the farms operated at a loss. In effect, this became a process of ongoing confiscation, but it served Stalin's purposes. He was able to extract manpower and funds for investment in basic industries in the cities. In this way Stalin quickly built up an impressive steel and heavy industrial infrastructure.

With enough determination, Stalin proved that a country could lift itself up by its bootstraps, even if its feet were bloodied in the process. No other system seemed able to mobilize so much capital in such a short time. That as much as anything explains why, without exception, every country that subsequently became Communist adopted the same growth strategy. For a country that was predominantly agrarian and where the population was largely illiterate and unacquainted with urban and in-

2. Ibid., pp. 139-40.

tellectual life, there seemed to be no better way to industrialize.

It was also necessary, of course, to create an entity that could take those cumulative resources and direct them systematically to the high-priority needs of the state. Gosplan and the central plans were created for that purpose. Like collectivization, they seemed ideally suited to the task of developing heavy industry and absorbing and converting the enormous influx of unskilled and unsocialized peasants into the industrial work force. It helped, of course, that the technology of the time was pretty simple and slow moving. Not surprisingly, the quantity of output was poor, but given the magnitude of the transformation and the speed with which it was undertaken, the results were impressive. Little was set aside for frivolous pleasures or consumer luxuries. Thus even basic needs such as comfortable housing or uncrowded transportation or a selection of consumer goods were frequently neglected. But the Soviet Union went from producing 4 million tons of steel in 1928 to 18 million in 1940, to 116 million in 1970. By 1974, it produced more than the United States. The Soviet Union had indeed overtaken and surpassed the United States not only in the production of steel but also in such goods as petroleum and machine tools.

PROBLEMS BEHIND THE SUCCESS

In the mid-1960s, some Soviet economists began to warn that despite what the statistics might show, not all was well with the Soviet economy. Collectivization and central planning may have facilitated the mobilization of capital in a poor society and the mastery of relatively simple technology, but such growth was dependent largely on the introduction of more and more labor and capital. But labor and cap-

ital were becoming harder to find and technology was beginning to change. Centralized control was not as well suited for mastering more sophisticated technology. That seemed to require more decentralized decision making in order to move more quickly and flexibly. Moreover, after so many decades of sacrifice, the work force had become more demanding. The workers were no longer uneducated or recently arrived from the village fields. More and more, they were highly trained and sophisticated. It was not only that they were beginning to resent the inflexible nature of the planning system, but their innovative potential was lost since the system served to squelch, not stimulate, creativity.

One of the first Soviet analysts to acknowledge what was happening was Tatiana Zaslavskaya. In a classified report, she noted that "an overwhelming number of workers in industry had only recently left their villages and had only a weakly developed sense of their rights" in the 1930s. Moreover, "the links between branches, enterprises, and regions were as yet easily 'overseen' from the center and could be regulated 'from above.'"[3] But she goes on to note that the worker's "level of education, culture, general information, and awareness of his social position and rights has grown incomparably."[4] Not surprisingly, not only did the rate of Soviet economic growth begin to slip, but the economy began to produce a less and less suitable mix of goods for increasingly demanding consumers. In turn, indifference to their needs caused the workers to adopt a similar indifference to their work. Ultimately this was reflected in the attitude that "they pretend to pay us; we pretend to work." That is one important reason why the Brezhnev era was so stagnant.

3. *Survey,* Spring 1984, p. 90.
4. Ibid., p. 71.

THE BEGINNING OF REFORM

It took someone as daring and sensitive to what had been happening as Mikhail Gorbachev to decide to change the system. Efforts at reform had been made before, most notably the so-called Liberman reforms of the 1960s,[5] but they were too little and too late. For that matter, while the economy in 1985 was in more serious need of reform than it had been two decades earlier, Gorbachev's initial prescriptions were similarly inadequate. At first he stressed more discipline, less corruption, and what he called intensification and acceleration. This involved the consolidation of a few industrial ministries and harder work by the workers, but little more. Only gradually did Gorbachev come to see that considerably more far-reaching measures were necessary.

Under the influence of critics like Zaslavskaya and through his own insight, Gorbachev came to realize that instead of being the solution, central planning had become the problem. What the Soviet Union desperately needed was to stimulate individual initiative and enthusiasm. It was no longer possible to determine all economic questions in Moscow. The society had become too large, too complex, and too fast moving for that. Nor would the problem be solved by merging or closing down a large number of ministries. To the extent that the center sought to hold on to its controls, Soviet economic growth would be constrained, simplified, and retarded.

But how does one go about decentralizing a centrally administered economy or at least do it in such a way that there is an increase in economic growth and no encumbrance for the future? As Alexander

Gerschenkron has noted, all too often in Russian history, efforts to westernize or advance the Russian economy have been accompanied by measures that ultimately preclude self-sustaining growth.[6] For example, Peter the Great's attempt to modernize Russia brought with it serfdom, just as Stalin decided he would have to collectivize Soviet agriculture in order to fund the industrialization of the five-year plans that were his first priority. Nonetheless, both serfdom and collectivization later served as a brake to self-sustaining growth.

It is easy to centralize an economy — just set up ministries or state agencies and order all businesses, both private and those nationalized, to follow state orders. But no one has been able to do the reverse. The Hungarians seemed to have made some progress in the early stages of their reform, but after a few years of promise, new problems developed. Amid growing inflation, foreign trade deficits, and a decline in per capita income, there were renewed calls for the reinstitution of centralized decision making. Much the same thing happened in China.

To some extent, the sudden transition from central planning to market self-determination is complicated by the absence of institutions on which market economists depend to provide indirect controls. In doing away with centralized control organizations such as Gosplan and the ministries, the reformers in Hungary and China neglected to replace them with less centralized but nonetheless essential coordinating and regulating institutions like our Federal Reserve Bank, Council of Economic Advisers, and the Department of the Treasury, which we use to guide our economy. In moving from strict centralized administrative control to a market decentralized system, economists in Hungary, China, and the Soviet Union often find themselves

5. Marshall I. Goldman, "Economic Controversy in the Soviet Union," *Foreign Affairs*, Apr. 1963, p. 498.

6. Ibid., pp. 135-37.

inside a twilight zone. They no longer have their strict centralized orders that used to determine what they were to do, nor do they have indirect guidelines or institutions with the experience to issue such guidelines. It takes time to evolve such institutions and policy, and so far there is nothing there. That helps to explain why at times the Chinese economy has seemed to be out of control and why to curb it, the Chinese authorities have had to retreat to centrally issued orders and decrees.

Central planning and control also color individual attitudes toward the markets to complicate the process of reform further. This is reflected in the attitudes of many of the Russians who have recently immigrated to Israel and the United States. It is hard for these émigrés to comprehend that the state does not provide for all their needs or guarantee them a job. There have been many instances when some of these new arrivals have decided to open up their own businesses only to complain that the state did not send them enough customers to generate the necessary sales.

This same attitude has been demonstrated dramatically in the Soviet Union. Gorbachev has sought to wean managers of the state enterprises away from complete dependence on Gosplan and the ministries. Beginning in 1988, state enterprises producing about 50 percent of the Soviet Union's industrial output were told that they would only have to designate about 70 percent of their output for state orders (*goszakazy*) issued by the central authorities. This was part of a new Law on the State Enterprise, which decreed that by 1989 all state enterprises would be free to sell about 30 percent of their output outside the state order framework.

It turned out, however, that, at least initially, the new procedures hardly varied from the old system of almost 100 percent control over enterprise output. On the one hand, the state ministries refused to loosen their control. They continued to insist that the enterprises provide them with close to and sometimes more than 100 percent of their output. On the other hand, few of the enterprise managers rose to the new challenge. Many of them found it safer to stay within the old system. Certainly it was less risky. Anyone exercising the option not to fulfill the state order had to find customers willing to buy his or her products. This could be a difficult thing to do since there were no well-established wholesale markets. Thus there was no ready-made forum where prospective sellers and buyers could meet. Those who could find customers might be able to sell their goods at a higher price. That might bring higher bonuses. Offsetting these potential gains, however, was the danger that there might be no customers. In addition, those who sold outside the framework of the state order were no longer guaranteed that they would receive delivery of the raw materials and components they needed to produce the goods they sought to sell on those wholesale markets. Not surprisingly, most managers concluded that the gains were not worth the risks and uncertainties.

This affinity for security and aversion to risk is underpinned by an underlying resentment of income inequality. The Russian people seem to prefer what the authorities call leveling or what the Chinese call sharing from the same big iron pot. This attitude was fostered during the seventy years of Soviet socialism and the stress upon, if not the existence of, equality. But such attitudes also stem from Russian cultural traditions, particularly the Russian commune (*mir*) of the prerevolutionary period. After the emancipation of the serfs, most of the Russian peasantry were linked together in the village commune. It was the commune that was responsible for obtaining the emancipation of all the peasants in the village. Under the circumstances, no one could become wealthier than anyone else. Moreover, the land in the commune was periodically redistributed to ensure that no one had long-run use of land that was more fertile than that cultivated by his or her neighbor.

The combined impact of both the pre- and postrevolutionary traditions is reflected in a story the Russians tell about themselves. It also explains the reluctance of many Soviet people, especially the Russians, to step out from underneath the security blanket of the central plan and collectivized farm:

A genie appears with three wishes. The Englishman declares he wants a cottage overlooking the sea. The Frenchman opts for a vineyard and his mistresses. The Russian complains that his neighbor has a goat but he himself lacks one. His wish? "Kill my neighbor's goat."

REFORM REVISED

Undeterred by the cultural and sociological shackles of the Russian and Soviet traditions, as well as the lack of success thus far, Gorbachev seems determined to move forward toward the market and privatization and away from the stultifying effects of central planning. After several early false starts where he mistakenly put stress on more effective central planning, consolidation of overlapping industrial ministries, and the increased production of machine tools, Gorbachev came to realize that he had inverted his goals. Thus, beginning in 1987, he decided that he should shift his priorities. Thereafter he began to rely more on the market and an emphasis on consumer goods, while reducing the power of the industrial ministries.

Implementing that policy shift, Soviet authorities halted a crackdown on private trading activity they had instituted in 1986, and they decreed instead that as of 1 May 1987, private and cooperative businesses could be legally opened. The decision was also made to authorize peasants to break out of collective and state farms and set up family farms or lease land from the collective farms for up to fifty years. Similarly, the Law on the State Enterprise was passed, which, as we saw, established the timetable for the move away from an overdependence on central planning. In the same spirit, every Soviet enterprise was authorized as of 1 April 1989 to do its own importing and exporting. Under the new regulations, no longer were Soviet enterprises required to subordinate their foreign trade activities to Foreign Trade Organizations under the Ministry of Foreign Trade. This also fit in with the decision to reallow joint ventures to establish themselves on Soviet territory. The decision was made in late 1986 and, by early 1989, approximately 400 joint ventures had been officially approved.

All of these moves are steps in the right direction, but they do not appear to be generating the structural changes Gorbachev seems to be seeking. Admittedly, at this writing, Gorbachev has only just marked his fourth anniversary as Soviet leader, and so it may be too early and thus unfair to make a judgment about the nature of his efforts. But thus far, they do not portend any major improvement, and indeed the results have been very disappointing. In fact, there are signs that the situation has actually deteriorated and continues to do so.

RESULTS NOT HOPED FOR

Part of this deterioration is a natural consequence of any effort at reorganization. Change always generates confusion.

For a time, at least, no one knows who is in control or what procedures to follow. But much of what is happening also illustrates many of the inevitable difficulties associated with a move from central planning to the market that we discussed earlier.

Gorbachev made a critical mistake. In 1985, when he began the reform process, he decided to concentrate first on the machine tool industry. This brought an initial increase in output, but nothing that was noticeably different from what had occurred under earlier Soviet leaders. More important, there were no tangible benefits for the ordinary Soviet workers. Inevitably, this affected the credibility of the reform efforts. Letters appeared in the Soviet press from workers asking why the reform process always begins by asking the worker to work harder and why there never seemed to be any accompanying increase in consumer goods. The lack of beneficial results colored almost everything that was to follow.

In contrast, the decision to legalize private and cooperative trade has had an impact. Because of the perennial neglect of consumer needs, there is an enormous demand for consumer goods and services. This has long been reflected in the scale and ingenuity of the underground and the second economy. If nothing else, it made sense to legalize the underground economy. In part, that is what happened. Black-market jeans, some manufactured by the cooperative along with some produced elsewhere and diverted to the cooperative enterprises, but with its higher prices, are now sold legally, often for R100 or more — that is, about $165. Of course, many activities have been newly created. Thus cooperative restaurants have sprung up in most Soviet cities, something that would have been difficult to accomplish earlier, when there was only the black market.

Introducing cooperatives or private businesses in an environment of central planning is all but guaranteed to cause problems, especially if these new businesses are successful at what they do. That may sound like a paradox, but it is not. Cooperatives are supposed to fill gaps, generate competition for state enterprises, and at the same time bridge the gap between the unnaturally low prices of the state shops and the high prices of the black market; in effect, they are to function as arbitrageurs.

Unfortunately, the higher prices charged by the new private businesses have been a source of enormous resentment and bitterness. Even Gorbachev has criticized the cooperatives for this.[7] Such criticism ignores the fact that it is the higher prices and, by extension, the resulting higher profits that serve to attract others into going into business. When there are enough new competitors, the prices will fall. Restricting operations by limiting prices is an effective way to perpetuate monopoly pricing and thus discredit the whole process.

Certainly, when competition from the cooperatives does begin to have an effect, it is bound to upset the traditional state enterprises. That is exactly what happened with health care. A relatively large number of doctors set out on their own to establish cooperative clinics and health care centers. Eventually their efforts became effective enough to attract a large following of patients, many of whom were in the lower income groups.[8] It turns out that upper income groups and party officials could always use bribes or political clout to obtain

7. Moscow Television, Vremia, 12 Sept. 1988, reported in *Foreign Broadcast Information Service*, 13 Sept. 1988, p. 40; *Foreign Broadcast Information Service*, 23 Jan. 1989, p. 49.

8. *New York Times*, 5 Mar. 1989.

the treatment they wanted while ordinary patients lacked that ability.

The very success of such clinics, however, brought about their demise. The doctors in the state clinics resented the competitive pressures that were forcing them to be more accommodating to the masses. They also resented the higher prices and profits collected by their one-time compatriots. As a consequence, the Soviet government announced in December 1988 that cooperative medical groups, as well as other cooperative activities, would be closed or severely limited in their operations.[9] Similar restraints were applied on other cooperatives as well. Other limitations included the imposition of price ceilings.

If these problems were not enough, the cooperative and private business movement has also become too closely identified with an unsavory or seamy segment of the Soviet population. Official Soviet statistics indicate that the cooperative movement has been much more widely adopted in the different minority republics and among other minority groups such as the Jews. The movement has also attracted a criminal element, those who used to operate underground. It has also given rise to a brand-new class of racketeers who see cooperatives and private businesses as a lucrative source for extortion. All of this tends to obscure the positive contributions of the cooperative movement and hampers its growth.

Similar counterreactions hamper almost every aspect of the reform process. We have already seen what happened to the enterprise law. Much the same reaction has crippled the move to allow independent importing and exporting. Soviet officials began to worry that unbridled importing and exporting might lead to the importation of frivolous products and a general loss of control. In truth, that is probably exactly what would have happened — much as it did in China, when similar restraints were removed and people began to utilize the money they earned to satisfy their needs. To prevent that, the Soviet authorities have announced the imposition of a new set of regulations. Under these new rules, importers and exporters would be required to obtain licenses and permits to import most products.[10]

It may well be that these setbacks are all temporary and that with a little more time, Gorbachev's reforms will become firmly established and produce the anticipated results. For the time being, however, that does not seem to be happening. While the number of cooperatives now exceeds 40,000 and the number of joint ventures is close to 700, they have not brought with them an increase in consumer well-being in the country, and, in fact, the real standard of living has declined while the rationing of basic commodities such as sugar has become widespread, even in Moscow.[11] In the meantime, inflation has become a serious matter along with strikes by workers seeking to maintain their relative living standards.

No one ever argued that the process of privatization and marketization would be easy. It is doubtful, however, that anyone ever thought it would be quite this hard.

9. *Ekonomicheskaya gazeta,* Jan. 1989, no. 1, p. 4; *Moscow News,* 1989, no. 3, p. 13; ibid., no. 5, p. 4.

10. *Pravda,* 17 Feb. 1989, p. 2; "On Measures for State Regulation of Foreign Economic Relations," *Foreign Trade,* Apr. 1989, special insert.

11. *Moscow News,* 1989, no. 19, p. 12.

ANNALS, *AAPSS,* **507,** January 1990

Economic Reform of Socialism:
The Soviet Record

By GERTRUDE E. SCHROEDER

ABSTRACT: For more than three decades, the Soviet Union has been engaged in an almost continuous process of reforming the centrally planned economy inherited from Stalin. The objective of the reform programs of all Soviet leaders from Khrushchev to Gorbachev has been to make the economy more efficient and responsive to consumer wants, while retaining its socialist character. The reforms made by Khrushchev and Brezhnev came to naught, because they left the essential features of the Stalinist economic system in place. Although Gorbachev's reforms enlarge the scope for the private sector, they, too, leave much of the old system in place. Far more radical moves toward privatization and marketization will be required to achieve the goal of creating a socialist regulated market economy that can satisfy consumers and keep up with the West.

Gertrude Schroeder, a past president of the Association for Comparative Economic Studies, is professor of economics at the University of Virginia. She holds master's and doctoral degrees from the Johns Hopkins University. Before entering teaching, she spent many years as senior economist with various agencies of the federal government. She is the author of a book and numerous articles on the Soviet economy, with a focus on economic reforms and living standards.

F OR more than thirty years, the Soviet Union has been engaged in an almost continuous process of reforming the Stalinist system of socialist central planning. While that system proved able to generate fairly rapid economic development in accord with political priorities, it did so with enormous waste of resources and inattention to consumer wants. All of the reforms introduced by successive leaderships — from Khrushchev to Gorbachev — aimed to remove those weaknesses of the system without diminishing its strengths or altering its socialist character. All the reform programs have moved in the direction of administrative decentralization, but only under Gorbachev do they really move appreciably toward privatization and marketization of the economy.

KHRUSHCHEV'S INNOVATIONS

Nikita Khrushchev initially believed that the economy could be made more efficient through administrative decentralization.[1] To that end, his 1957 reforms abolished the dozens of central ministries responsible for industry and construction and subordinated their enterprises to newly created regional economic councils (*sovnarkhozy*). As justification for this drastic shake-up of the bureaucracy, its architect argued that far too many decisions were being made in Moscow, that regional interests were being neglected, and that the ministries were empire builders concerned only with their own enterprises, to the detriment of efficiency and the welfare of the economy as a whole. This innovation soon created serious problems in coordinating the production and deliveries of supplies among enterprises; the result was a downturn in economic growth and productivity. The government's response was to amalgamate regional councils and create one coordinating agency after another. Similar organizational ferment took place in the agricultural sector.

But Khrushchev had launched his own version of *glasnost* — known as the "thaw" — with his speech attacking Stalin and his relaxation of restrictions on intellectuals. Discussion of economic problems became more open, and "radical" remedies were proposed, including the creation of a "socialist market" in the Soviet Union. The economist Evsei Liberman was permitted to publicize a proposal for reform at the level of the firm by according it more leeway to deal directly with customers and by using profitability as a criterion for assessing performance. Khrushchev allowed a variant of this scheme to be tested experimentally in a few enterprises in light industry. His successor, Leonid Brezhnev, expanded these experiments to some other sectors but moved quickly to end the unpopular and unproductive experiment in regional administration.

THE KOSYGIN REFORMS

In September 1965, Premier Alexei Kosygin unveiled a comprehensive reform program that was labeled a "revolution" by some observers in the West[2] and as "the third great reform in all Soviet history" by a Soviet writer.[3] It was launched by a leadership increasingly aware of the economy's technological backwardness relative to the West and of the imperative need

1. Khrushchev's innovations are well described in Eugene Zaleski, *Planning Reforms in the Soviet Union, 1952-1966* (Chapel Hill: University of North Carolina, 1967).

2. Marshall Goldman, "Economic Revolution in the Soviet Union," *Foreign Affairs*, 45(2):319-31 (Jan. 1967).

3. A. M. Birman, "Thoughts after the Plenum," *Noviy mir*, Dec. 1965, p. 194.

for greater productivity as a source of future economic growth. The program put the wager on the efficacy both of increased centralization through reorganization of bureaucracies and of the devolution of greater decision-making authority to enterprises.[4] With respect to organization, the reforms replaced the system of regional councils with their predecessors — the numerous industrial ministries — which, however, were enjoined to "work in a new way" and to eschew "petty tutelage" over subordinate enterprises. In addition, new centralized agencies were created to manage prices, the rationing of supplies and equipment to firms, and the coordination of research and development activities. Although the reforms called for steps to be taken to organize "wholesale trade in the means of production" and for the use of "economic levers" — prices, profits, interest rates, and incentive funds — to influence enterprise behavior, no real markets were created by those features. Firms were given fewer plan targets and accorded more decision-making authority in managing their work force and small investment projects. They also were authorized to establish profit-based incentive funds. Enterprise success and managers' bonuses were to depend on meeting plans for sales and profitability rather than on gross output as before. A larger share of investment was supposed to be financed from profits and bank credits rather than by budget grants. Under these market-sounding arrangements, socialist firms were expected to start behaving like those in a private-enterprise market economy: they were to try to please

customers with new and high-quality products, minimize costs, strive for profits, and, above all, welcome innovation and new production technology.

The reforms were extended gradually throughout industry and in some other sectors during the years 1966-70. But in exercising their increased freedom of action, enterprises responded in ways that the central authorities did not like, such as some distributions of bonus funds and undertaking some kinds of investment projects. Moreover, the hoped-for gains in labor productivity and product quality failed to materialize. In short, firms continued to behave much as before, because the reforms did not alter any of the essentials of Stalinist central planning.

THE TREADMILL OF REFORMS

The government's response to these developments is a saga of almost continuous efforts over some 15 years to reform the reforms.[5] The objectives were the same — creating more effective forms of organization and altering the behavior of enterprises. A decree adopted in 1973 launched a drive to merge enterprises into various forms of large associations with the objective of reaping assorted economies of scale: by 1986, associations managed enterprises accounting for 50 percent of total industrial output and 53 percent of employ-

4. A large literature exists on the 1965 reforms. See, for example, Karl W. Ryavec, *Implementation of Soviet Economic Reforms* (New York: Praeger, 1975); Gertrude E. Schroeder, "Soviet Economic Reforms: A Study in Contradictions," *Soviet Studies*, 20(3):1-23 (July 1968).

5. For details, see Gertrude E. Schroeder, "Soviet Economy on a Treadmill of Reforms," in *Soviet Economy in a Time of Change*, by U.S. Congress, Joint Economic Committee (Washington, DC: Government Printing Office, 1979), pp. 312-40; idem, "Soviet Economic Reform Decrees: More Steps on the Treadmill," in *Soviet Economy in the 1980s: Problems and Prospects*, by U.S. Congress, Joint Economic Committee (Washington, DC: Government Printing Office, 1982), pt. 1, pp. 65-88. Also see Morris Bornstein, "Improving the Soviet Economic Mechanism," *Soviet Studies*, 37(1):1-30 (Jan. 1985).

ment. But bureaucracies proliferated: during the years 1966-85 the number of industrial ministries increased from 31 to 57, and total employment in state administration rose by 82 percent.

With regard to industrial firms, mandatory targets for growth in labor productivity were reimposed in 1971, and managerial bonuses were tied to them. In 1973, targets for raising product quality were established and linked to incentives. In 1976, ministries were given more discretion in deciding bonus-determining targets for firms, and in 1977, an attempt was made to link bonuses to fulfillment of contracts for product deliveries. An omnibus decree issued in 1979 directed the ministries to introduce gradually the requirement that enterprises finance all expenditures, including investment, from their own funds, thus eliminating the widespread practice of subsidizing loss-making firms through budget grants and intraministry redistribution of profits. This decree also made still more revisions in the rules governing enterprise incentive funds and managerial bonuses. In 1980, mandatory employment ceilings were reimposed on enterprises, and in 1981, another decree introduced a complicated set of measures to impose on enterprises targets for saving raw-material resources and tie incentives to meeting them. Agriculture was also affected: farms were merged, and various innovations with organizational forms and incentives were introduced, the most notable being the establishment of regional agro-industrial associations as part of Brezhnev's omnibus food program adopted in 1982. Major industrial price revisions were made in 1967 and 1982, but the prices for all important products remained centrally fixed.

After Brezhnev's death in November 1982, his successor, Yuri Andropov, sought to halt the deterioration in economic performance by replacing managers in the party and bureaucracy and by launching a campaign to impose discipline on one and all. On the reform front, he initiated an experiment in 5 ministries to test new rules of the game for enterprises, which amounted merely to another attempt to implement the 1979 decree. Konstantin Chernenko's contribution was to extend the new rules to 20 ministries beginning in January 1985.

GORBACHEV'S FIRST TWO YEARS

Upon becoming party general secretary in late March 1985, Mikhail Gorbachev moved vigorously to alleviate what he termed the "pre-crisis" state of the Soviet economy and society. Economic growth rates were on a long-term slide, productivity was declining, improvements in living standards had slowed to a crawl, consumer markets were in massive disarray, Soviet manufactures were virtually unsalable on Western markets, and the technological gap with respect to the West was widening. Gorbachev rightly perceived that the economy's plight threatened the USSR's status as a superpower and its image as a successful socialist state. He vowed to turn the situation around. Apparently, he believed that quick results were possible.

His first moves resembled those of his immediate predecessors — replacing cadres, trying to enforce discipline, inaugurating draconian measures to reduce consumption of alcoholic beverages, and expanding the ongoing experiments with enterprise self-finance and revised incentive rules. Several measures addressed the stagnant agricultural sector by establishing a new bureaucracy — the State Committee for the Agro-Industrial Complex — and tinkering with marketing arrangements and price incentives. Laws adopted in 1986 initiated yet another reorganization of the perennially malfunctioning construction sector and one more round of ostensible devolution of decision-making authority to the union republics and local soviets. Finally, a crash program to modernize the industrial capital stock was inaugurated through a massive shift of investment in favor of the machinery industries and the renovation of existing facilities throughout the economy.

As Gorbachev's perception of the severity of the economy's problems deepened, however, his prescriptions for remedies became less traditional. At the Twenty-Seventh Party Congress in February 1986, he declared the need for "radical reform" of the economic mechanism, including a reexamination of the nature of property ownership under socialism, an issue long proscribed. He spoke of the need to make each worker feel like an owner of his or her firm and, contrary to established ideology, suggested an expanded role for producer cooperatives.

In line with these ideas, measures taken during 1986 also became less traditional. A law adopted in 1986 enlarged the permissible scope of private economic activity, albeit simultaneously with another one aimed at curtailing corruption and so-called unearned incomes. Actions were taken to encourage groups of individuals to form cooperatives to produce consumer goods and provide services. With the aim of increasing pay differentials for skilled and efficient workers, a sweeping reform of the wage and salary system was introduced, with its financing linked to a firm's ability to pay the higher wages from its own earnings. Still another novelty was the initiation of reforms in the conduct of foreign trade that broke the state monopoly in that area by permitting a few ministries and enterprises to engage independently in foreign trade; this law also authorized joint ventures between Soviet and foreign partners on Soviet soil. In contrast to these reformist moves, however, the government chose to attack the chronic problem of low product quality by stationing teams of state quality inspectors in many major factories, particularly in those producing machinery.[6]

THE RADICAL REFORMS
OF 1987-88

In June 1987, the Communist Party Central Committee endorsed a set of General Guidelines for a comprehensive economic reform. That document, along with a new Law on the State Enterprise, 10 decrees governing various aspects of the reform package, new laws in 1988 dealing with cooperatives and foreign trade, and the measures taken in 1985 and 1986 make up Gorbachev's self-styled radical economic reforms.[7] All of these measures are now in various stages of implementation. They modify in greater or lesser degree each of the major pillars of the traditional system of socialist central planning. With regard to property ownership, the laws expand the scope for private and particularly for cooperative ventures, thus taking a small step toward privatization. Centralized planning is retained, but its directive scope is supposed to be reduced gradually and substantially by the early 1990s. Central bureaucracies are to be reduced in size and number. Rationing of supplies and machinery is gradually to be replaced by

6. For details on Gorbachev's first two years, see Gertrude E. Schroeder, "Gorbachev: 'Radically' Implementing Brezhnev's Reforms," *Soviet Economy,* 2(4):289-301 (Oct.-Dec. 1986).

7. For details, see Gertrude E. Schroeder, "Anatomy of Gorbachev's Economic Reform," *Soviet Economy,* 3(3):219-41 (July-Sept. 1987).

wholesale trade. State-set prices are to be revised, and contract prices are to be employed much more extensively.

The reforms greatly enlarge the autonomy of state-owned firms. They now formulate their own plans, based on centrally set guidelines, mandatory state orders for a part of output, and contracts with customers for the remainder. The state continues to regulate the growth of wages and the distribution of profits. Firms must finance all expenditures from their own revenues and can be closed down if they persistently make losses. Each firm's workers are required to elect a work council with considerable decision-making authority and also to choose the managers of the firm. All of these innovations are supposed to elicit a "proprietary attitude" from everybody toward the firm's property, with efficient production of high-quality goods and innovative behavior being the expected outcome.

The enterprise reforms took effect in most of industry and in some other sectors in 1988 and were extended throughout the economy in 1989. Central and regional bureaucracies were reorganized and reduced in size. The scope of state orders was cut from some 86 percent of total industrial production in 1988 to about 40 percent in 1989, and the volume of wholesale trade was planned to triple compared with 1988. The wage reforms affected over 30 million workers at the end of 1988, and some 2 million persons worked privately or in cooperatives.

Despite this formal progress, the reform process thus far has produced few if any benefits and has contributed to serious economic difficulties; indeed, the economy is in worse shape now than in 1985. In an environment of universal shortages and general confusion, firms used their newly found freedom by engaging in what was quickly labeled "anti-social" behavior. Specifically, they reduced planned output, demanded conditions viewed as extortionary for renewal of contracts, dropped low-priced products from production, declined to accept unprofitable state orders, and raised prices under the guise of new products. All this added to inflation and exacerbated the perennial shortage of consumer goods. Even worse, enterprises hiked wages far in excess of productivity gains. Newly minted cooperatives were able to raise prices also, along with their own incomes.

The difficulties created by the reforms themselves were exacerbated by a series of policy mistakes over several years. An ill-conceived antidrinking campaign deprived the state budget of billions of rubles in tax revenue and retail stores of billions in sales. It also produced long queues, a burgeoning moonshine industry, and rationing of sugar. In response to the fall in world prices for oil, the government reduced imports of highly taxed consumer goods, further depriving both the budget and retail stores of revenue. Meanwhile, the growth of state budget expenditures accelerated in response to a surge in investment and subsidies. The result was an enormous budget deficit, projected at some R100 billion, or about 11 percent of gross national product in 1989. With continuously rising incomes, shortfalls in planned production of consumer goods and services, and much publicity about a possible reform of retail prices, people have gone on a buying spree. Empty shelves, longer queues, and increased distribution through special channels have become widespread.

RETRENCHMENT

By and large, the government has responded to these difficulties in traditional ways that violate the spirit of the reforms and are strongly reminiscent of actions following the 1965 reforms. Ministries have intervened to correct undesired actions of firms and to bail out those in financial trouble at the expense of profitable firms. Central authorities also have interfered in the contract-signing process between firms. State inspection of product quality has been expanded. To deal with the situation in consumer markets, the state imposed on all enterprises mandatory targets — state orders — for the production of consumer goods and services. Centrally set ratios — normatives — relating the growth of wages to that of productivity have been mandated. The freedom of firms to determine prices set in contracts has been curtailed, and local governments are authorized to set ceilings on various kinds of prices. Finally, in response to a public outcry about the "abuses" of cooperatives, the list of permissible activities has been reduced and controls placed on prices. Also, local authorities have been given the right to set taxes on the income of cooperatives, and a progressive income tax on all incomes, with a top surtax rate of 50 percent, has been proposed.

The key to the success of marketization is price reform. Although revised state-set prices for industrial products and for state purchases of agricultural products were scheduled for introduction in 1990, retail price reform has been postponed — "for two or three years," according to Gorbachev. This action, taken in response to strong public opposition, will make it nearly impossible to end the budget deficit. Food subsidies now account for about 20 percent of total budget expenditures. Moreover, postponement violates the reform's declared intent to make consistent changes in the three kinds of prices, as would occur automatically in a market economy. By this delay and the imposition of administrative price controls, the government perpetuates the traditional approach of dealing with shortages only by trying to increase supply. Thus the grossly distorted pattern of consumer demand will be preserved, as will the inefficient signals provided to producers.

Two major reform documents were unveiled during the first half of 1989. Neither is in the least radical. One relates to the republics. To head off demands for regional economic autonomy, notably from the Baltic republics, the government published a draft decree spelling out new republican rights and responsibilities. In brief, the republics are to have primary authority for managing agriculture and the consumer sector, while all authority over raw materials and heavy industry has been transferred to Moscow. The decree also increases the republics' authority over their budgets, although a complex set of arrangements with the central budget is retained. Since the scope of central authority remains large and central so-called coordinating agencies remain in place, the decree amounts mostly to yet another administrative decentralization of authority to regions. The outcome is unlikely to please the localities or to further the reform process.

The other document, a package of agricultural reforms, was adopted in March and is far from bold. While sanctioning the legitimacy of all forms of property — state, cooperative, leased, peasant farms, private plots — it leaves the state and collective farm structure in place. Individuals and groups are to be encouraged to lease parcels of land and to contract with the farms for sale of the output on mutually agreeable terms. Experiments with such "strictly voluntary" forms are to be conducted during 1989, and a new law on leasing reflecting the results is to be submitted to the Supreme Soviet by 1 July 1990. State purchase quotas are to be imposed on procurement agencies rather than the farms, which sign delivery contracts on a "voluntary" basis. At the center, authority is vested in a new State Commission for Food and Procurement, and assorted reorganizations are made in the regional bureaucracies managing agriculture. State and collective farms also are bound respectively by the Law on the State Enterprise and the Law on Cooperatives, thus bringing them under the general provisions of the reforms. Finally, loss-making farms are to be liquidated or merged.

CONCLUSION

We are now witnessing the latest round of almost continuous attempts over some three decades to reform the system of Stalinist central planning, so as to improve economic performance. Previous rounds had failed because they left the pillars of that system essentially unchanged. Gorbachev's package of reforms goes considerably beyond those of his predecessors in the direction of privatizing and marketizing the economy. Even so, the provisions of the reforms as now laid out are a series of half-measures that also will retain much of the essence of the traditional system, even when the program is fully in place in the early 1990s. Perhaps the most promising feature is the legislation permitting and encouraging private and cooperative economic activity, including a strong push for expansion of private plots and of leasing arrangements on farms. But privatization has gotten off to a rocky start, with some pullback already. The reform legislation pertaining to the socialist sector, while imbued with a strong thrust toward creating markets and modifying property rights, contains inconsistencies and contradic-

tions that will greatly impede that process. Indeed, they are already doing so, leading the authorities to reimpose administrative controls.

The current difficulties might be viewed as an unavoidable part of the growing pains associated with the transition to a new order of things, where both the population and business firms would have learned how to function in a market arena. But the present difficulties will multiply, unless serious flaws in the reform program are removed. In particular, orderly markets will never arise while bureaucracies charged with the responsibility for production are retained. Moreover, efficient markets require flexible prices — for products as well as for labor and capital — that reflect reasonably well their relative costs and scarcities. Without such prices to guide them, enterprises cannot make efficient decisions about what and how to produce, and profitability will be a poor indicator of whether a firm is working well or poorly. Distorted prices will produce distorted — socially undesirable — outcomes, providing good excuses for administrative intervention to correct them. Without major alterations, Gorbachev's reform program cannot produce his vision of a socialist regulated market economy capable of satisfying people's wants and closing the technological gap with the West.

Even if a thoroughgoing reform program that replaces present institutions with those suited to a market economy is adopted, the obstacles to its effective implementation are formidable. Workers and consumers will protest the unemployment, job insecurity, widened income differentials, and inflation that are inevitable in the transition. Politicians and bureaucrats will resist the erosion of their power, authority, jobs, and privileges. Both workers and managers lack the experience and the requisite skills for functioning in a competitive market economy. Creation of competition will be fettered by the monopolized production structure that is a legacy of the centrally administered economy. An even worse legacy is the huge capital stock that is technologically obsolescent, poor in quality, and inefficiently located. These legacies will take many decades to overcome.

Although economic reform has resurged spectacularly during Gorbachev's first four years, signs of retrenchment are already visible. To achieve its objectives, moreover, his program will have to be redrawn and made far more radical than what is now being implemented. Whether that can be accomplished politically remains to be seen. If it cannot, the present round of reforms will come to be viewed as continuing the treadmill. As of now, however, Gorbachev continues to pursue his reform program with zeal.

Sub-Rosa Privatization and Marketization in the USSR

By GREGORY GROSSMAN

ABSTRACT: In the USSR, conditions for private underground activity have been highly propitious, given the barring, until recently, of nearly all lawful private business, chronic excess demand with fixed prices, high excise taxes, and both pervasive bureaucratic regulation and widespread corruption. State property is vastly misappropriated and exploited, particularly by camouflaged cryptoprivate firms. The underground, generally employing money as the main medium of exchange and functioning through markets, touches very many and on average provides large supplements of goods and — together with bribes, theft, and fraud — income to the public. In the larger operations, illicit money flows up informal structures, often to very high officials. Underground money and aboveground political and administrative power tend to fuse and to spawn, or exploit, organized crime. Vested interests so created are a significant aspect of conservative opposition to *perestroika*. Under Gorbachev, the underground economy has increased markedly, despite measures both to suppress and to legalize it.

Gregory Grossman, professor of economics at the University of California at Berkeley, received his Ph.D. at Harvard University while a student fellow at the Russian Research Center. He has been studying the Soviet economy for some forty years, lately focusing on the second economy and on financial and monetary aspects of perestroika.

NOTE: The author gratefully acknowledges funding by Wharton Econometrics Forecasting Associates.

A N international committee of experts seeking to define the social conditions that maximize the scope and size of a country's underground economy would in effect rediscover Soviet-type socialism. Of course, the underground economy in some form or other—the aggregate of a country's ongoing illegal economic transactions and supporting activities—is a universal and venerable phenomenon that spares no social system. One exists wherever there are taxes to be evaded, price or wage controls to be violated, a principal's property and prerogatives to be abused by the principal's agents and employees—especially when the principal is the state—and other legal norms regulating economic behavior to be infringed—which is to say everywhere, and not the least in a Soviet-type society.[1]

The specific features of a particular underground economy are largely a reflection of the ambient socioeconomic, legal, and political institutions. Change the ambient system and the underground economy will adapt and change, but it will hardly disappear. Moreover, its vigor and vitality are probably not unrelated to the culture and prior history of the population, though, with time, cultural resistances to corruption and "economic crime"—to introduce a Soviet phrase—may be expected to recede before the force of economic self-interest working within the given institutional setting and economic conditions, as seems to have happened in once relatively clean East European countries, such as East Germany—Prussia—and the Czech lands.

In addition, it seems to be virtually impossible to extirpate an underground economy or its inevitable concomitant, corruption, by police methods alone, not even under a Mao or a Stalin.

Underground business is usually conducted on private account—though governments and their subdivisions have been known to trade in violation of their own, not to say other countries', laws—and because it operates out of reach of all administrative authority, its prices and markets are necessarily free.[2] It is also likely, except in the case of relatively small transactions, to employ money as the main medium of exchange, rather than to transact by barter. Hence, in capitalist market economies, the distinction between the underground and the aboveground economy is more legal than systemic. On the other hand, in the Soviet-type system, it is precisely the cited attributes, in addition to the legality criterion, that set the Soviet underground economy off from the ambient—that is, official, Stalinist—economy, which at least until very recently was almost entirely nonprivate and devoid of free markets and free

1. Among collective volumes addressing, as it were, the other economy in various countries and from several standpoints one might mention the following: Vito Tanzi, ed., *The Underground Economy in the United States and Abroad* (Lexington, MA: D. C. Heath, 1982); Sergio Alessandrini and Bruno Dallago, eds., *The Unofficial Economy: Consequences and Perspectives in Different Economic Systems* (Aldershot, England: Gower, 1987).

2. Given the nature of the subject matter and the elusiveness and opaqueness of the underlying data, a few words about our sources and information are in order. Official statistics give some, though mostly indirect, indication of the nature and dimensions of sub-rosa activity. Even before *glasnost,* the media and other published Soviet sources carried a great deal of anecdotal information, especially of a criminal kind, that has been informative in regard to many details and suggestive at large, although of uncertain validity or representativeness. Journalists and other Western visitors to the Soviet Union have been bringing out similar information. Serious scholarly work estimating the magnitude and analyzing the causes and consequences of the "shadow economy," as the phenomenon is now termed in the USSR, is only beginning there, however. In contrast, in Hungary and Poland, scholarly work on the respective second economies has been going on much longer and is often of high quality.

prices and in which money has played largely a passive role.

An interesting question, therefore, implicit in this article's title, is whether the Soviet sub-rosa economy may not, in some manner or other, perform a significant constructive role in the course of the Gorbachevian economic reform, which reform, as we know, aims to introduce substantial — and, of course, legal — privatization of business activity; to marketize the economy, that is, to supplant the command system with a market mechanism of sorts; and to increase the overall use of money as the economy's primary exchange medium. We shall return to this question; but first a quick glance into history and a closer look at the Soviet sub-rosa economy.[3]

A GLANCE BACK

One need hardly stress that the USSR's underground economy is as old as Soviet rule — indeed, much older. Gogol's *Inspector General* (1836) and *Dead Souls* (1842) depict official corruption and elaborate schemes of bribe extraction that might as well be taken from contemporary Soviet

reality. Writing about the first years of Soviet rule, Thomas Remington has vividly described the dependence of the young revolutionary regime, as well as of the population, upon black markets during the period of so-called war communism (1918-21), a time of extreme shortages and privation and of severe repression of private economic activity. Moving on to the late 1920s, we find in I. Il'f and E. Petrov's *Twelve Chairs* (1928) and *Golden Calf* (1931) the fictional but almost believable images of the flamboyant con man Ostap Bender, making the most of the partly capitalist era of the New Economic Policy, and — presciently — of the reclusive Koreiko, already scheming how to snatch private riches from the emergent Stalinist economy by exploiting its weaknesses and rigidities from within. Turning from fiction to the Communist Party's own archives, we find, with Fainsod, conclusive evidence of official concern with illegal economic activity during the early 1930s.[4]

Nonetheless, historical information on the Soviet underground economy is scant and spotty. It would seem that its main growth occurred after World War II, when it swelled, ramified, and matured into the major and highly complex and potent social, political, and economic phenomenon that it came to be in more recent decades. Khrushchev's campaign against "economic crime" in the early 1960s, to the point of reintroducing the death penalty, appears to have produced only a brief setback, judging by private eyewitness information. The Brezhnev-Chernenko period was doubtless a great boon to underground

---

3. Clearly, there is a very major barrier to serious study of the underground economy within any given country: the reluctance of the criminally implicated actors to reveal themselves and their acts while within the reach of the law. In this regard the emigration of hundreds of thousands of persons from the USSR in the past twenty years has made a crucial difference, permitting scholars in the West to tap this rich source of information by means of questionnaire surveys and in other ways, outside the reach of Soviet authorities. For some years now, I have been engaged in such an endeavor — the Berkeley-Duke Project on the Second Economy in the USSR — with Professors V. G. Treml of Duke University and Michael Alexeev of George Mason University. We have drawn on personal interviews with emigrants, questionnaire surveys, published and unpublished émigré literature, and a broad range of Soviet-published information. The preliminary results of this project underlie the present article.

4. Thomas F. Remington, *Building Socialism in Bolshevik Russia: Ideology and Industrial Organization, 1917-1921* (Pittsburgh, PA: University of Pittsburgh Press, 1984), chap. 6; Merle Fainsod, *Smolensk under Soviet Rule* (New York: Random House, 1958), pp. 200-206.

economic activity, corruption, and various related phenomena and their consequences.

THE FAVORABLE CLIMATE

Returning to the opening sentence of this article, we proceed to take a brief look at the extremely favorable conditions for underground economic activity and other types of illegal personal gain in the USSR as of, say, the eve of Mr. Gorbachev's accession to the general secretaryship of the Communist Party of the Soviet Union in March 1985. The developments since this event will be discussed later. The narrative in the next several paragraphs proceeds in the present tense inasmuch as the situation has changed little to date except in the direction of greater propitiousness.

The favorable circumstances include various systemic features: for example, money is in excess supply while nearly all prices and wages are administratively fixed or controlled; markets are more the exception than the rule; nearly all productive assets — including inventories, of course — are officially owned; decision making is highly centralized and bureaucratically executed; shortages abound; quality and service in the official sector are miserable; nearly all producer goods and resources and some important consumer goods and services are bureaucratically allocated or rationed; and virtually all independent private gainful activity is forbidden, except in agriculture. Confronting this situation is a cynical population starved even for material necessities, educated above its economic reach, and with a modern existence mostly beyond its grasp. Confronting the population is an inert and heavily corrupted apparatus of rule and enforcement.

In the very few areas where individual private activity has been traditionally permitted, it has been hemmed in and discouraged by administrative and ideological hostility, high taxes, extortion by sundry officials, supply shortages, a bar on hiring labor, and so forth. It is small wonder that on the eve of the Gorbachev era only some 70,000 persons — about 1 per 4000 population — were legally pursuing, as individuals, the permitted trades and professions and paying direct taxes and that only about 150,000 were legally renting out private space in a country with a fearsome housing shortage. But, per contra, millions were so engaged illegally, though often on sufferance and with palm greasing, paying no income taxes, and depending heavily on materials stolen and equipment borrowed from the socialist sector.

Overlooking the damage to the state and to the fisc and taking the overall system as is, much of this sub-rosa activity is, of course, most useful in that it supplies goods and services of great variety and often relatively superior quality, which the official sector cannot provide properly, if it provides them at all, or cannot provide as cheaply, because the goods are massively stolen from that same official sector, as happens with gasoline, or because taxes on them are avoided, as in the case of home brew. Incidentally, the underground economy supplies goods and services not only to households and to the private sub-rosa production sector but to the official production sector as well.

Furthermore, millions of individuals buy scarce and cheap and sell dear, a practice called "speculation," which is a criminal offense; millions steal and embezzle from the state or defraud it by overstating their production accomplishments;[5] mil-

5. It should come as no surprise that defrauding the state can be particularly lucrative. The largest such scheme yet to surface is the cotton affair, in which during the late 1970s and early 1980s enormous quantities of nonexistent cotton were sold from Central

lions defraud the buying or selling public; millions abuse their official positions, take graft, tribute, bribes, kickbacks, outsize tips and gifts—all of which opportunities abound at every step. Much of this criminal—or at least gray—activity is taken for granted by the public, whether it approves of it on moral grounds or not.

SOME TECHNICALITIES

The crucial importance of theft from the state for the Soviet underground economy cannot be overstated. We note again that in the Soviet Union—and, with some exceptions and modifications, in all other Soviet-type economies as well—nearly all of the natural resources, capital equipment, and nonconsumer inventories have been owned by the state or at least by entities under its closest control and that of the state's boss, the Communist Party. The formal custodians of these assets have too often been incompetent and/or negligent, venal, crooked, or, at any rate, ineffectual, while public respect for socialist property has been very low. Consequently, a considerable portion of socialist—mostly state-owned—assets has been routinely and widely misappropriated or misapplied for private benefit, often on a large scale and not least by the ostensible custodians themselves. If not turned directly to personal use, the goods and services pilfered from the socialist sector, as well as labor and equipment time stolen from the socialist employer, feed massively into underground production and black markets.

Asia—mainly Uzbekistan—for a take of billions of rubles—the exact amount is still unclear—with the help of massive bribery extending up to Brezhnev's son-in-law Iurii Churbanov, deputy minister of internal affairs, that is, of the police. Nearly all the Party and government leadership of Uzbekistan was implicated.

Indeed, a considerable, though unascertainable, part of black production on private account takes place within the very walls of socialist firms. In turn, a considerable proportion of that is what we call cryptoprivate, that is, private production concealed behind the socialist firm's facade and masked to the point that it is identical in physical appearance and price with the officially produced goods in the same facility at the same time. The privately produced portion is, of course, not reported to the competent authorities. The profit to the underground operators derives from the fact that all inputs, labor included, used in the production of the private portion as well as of the officially reported portion of the output belong to or are paid for by the state. In other words, the secret of success of this ingenious stratagem is that cryptoprivately produced goods are absolutely indistinguishable from those produced for the plan, either to customers or to authorities—except the authorities who are in on the deal and abet it by channeling extra supplies and other inputs to the operation.

Several aspects of the cryptoprivate mode of illegal activity should be mentioned. First, because it can potentially draw on the very large resources of the state for private gain, it is able to generate very large underground profits, though it is not the only underground operation capable of doing so. Second, it does so not without a great deal of large-scale bribery in a variety of planning, administrative, supervisory, and other offices, thus strongly contributing to the overall corruption of the system, though in this regard the cryptoprivate technique is certainly not alone. Finally, the cryptoprivate segment of the underground economy is not a candidate for privatization through legalization precisely because it is nominally part of the official sector, that is, it is ostensibly already legal. It may be, however, under certain conditions, a rather logical area for limited privatization through private leasing from the state. Nor is there much private — underground — capital sunk into production capital in cryptoprivate ventures; rather, it is sunk primarily, and often in large amounts, into the form of bribes and protection money, so that there is very little by way of tangible assets for which one's property rights can be formally legalized.

EFFECTS AND CONSEQUENCES

A questionnaire survey conducted by the Berkeley-Duke study among emigrants from the USSR suggests that in the late 1970s the urban population alone, which constitutes 62 percent of the total population, derived on the average about half again as much income from all nonofficial sources, including some legal ones, as it did from official sources, such as wages, salaries, pensions, and stipends. Even more important is the contribution of informal sources to personal wealth. In interpreting ratios such as the just-cited 0.5:1.0, however, it should be borne in mind that the levels and distribution of legitimate income from official sources would be considerably different in the unlikely absence of substantial informal income. For instance, many jobs are officially paid very little precisely because they provide good opportunities for illicit supplementary earnings — for example, jobs in retail trade. Lucrative positions are not infrequently sold and purchased for money up front plus a periodic tribute. A Soviet specialist has estimated the annual value of illicit consumer goods and services for the mid-1980s at R80-90 billion, which would add

about a fourth to the value of the goods and services sold to the public by the state.[6]

Except in the very common case of illegal activities that involve only one person and that are not very visible, the gain from underground operation does not generally stay with the direct, or initial, receiver, say, the retail sales clerk who short-weights his customers or collects under the counter or both. Rather, a large part of it is often passed upward through an elaborately organized money pyramid. The direct payees' take is shared with their superiors, and likewise all the way up, which may be a very high level indeed, judging by stories in the media and by private information. Simultaneously, at each level of the pyramid, part of the money flow is diverted toward various power holders — "necessary people," in Russian parlance — officials of the Party and the government, police, inspectors and auditors, crucial suppliers, and, these days, also increas-

6. In the Berkeley-Duke project, mentioned in fn. 3, informal — including illegal — income is a much broader concept than income from the underground economy; it also includes income from legal gainful private activities, transfers from private individuals, and gain from ordinary crime such as fraud, bribes, and theft. Any very large incomes, and especially very large wealth, almost always derive from illegal sources, however. The cited ratio, 0.5:1.0, varies very greatly between regions — the further south the higher — and, of course, between persons within a region. But note also that the levels and distribution of legitimate incomes would be quite different in the absence of a significant underground economy. The Soviet figure was estimated by T. I. Koriagina of the Economic Research Institute of the USSR State Planning Commission, as cited in *Financial Times* (London), 13 Aug. 1988. Some Soviet observers, however, deem it to be low. Dr. Koriagina estimates also that illicitly obtained personal wealth currently amounts to R200-240 billion. For the report of the round-table discussion at which Koriagina presented this figure, see *Moskovskie novosti*, 20 Aug. 1989. The figure may represent 20-25 percent of all personal wealth, including money holdings.

ingly to professional extortionists and blackmailers—illegally acquired wealth is a relatively safe target for the criminal. Many people, including many at the pyramid's base, are trapped in the system—in fact, doubly trapped: they need their illegal take to make ends meet, and they dare not drop out of the system for fear of reprisal.

Spending and earning, surviving and succeeding in an underground economy that ranges through various shades of gray to black is a way of life for the Soviet people, as it is for the people of many other countries as well. But the underground economy is and does more than that. It incriminates and thus renders vulnerable a large part of the population. It is a crucible of moral values. It shapes the public perception of reality against which official versions are judged. It tests the regime's mettle and ultimately its legitimacy. It provides visions of social alternatives. Finally, and more concretely, it furnishes the material foundation for existing alternative social structures.

Indeed, at least two alternative social structures rest on the second economy. The first, better known abroad but much the smaller in size, is the world of political dissidents, ethnic and religious activists, refuseniks, opters-out, nonconformist writers and artists, and *samizdat* publishers. To this countersociety and counterculture, the second economy—in itself a counterphenomenon, an implicit indictment and rejection of the official system— has furnished much material support, especially in the pre-Gorbachev years.

The second, and very different, edifice is the all-permeating but shadowy structure of formal-informal alternative power, the world of political and social realities, of corruption, unofficial networks, patronage and clientelism, extortion, intimidation,

large payoffs, organized crime, and purposive violence. It is a world of surviving or newly fostered "neotraditionalism"[7]— as it were, satrapies in which near absolute power derives at once from formal hierarchical status and tacit official sanction from above, and from the informal realities—often mingled with ethnicity, territorial considerations, even religion. In this world of the "Mafia," as the Soviets now call it, there is no demarcation between underground and aboveground.[8]

THE UNDERGROUND AND *PERESTROIKA*

With its own sub-rosa private enterprise and free markets, the underground economy has probably been both a boon and a bane for Gorbachev's attempts to move the legal, aboveground Soviet economy along its rocky road of privatization and marketization. First let us examine the boon, where the most important effects have probably been intangible, perceptual, and even ideological, accumulating over decades. By its vigor and vitality, its flexibility and resourcefulness, the second economy has vividly underscored the negative lesson of the ineffectualness and wastefulness of the traditional, Stalinist "command economy," as it is now called in the USSR, too. The positive lesson—the

7. The term comes from Kenneth Jowitt, "Soviet Neotraditionalism: The Political Corruption of a Leninist Regime," *Soviet Studies*, 35(3):275 (July 1983), a political scientist's trenchant analysis that anticipated the post-Brezhnev revelations of spectacular corruption.

8. The problems of organized crime and the Soviet Mafia, and their links with the formal power structure, especially at very high levels, have been the objects of grave and rising concern in the Soviet media and from the public at large in the last few years. These problems were also addressed from the podium of the newly formed Congress of People's Deputies in May and June 1989.

potential superiority of a significantly privatized and marketized economy over the traditional version—may not have been learned as widely. The idea of market socialism with substantial privatization, not to say out-and-out capitalism, and of corresponding economic insecurities and inequalities holding sway in the USSR does not seem to have had in 1985, or four Gorbachevian years later, anything like overwhelming popular acceptance.

The underground economy has doubtless been a school of enterprise, initiative, better work habits, pecuniary calculus, risk taking, and other attributes of a market-oriented economy. But the students in this school have been predominantly small, individual tradesmen and—less so—professionals. Its curriculum may not have been well suited to produce market-oriented managers for considerably larger business undertakings, sophisticated bankers, or effective vice-presidents for marketing. Moreover, much of the underground economy has been a zero-sum game: the state or the buyer loses, the individual wins—not a healthy outlook for marketization.

Yet, according to our informants who came out of that milieu, there is also a remarkable amount of integrity among and mutual trust between underground operators—indispensable qualities where business understandings cannot be committed to paper for security reasons. Our expressions of surprise were met by surprise: "After all, we were businessmen, not Party crooks!" More generally, we do not subscribe to the assumption that potential entrepreneurial and managerial abilities hardly exist in the Soviet population. We suspect they are there all right, albeit unschooled and underskilled, and if they do exist, the credit in part belongs to the second economy.

If the underground is a drag on the economic reform, this is largely for two reasons. First, it fosters a great deal of politico-economic conservatism in the anti-*perestroika* sense. Millions of people have cultivated their little illegal or gray niches and rackets and would rather keep the known risks than face the unknown brave new world. More significant, as we have seen, the big-time underground and the organized underworld that it has spawned have melded with a part of the official political—and administrative and police—pyramid of power. Here the stakes are enormous—not just vast wealth and great power but also personal security and even one's head. The last several years' purges, prosecutions, convictions, executions, and suicides of the once mighty drive the lesson home. True, every economic system creates its countereconomy; so will *perestroika* if it succeeds. But the grandfathers will be new, as will be their political patrons and partners. Hence a good part of the old establishment's resistance to economic reform, to the legitimation of privatization and marketization.[9]

In the event, during the four-plus years since Gorbachev's coming to power, the underground seems to have prospered and swelled further, despite both a major renewed campaign against it and the newly enacted opportunities to turn legitimate. Major reasons are to be found in the evolution—or lack of it—of the official economy, namely, the rapid expansion in the money supply with prices still largely, but not firmly, fixed, and therefore a rapid increase of excess demand by both consum-

9. For more extensive discussion, see Gregory Grossman, "The Second Economy: Boon or Bane for the Reform of the First Economy?" in *Economic Reforms in the Socialist World,* ed. C. O. Kim and S. Gomulka (New York: Macmillan, 1989).

ers and producers, aggravated shortages, and other windfalls to black production and markets. The continuous confusion engendered by *perestroika* probably helped, too.

The drastic anti-alcohol measures promulgated in May 1985 were followed by sharp increases in official prices of liquor and wine and inevitably by an explosion of bootlegging and home brewing and by a serious drop in tax revenue. The campaign against economic crime — "nonlabor income" — was announced in May 1986, in prophylactic anticipation of the widening of the scope of legitimate private activity, which was promulgated in November 1986, but the campaign quickly caused so much disruption in the economy, especially in informal food supply, that its enforcement was relaxed and has been tapering off since.

We cannot dwell here on the limited and ambivalent legitimation of private activity by individuals and producer cooperatives, legitimation that had embraced over 2 million persons, including part-timers, by mid-1989. To some extent this new private sector must have brought underground producers and traders into the open, but many

of the now lawful operations doubtless combine illegal activities behind the new facades and, in fact, seem to have stimulated additional underground activity around themselves. Any rumors of the economic underground's early indisposition, let alone demise, or of the wasting away of corruption and organized crime are definitely premature.[10]

10. In the round-table discussion mentioned in fn. 6, Dr. Koriagina also offered the estimate that in 1988 some 800 million rubles' worth of the "shadow economy," as she termed it, was legalized, offset by an increase of some 1400 million rubles' worth of various illegal activities. In regard to the Gorbachev era, see the following: Misha Belkindas, "The Campaign against Unearned Income," *Berkeley-Duke Occasional Papers on the Second Economy in the USSR,* 14:1-89 (Apr. 1989); idem, "The Development of Private Cooperatives," ibid., pp. 90-97; Stanislaw Pomorski, "Notes on the 1986 Law on Individual Enterprise," ibid., 13:1-22 (Oct. 1988); V. G. Treml, "Gorbachev's Anti-Drinking Campaign: A 'Noble Experiment' or a Costly Exercise in Futility," in U.S. Congress, Joint Economic Committee, *Gorbachev's Economic Plans,* (Washington, DC: Government Printing Office, 1987), 2:297-311; idem, "Alcohol Underground in the USSR," *Berkeley-Duke Occasional Papers on the Second Economy in the USSR,* 5 (Dec. 1985).

ANNALS, *AAPSS*, 507, January 1990

Obstacles to Economic Reform
of Socialism:
An Institutional-Choice Approach

By BARRY W. ICKES

ABSTRACT: Marketizing reforms are often suggested as remedies for the problems that plague socialist economies. Introducing market reforms is a complex problem. This article examines the obstacles to such reforms. It employs an institutional-choice perspective to study the conditions that are necessary to make marketization effective and discusses the likely outcomes of incomplete marketization.

Barry W. Ickes holds B.A. and M.A. degrees in economics from the University of California, Los Angeles, and earned his Ph.D. in economics from the University of California, Berkeley, in 1984. He has been assistant professor of economics at the Pennsylvania State University since 1983. His published articles include "Cyclical Fluctuations in Centrally Planned Economies," in Soviet Studies; *"On the Economics of Taut Plans," in the* Journal of Comparative Economics; *and "A Macroeconomic Model of Centrally Planned Economies," forthcoming in the* Journal of Macroeconomics.

THE notion of introducing markets into socialist economies dates back at least as far as the famous articles of Oskar Lange and Fred Taylor.[1] As a practical matter, however, the marketizing of socialist economies is a recent phenomenon. The most notable efforts have been in Hungary — initially in 1968, with a lull until 1982 — and in China. There is much talk these days, inspired by the promise of *perestroika,* of introducing the benefits of markets in planned economies.

Despite the rhetoric in favor of markets, there are good reasons for remaining skeptical about the likely success of this venture.[2] One might naturally ask whether it is really in the interests of political leaders to implement such reforms.[3] The purpose of this article, however, is to focus on institutional obstacles to marketization. Consequently I will assume throughout an interest on the part of the leadership in implementing such reforms. This will allow us to focus on the economic problems the reformers will face.

The experiences of previous attempts at economic reform in planned economies suggest that attempts to introduce markets will likely encounter difficulties. These efforts have been likened to a "treadmill of reforms," where reformers must continually initiate new measures to prevent the system from sliding back to orthodoxy.[4] It seems as if the socialist system rejects measures of reform much as an organism may reject transplanted tissue. The purpose of this article is to offer an explanation of why this rejection occurs from the perspective of institutional-choice theory.

Institutional-choice theory is a branch of economics that studies the advantages of markets relative to hierarchical organization, within the context of capitalist economies.[5] The purpose is to explain the economic rationale behind mergers, vertical integration, and long-term contracts. The basic theme of this literature is that organizational forms are the responses of agents to the relative efficiencies of alternative institutional structures. Altering the institutional structure may affect the transaction costs associated with various economic activities. Vertical integration, for example, may be an efficient institutional adaptation to a situation in which one firm must make an investment specific to the needs of another, such as Fisher Body and General Motors. By vertically integrating, the two firms avoid the contracting difficulties that would arise to protect the former from being held hostage by the latter after the investment is made.

It might seem strange to use the institutional-choice approach for the study of socialist economies, where the institutional

1. See B. Lippincott, *On the Economic Theory of Socialism* (Minneapolis: University of Minnesota Press, 1938).

2. For a more optimistic appraisal of market socialism, with respect to China, see Gregory Chow, "Market Socialism and Economic Development in China" (Econometric Research Program Research Memorandum no. 340, Princeton University, Dec. 1988).

3. The politics of economic reform in the Soviet Union are discussed in Timothy J. Colton, *The Dilemma of Reform in the Soviet Union* (New York: Council on Foreign Relations, 1986); Jerry Hough, *Opening up the Soviet Economy* (Washington, DC: Brookings Institution, 1988). Hough argues that the "biggest obstacle to radical economic reform in the Soviet Union is not political or bureaucratic opposition, but the immense inherent difficulty of achieving the goals of reform itself." Ibid., pp. 45-46.

4. Gertrude E. Schroeder, "Soviet Economic Reform Decrees: More Steps on the Treadmill," in *Soviet Economy in the 1980s: Problems and Prospects,* by U.S. Congress, Joint Economic Committee (Washington, DC: Government Printing Office, 1982), pt. 1.

5. For an excellent introduction to this literature, see Oliver Williamson, *The Economic Institutions of Capitalism* (New York: Free Press, 1985).

structure is determined by the leadership. But economic reforms involve questions of the optimal organizational structure of an economy, and an approach that sheds light on this question turns out to be quite useful.

The rest of this article is organized as follows. The first section discusses the meaning of marketization. The second then outlines the institutional-choice framework for application to socialist economies. In the third section, I use this framework to study the obstacles to marketization. The fourth section offers some concluding comments.

MARKETIZATION

The impetus for the introduction of markets into socialism is the recognition of the inefficiencies associated with central planning. In particular, central planning is viewed as a system wasteful of resources. The basic problem is the excessive informational requirements necessary to plan an economy centrally. In the process of collecting, transmitting, and processing information about preferences and production possibilities, the limits of our computing powers inevitably introduce errors into the system. Since the essence of socialism is social ownership of the means of production, rather than planning itself — though Marx spoke frequently of the chaos of the market — it is suggested that markets can be utilized, through a trial-and-error process, to solve the millions of equations that are the essence of formulating a consistent plan.

There are really two distinct trends toward the introduction of markets in socialist economies. The trend that captures the most attention, and that is the subject of this article, is the use of markets to coordinate activities within the production sector of socialist countries, that is, the replacement of the plan by the market. The other trend is the cooperative movement, which appears to be the most successful element of *perestroika* to date. This is a new and important development, but as yet its scope is limited. In particular, the capacity for cooperatives to form in the production sector is, at present, still quite limited.

Marketization, in the spirit of Lange, is seen as a substitute for the annual plan. Markets can help coordinate the actions of agents in the economy more efficiently than a planning system. It is also argued that since managers know more about the conditions of production, they should have more autonomy. Indeed, marketization without reform of the price system is really nothing more than a call for greater managerial discretion. What is important to grasp is this identification of marketization with decentralization and with the replacement of one method of coordinating activities with another.

This view of marketization is consistent with viewing economic systems along a spectrum from the most centralized at one end, to the pure market economy at the other. Marketization is then thought of as any move away from the planning axis. What this characterization captures is the notion that one can choose any point along the spectrum, from the pure command economy to the fully decentralized market, and that this choice is independent of other changes in the economy.

Notice that with this characterization, a reform that grants enterprises greater autonomy — for example, the Law on the State Enterprise — but does nothing about the price-formation mechanism is still viewed as marketization. One normally views the market as a mechanism through which prices are formed. This is not the case, however, in the typical reform process, where marketization and reform of the price system are typically treated as distinct processes. In practice, marketization means an alternative to the central direction of the economy, and it means more autonomy for managers. It is frequently associated with no change in the mechanism of price formation.[6] This has important ramifications, since the efficiency of the market system depends critically on agents' reliance on prices that reflect opportunity costs.

INSTITUTIONAL CHOICE AND SOCIALISM

The theory of institutional choice was formulated to deal with market economies. The idea is to explain why agents choose to form firms or use markets to conduct their transactions. The theory has proved quite successful in explaining how the location of decision rights — in particular, those over the structure of the organization itself and the disposal of its assets — affects the efficiency of alternative ways of carrying out economic activity.

Of what use is this approach to the study of Soviet-type economies (STEs)? In STEs, organizational forms are exogenous. Enterprises are established by central authority. They are imposed on agents from above, rather than evolving from the individual decisions of the agents involved. Institutional-choice theory treats economic organization as endogenous. In studying socialist countries, the opposite view is often taken. Institutional structure is taken as exogenous, and the performance of the system given that structure is studied. Since the economic structure is imposed from above in socialist economies, this seems like a sensible approach.

The exogenous nature of economic organization in STEs is of central importance to any analysis. The essence of socialism is to replace the endogenous structures that evolved into capitalism with a socialist system. The central idea of socialism is to design the economic system in accord with socialist ideals. Even the very notion of reform presupposes an exogenous institutional structure, since reforms involve a discrete rearrangement of that structure. Yet agents in STEs pursue their own self-interest and act to exploit the opportunities they face. The fact that forms of organization do not evolve to minimize the dysfunctional aspects of this behavior does not mitigate the importance of these considerations for the performance of STEs. Moreover, even if economic organization is exogenous, agents will adapt, within the constraints they face, to the presence of transaction costs. The key point is that if organization is fixed, it is behaviors that will evolve — often in ways viewed as counterproductive by the designers of the system.

It may be useful, then, to think about how the institutional structure of STEs is a response to the transaction-cost problems faced by agents in such economies. The fact that the coordination of economic activities takes place via a central plan implies that the solutions that agents devise to their transacting problems will often be different from those in market economies.

6. For examples in the Soviet case, see Ed Hewett, *Reforming the Soviet Economy* (Washington, DC: Brookings Institution, 1988), p. 330; for Eastern Europe, see J. C. Asselain, *Planning and Profits in the Socialist Economies* (New York: Routledge & Kegan Paul, 1984), pp. 145-61. The same appears to be the case with respect to *perestroika* as well. Prybyla emphasizes the distinction between a price adjustment — which involves a one-time correction of relative prices, leaving the system of price determination unchanged — and a reform of the price-formation mechanism. The latter involves a change in the way prices are determined. Jan Prybyla, *Market and Plan under Socialism: The Bird in the Cage* (Stanford, CA: Hoover Institution Press, 1987), pp. 49-53.

This is because the choice of coordination mechanism — that is, plan versus market — affects the relative cost advantages of different forms of organization. It follows that an organizational structure suited to a planned economy may not be well suited to the introduction of markets.

Consider, for example, the costs associated with central planning. The costs of constructing the central plan increase as the number of enterprises grows. This is due to increased communication costs, plus the extra complexity introduced by greater numbers. Hence there is a strong tendency in planned economies toward large enterprises and fewer numbers than in comparable market economies. This is an example of how coordination costs affect the industrial structure of a planned economy.

The case of large enterprises is an example of the planners' imposing an organizational structure to minimize coordination costs. An alternative form of behavior is for agents to adapt to their own particular transaction-cost situation. For example, consider the prevalence of self-supply in Soviet industry. This is clearly a response to the uncertainties of the supply system. Given the costs to managers of failure to fulfill plan targets, enterprise managers practice universalism. They try to make the enterprise self-sufficient in terms of important inputs. Hence vertical integration in Soviet industry is often a response to the particular set of coordination and transaction costs facing agents.

The existing institutional structure of an economy may then be thought of as the solution to the problem of choosing an economic structure, given central planning, the incentive system of a socialist economy, and the problems that result from hidden action and hidden information. Of course, the mechanism that results need not

be optimal, hence the need for economic reforms. The key point, however, is that the economic structure that is to be reformed is conditioned by the interaction of transaction, technological, and coordination costs. Consequently, when economic reforms are attempted that tend to involve altering one of the constraints — the coordination mechanism — while leaving the organizational structure unchanged, it is not surprising that the reformed system tends to be dysfunctional. Agents are taking advantage of the new altered structure.

This suggests that simply introducing markets into socialist economies is less dramatic a reform than is conventionally assumed. As long as organizational structure is chosen exogenously, replacing the plan with markets is a limited measure that treats only the coordination mechanism. Moreover, such a program is likely to be unstable, as the historical record illustrates. With an unchanged organizational structure, markets are unlikely to function effectively, resulting in pressures to reverse the reforms and move back to the orthodox system.

The contrast between exogenous and endogenous systems illustrates another important characteristic of economic reform. By its very nature economic reform is peculiar to exogenous systems. In market economies — endogenous systems — change occurs all the time with no central direction. But economic reform is precisely a program imposed from above; it is simply the replacement of one imposed design with another. The fact that reforms are products of design rather than experiment is recognized by Gorbachev:

"It is impossible to move forward successfully by the method of trial-and-error. . . . The art of political leadership demands the ability to uncover and effectively resolve contradictions —

not to suppress them and let them accumulate, but to turn them into a source of progress and self-development."[7]

The problem with this process is the inherent difficulty in designing an effective organizational structure for an entire economy from above, what Hayek terms the "fatal conceit."[8]

The introduction of markets in socialist economies is often then merely the replacement of the coordination mechanism. Essentially the same structure remains: the same plants and enterprises and even ministries as before, plus the same decision makers occupying the same positions within the hierarchical structure of the economy. Even though the reform eliminates some of the hierarchical flows of information, it does not alter the selection mechanism for choosing enterprise managers. The system remains hierarchical in that important sense. The implication is that agents in the marketized system will make decisions based not on the bottom line but rather on how their superiors will judge their actions. This weakens the force of market signals and tends to reintroduce old patterns of behavior. The only exception to this would be a change of the system itself, from an exogenous system to an endogenous one. But such a reform would be essentially an abandonment of socialism itself.

The exogenous-endogenous distinction is also useful in illuminating differences in the process of organizational change in economic systems. As mentioned previously, since organizations are imposed under socialism, they are the product of design. Market economies, on the other hand, are essentially experimental. The market system is a trial-and-error process of various types of economic institutions. Successful variations are imitated, and in this way innovations diffuse throughout the economy. Under socialism, changes are imposed from above. Designs are chosen and implemented over the entire economy. Change in market economies is piecemeal and continual. In socialist economies, on the other hand, the structure is static until a reform is instituted. Inefficiencies accumulate until the leadership deems it necessary to impose a new design. Economic reform is thus the counterpart for exogenous systems of the recurrent piecemeal change that takes place in endogenous systems.

The relevance of this contrast is apparent when we consider the resulting institutional structure of the economy. When chosen by design, the likely outcome is a homogeneous solution, that is regimewide. A law such as the Law on the State Enterprise is promulgated to govern the structure of all enterprises. This means that all economic transactions are treated as similar, even if the actual situations differ. In market economies, the trial-and-error process results in a heterogeneous solution, precisely because the transaction costs of various activities differ. Agents choose structures that minimize those costs for their particular activities. To the extent that the factors that induce such variation are important, the implementation of a homogeneous design means that for important elements of the economy it will be inappropriate.

There is good reason to expect differences in transaction costs — transaction costs to be interpreted broadly to include those induced by the nature of the planning system — to be important under socialism. These costs are to a large extent the "legacy

7. Quoted in Hough, *Opening up the Soviet Economy*, pp. 46-47.

8. F. A. Hayek, *The Fatal Conceit: The Errors of Socialism* (Chicago: University of Chicago Press, 1989).

of central planning."[9] Attempts to introduce marketization — and/or other reforms — will succeed or fail depending on how well suited they are to the specific environment in which they must operate. Reforms do not operate on a clean slate. For these programs to be effective they must be suited to the particular institutional structure that is inherited. Otherwise the initial impact of the reforms will be deleterious, and the reform program jeopardized.

It is not only with respect to the impact of reform that institutional structure is important. It is also crucial that a marketized socialist economy possess the necessary features of the institutional structure that make markets effective.[10] Most critical in this regard are exit and entry. These processes, which are the essential elements of endogenous systems, play a central role in allocating resources efficiently. Without exit and entry, marketization may result in the preservation of loss-making enterprises coexisting with enterprises earning monopoly profits.

THE DILEMMAS OF
MARKETIZATION

Market economies are endogenous systems. With no central authority imposing designs from above, actors voluntarily form coalitions that they expect will promote their self-interest. The introduction of markets into socialism, however, introduces an alternative coordination mechanism into what is essentially an exogenous system. Since the efficacy of markets depends on features associated with endogenous systems, how might this hybrid be expected to operate? That is the topic of this section.

As I noted earlier, entry and exit are crucial characteristics of an endogenous system. Under socialism both entry and exit are processes imposed by higher authorities. They are planning decisions essentially. A socialist market economy, by its very nature, would operate with enterprises established by the state, in order to avoid the reappearance of private property. Similarly, exit from an industry is a ministerial or planning decision. Neither entry nor exit is a decision made by the agents involved.[11] This points to the important fact that marketization reforms in exogenous systems invariably retain the economic ministries. Since the enterprises are not autonomous in the sense that they are in an endogenous system, it is imperative to retain authorities to monitor their performance.

The absence of an entry process in a socialist market economy is an important problem. Without entry, sellers are able to exploit monopoly power, if it exists. Rather than calling forth increased output, higher prices simply yield higher profits. This problem is exacerbated by one of the legacies of central planning, a highly concentrated industrial structure. To reduce the costs of central planning — that is, to reduce coordination cost — socialist economies tend to favor large enterprises. This reduces the communication costs of creating

9. The importance of the "legacy of central planning" in analyzing economic reforms in the Soviet Union is emphasized in Hewett, *Reforming the Soviet Economy,* p. 234.

10. "Economic outcomes in market economies appear to depend on detailed features of the institutional structure. . . . Given this, it would be absurd to prescribe for Hungary and other Eastern bloc countries merely that they should move towards a market economy, or market socialism. These terms are unacceptably vague and fail to specify how the above institutional features should be arranged." Paul Hare, "Economic Reform in Eastern Europe," *Journal of Economic Surveys,* 1(1):54 (1987).

11. The limitations on entry and exit contained in the Soviet Law on the State Enterprise are noted in Richard Ericson, "The New Enterprise Law," *Harriman Institute Forum,* 1(2):7 (Feb. 1988).

a central plan. Hungary, for example, undertook in the early 1960s a dramatic amalgamation of enterprises, creating a highly concentrated industrial sector, much more concentrated than in developed Western economies.[12] The amalgamation took the form of a widespread movement of horizontal mergers. This course of action makes some sense under a planning system, since there is no need to consider the effects of such a program on competition. The problem is what happens when such a system is marketized, that is, when enterprises are given greater autonomy to make decisions. The absence of competition reproduces the conditions of a seller's market, not necessarily due to fixed prices but due to the absence of free entry. The result is the same: low quality and insufficient incentive to support innovation.

In principle, this problem could be alleviated by a ministerial entry process. The relevant ministry could create new enterprises in sectors where insufficient competitors exist. The problem is the absence of an incentive on the part of the ministry to do so. Entry reduces the rents — profits — accruing to the incumbent enterprises. To the extent that these rents are absorbed by higher costs of production — that is, padded costs — entry of new enterprises will threaten incumbents with losses, if prices fall with entry. Moreover, if profits are an indicator by which the ministry is assessed, then monopoly power is a favored outcome. The resources with which new enterprises could be created are, in any event, in high demand by existing enterprises to expand capacity, and there is no constituency for new enterprises, with which they compete.

12. Bela Balassa, "The Firm in the New Economic Mechanism in Hungary," in *Plan and Market*, ed. M. Bornstein (New Haven, CT: Yale University Press, 1973), pp. 356-57.

The absence of an automatic exit process — bankruptcy — has been an even more important problem in reforms designed to foster marketization. At first blush this might be surprising. Bankruptcy is a device to encourage agents to make equity investments by reducing the downside risks of these activities. Under socialism there is no need to construct such a device. Moreover, the resource-allocation role of bankruptcy can be achieved through ministerial fiat — the ministry could simply close the enterprise down. In practice, however, this rarely works. The problem is that closing plants involves transferring resources from one ministry to another. Ministries resist reductions in their power. They are much more likely to subsidize the operation of such plants to keep them in operation, because this helps fulfill the ministerial output plans.[13]

The primary role of bankruptcy in socialist economies is to make credible the financial autonomy of the enterprise. The drive to make enterprises financially self-sufficient is a recurrent theme of reforms, manifesting itself in the Soviet case, for example, in the frequent calls for full *khozraschet* ("economic accounting"). Without bankruptcy, however, financial autonomy is a mere bookkeeping device; the state bank will always bail out any losses. Hence there is no change in the incentives managers face unless budget

13. Most reforms — for example, the Hungarian reforms or *perestroika* — maintain ministerial output plans, even though the enterprise plans are discontinued. In the case of *perestroika*, the Law on the State Enterprise retains ministerial responsibility with respect to "satisfaction of demand for their [that is, ministerial] products, for productivity increases, for product quality, product and process innovation in their branches, and for the maintenance of a progressive capital structure." Ericson, "New Enterprise Law," p. 8.

constraints are "hardened."[14] Bankruptcy is thus a mechanism that induces managers to care about the bottom line. It is only binding, however, when enterprises are in trouble; a bankruptcy constraint does not much affect the decisions of successful enterprises.

The absence of bankruptcy thus implies that marketization will not necessarily lead to an efficient allocation of resources. Further consequences depend on how prices are to be determined in the new system. Suppose, contrary to experience, that a substantial number of prices are allowed to be determined by the market after the reform. Then many enterprises will lose money at these new prices.[15] Since there is no exit process, the authorities must continue to finance the deficits of loss-making enterprises, fueling inflation by pumping excess purchasing power into the system. In the Chinese experience from 1985 to 1988, this has led to a retrenchment of the industrial reforms. Indeed, fear of inflation appears to be common to the authorities of socialist countries, and its outbreak can cripple reforms.[16] Despite their concern

with inflation, the authorities do not seem to recognize the role played by the absence of bankruptcy in its genesis.

The inflationary potential of marketization is exacerbated by another legacy of central planning, the large money balances held by citizens in socialist economies.[17] Excessive liquidity is the result of the chronic shortages of consumer goods combined with fixed prices. If price controls were relieved, it is almost certain that a burst of inflation would result. Although this would be only a one-time shock, the fear of the inflationary consequences has frequently — and critically — delayed price reform in socialist economies.

Alternatively, marketization may occur without any change in the way prices are formed. Prices may continue to be set at periodic intervals according to branch average costs. In this case, there is no reason to expect marketization to set off inflation and there is no need for bankruptcy, since with these prices it has little meaning. On the other hand, with prices failing to reflect opportunity costs, it is difficult to see what gains are to be had by marketizing.[18] If

14. The term is Janos Kornai's; see, for example, Kornai, "The Hungarian Reform Model," *Journal of Economic Literature*, 25(4) (Dec. 1986). In contrast, an enterprise with a soft budget constraint — the typical case in socialist countries — receives subsidies from the state to meet any losses.

15. Indeed, many lose money at existing prices, though the implications of this are hard to untangle, when prices do not reflect opportunity costs. Under the current price system it is probably a blessing that bankruptcy laws are not enforced — they are on the books in most socialist economies.

16. Harding, for example, notes that the fear of inflation on the part of the leadership in China stems from their memory of its effect on the Kuomintang in the late 1940s. Harry Harding, *China's Second Revolution* (Washington, DC: Brookings Institution, 1987), p. 279. Hewett notes with respect to *perestroika* that "unless far more attention is given to the use of competitive pressures to automatically control the natural inflationary pressures during the transition, the

resulting inflation will create enormous pressures for retrenchment that will not be without justification." Hewett, *Reforming the Soviet Economy*, p. 353. One might also note the contribution of price increases to unrest in Poland that eventually led to the birth of Solidarity.

17. For example, in the Soviet Union. See Gregory Grossman, "A Note on Soviet Inflation," in *Soviet Economy in the 1980s: Problems and Prospects*, by U.S. Congress, Joint Economic Committee (Washington, DC: Government Printing Office, 1982), pt. 1.

18. "Although the reform's vision of autonomous, self-financing, socialist business firms threatened with bankruptcy for failure conveys an aura of markets and competition, it is, in fact, an artificial accounting construct, both under present Soviet conditions and under those created by the reforms. ... The belief that large gains in efficiency will accrue from self-finance under such conditions (i.e. fixed prices) is a grand illusion." G. Schroeder, "Gor-

agents use incorrect prices to make their decisions, granting those agents more discretion seems unlikely to improve the allocation of resources. Marketization can improve resource allocation only if enterprise managers have good information about the value of resources. If this information is distorted via an unreformed price system, managers will be making decisions in an informational vacuum.

This is the central dilemma facing those who seek to reform socialist economies. Reformers have been reluctant to reform the price system, as opposed to prices, due to their fear of inflation. Granting autonomy to managers to make decisions without a properly functioning price system, however, leads to a situation in which the actions chosen bear no relationship to goals deemed important by central authorities. The idea of marketization is to give greater autonomy to those who have better information. But with an unreformed price system managers have very little information at all about the true economic value of most goods and services. If they are given greater discretion, it will inevitably be used in ways that will frustrate central objectives. Such a situation cannot, of course, last. A retrenchment is the likely outcome.[19]

This illustrates a more general point, that marketization is unlikely to have beneficial effects unless the structure of the economy is altered to make it suitable to markets. To take a concrete example, consider one of the successful cases of

marketization, agriculture in China.[20] In this case, the turn to markets was associated with changes in the organization of production in agriculture. Specifically, the Household Responsibility System (HRS) devolved decision-making authority to the peasant as lessor, a new organizational form. Thus the introduction of markets was "coupled" with a change in the nature of organization. In this case, it provided for "high powered incentives" for the decision makers in the HRS, and it left them with no market power to exploit on their own behalf.

In the case of industrial reforms, on the other hand, no such coupling has taken place. These reforms, as well as the Law on the State Enterprise in the Soviet Union, grant more autonomy to the directors of the same organizations. To follow the agricultural example, this would be like introducing markets into the pre-reform system, keeping the People's Communes but weakening central control over their operations. There is no reason to believe that such a system would have resulted in the increased effort and improved allocation of resources brought on by the HRS. Yet this is precisely what is asked for in the industrial reforms.

The success of the HRS is due, in large measure, to the fact that marketization was accompanied by a change in the organizational structure of agriculture. The decision maker in the HRS cares about the bottom line, because he is the residual claimant. This makes market signals important and, coupled with prices that reflect relative scarcities, encourages agents to use resources efficiently. The change of producing unit to the household meant that producers would not have market power. This

---

bachev's Economic Reforms," in *Gorbachev's New Thinking*, ed. R. D. Leibowitz (Cambridge, MA: Ballinger, 1988), p. 65.

19. To put it another way, central planning may be the most effective way to direct an economy when prices do not reflect opportunity costs. This might explain why the treadmill seems so steep.

20. See, for example, Prybyla, *Market and Plan under Socialism*, pp. 204-13.

prevents them from using their increased autonomy in ways that would frustrate social objectives. In order for marketization to have anywhere near the same success in industry, the program must be coupled with reform of the organizational structure, in particular the relationship between the enterprise and the ministries.

In a command economy, enterprises and ministries stand in a vertical relationship. The managers of the enterprises are the subordinates of the ministry. The ministries are responsible for the performance of the enterprises. Meanwhile, the ministries are responsible for the career advancement of managers. Managers thus make decisions based on how they expect their superiors will evaluate the consequences of their actions. Bargaining between superiors and subordinates is the dominant form of economic activity. One of the purposes of reform is to reduce this bargaining, so that decisions are made based on objective opportunities — market signals — rather than case by case.

When marketization is undertaken without a change in the ministerial system, its effect is attenuated by the retention of the superior-subordinate relationship. The manager's autonomy is, at best, like that of a division manager of a multidivision firm. The manager runs one part of a much larger economic organization. But the ministries are still operating in a nonmarket environment. They still have plans to fulfill, and they still make decisions according to noneconomic criteria. Hence the imperatives of ministerial responsibility attenuate the autonomy of the enterprise and limit the extent to which marketization alters incentives.[21]

21. "But the actual introduction of competition was not compatible with just any kind of industrial structure. It was clear that competition had no place in a hierarchical economy in which the associations supervised production in each sector and controlled

The analogy with a multidivision firm is apt for another reason as well. Like such a unit, the enterprise makes decisions based on what are, in effect, transfer prices. The prices are internal to the organization and hence not reflective of opportunity costs. But the division faces transfer prices for only a limited set of goods and services. Market prices form the bulk of the terms of trade the division manager deals with, in particular with respect to labor. The enterprise, on the other hand, deals almost exclusively with transfer prices, in the absence of reform of the price system. Hence the manager knows very little about the value of resources. Consequently, the ministry is loath to delegate real authority to the enterprise. It is one thing to delegate responsibility but quite another to delegate authority. Marketization seems often to be nine-tenths the former and one-tenth the latter.

CONCLUSION

The institutional obstacles to reform that I have discussed in this article result from insufficient, or incomplete, change in the system. The problem is that marketization is viewed as a reform independent of other changes in the economic system, such as price formation and the entry and exit process. When these other systemic reforms do not accompany marketization, the system does not achieve the desired results, and retrenchment ensues. Incomplete reforms tend to be the rule. A few comments are nonetheless in order about the implications of a complete reform.

One of the crucial elements of successful marketization is market valuation of

sales; the declared intention of promoting competition in Czechoslovakia from 1965 onwards was thus doomed to failure." Asselain, *Planning and Profits,* p. 145.

resources. If enterprise managers are to use their discretion wisely, they must possess information about the scarcity values of the factors of production. This, of course, requires markets for capital and labor. Such markets pose critical questions for a socialist regime.

It is difficult to see how a capital market can be introduced into a socialist economy while the latter retains the exogenous nature of economic organization. Introduction of a stock market involves a change in the nature of ownership relations that would create what would seem perilously close to a restoration of capitalism. Short of a market for corporate control, reformers must devise a mechanism to value capital goods without affecting ownership. The inherent difficulty of this problem is illustrated perhaps by the failure of any actual reform program to deal with it successfully.

A similar problem concerns potential reforms of the labor market. Granting real autonomy to enterprises would create free labor markets. Such a change would threaten one of the prime achievements of socialism, the guarantee of full employment. Given the legacy of central planning — many loss-making enterprises, greater than full employment and labor hoarding, and so on — radical reform may precipitate widespread unemployment, at least in the short run. Indeed, the threat of widespread unemployment has been one of the main reasons why bankruptcy statutes are not enforced. Accepting the conse-

quences for the labor market of real enterprise autonomy is a radical step that reformers have so far declined to take.

Reformers also face an implementation problem. This involves the sequencing of reforms. It is critical for the success of economic reform that the various elements be introduced at the proper time. A well-conceived reform can nonetheless fail if the various elements are introduced in the wrong order. Improper sequencing is often a prime cause of the disruptions that accompany serious reform. In particular, price reform and bankruptcy must accompany, or even precede, marketization. *Perestroika* appears to be following the opposite sequence — price reform has been significantly delayed — and the deleterious consequences of this are easy to forecast.

My purpose in this article was to discuss the obstacles to marketization in socialist economies. As we have seen, reformers face a difficult problem. Introducing markets in a socialist economy is a complex problem, as suggested by experience as well as theory. This does not suggest, however, that attempts at marketization are necessarily doomed to failure. Indeed, the best hope for socialist economies involves the introduction of market forces. The point is that for marketization to be successful, it must be part of a serious and comprehensive reform. The failure of any socialist economy to find a successful path to marketization is evidence of the difficulties involved, but it does not lessen the importance of continuing the search for it.

ANNALS, *AAPSS*, **507,** January 1990

Obstacles to Economic Reform
of Socialism:
A Property-Rights Approach

By JAN WINIECKI

ABSTRACT: This article sketches briefly an answer to the question of why economic reforms fail under the Soviet-type system in spite of the obvious interest of the respective ruling groups in improving the performance of their ailing economies. The author, applying a property-rights approach, points to the fact that all segments of the ruling stratum benefit from maintaining an undemocratic political system, but party *apparatchiks* and economic bureaucrats benefit also from the persistent interference in the patently inefficient economic system. Therefore they are most interested in maintaining the status quo in the economic system as well. Moreover, since the rulers turn to them for the design and implementation of reforms, their chances for preventing, distorting, and/or aborting reforms are all the greater.

Jan Winiecki is an independent analyst from Warsaw, Poland. He teaches in the Department of Economics at the Catholic University of Lublin.

NOTE: A more extensive treatment of the subject by the author may be found in *Economic Inquiry*, in press.

T HIS article sketches an answer to the question of why economic reforms fail under the Soviet-type system in spite of the obvious interest of the respective ruling groups in improving the performance of their ailing economies. I apply a property-rights-based explanatory framework, stressing modes of rent maximization of the ruling stratum as a crucial explanatory variable. All segments of the ruling stratum benefit from maintaining an undemocratic political system, but party *apparatchiks* and economic bureaucrats benefit also from persistent interference in the process of wealth creation through the *nomenklatura* and privileged access to goods in short supply that is possible only in the present inefficient economic system with its muddled property-rights structure. Consequently, the party *apparatchiks* and economic bureaucrats are most interested in maintaining the status quo in the economic sphere.

INCENTIVES FOR THE RULING STRATUM TO MAINTAIN THE STATUS QUO IN THE STATE SECTOR

In this article the distribution of wealth is the focus of attention. This approach does not neglect the distribution of power, in the sense that rulers of a Soviet-type system may regard control over the working population through a system of multilevel hierarchical commands and reports on plan fulfillment as satisfying their thirst for power. But without focusing attention on wealth distribution, it is difficult to explain why market-type changes — needed also by the rulers — have failed to materialize.

Wealth distribution depends, in turn, on the existing property-rights structure. If we accept the Darwinian dictum that in economic evolution low-cost organizations tend to supersede high-cost ones, then re-

arrangements of property rights, away from Soviet-type economic systems, should have taken place. Following D. C. North,[1] I search for the political constraints that block such a rearrangement.

North stresses the existence of a conflict in predatory — prerepresentative — states between efficient property rights designed to maximize wealth and property rights designed to maximize rent to the ruling stratum. Under the circumstances, the rulers will avoid offending those powerful segments of that stratum who benefit most from the status quo.

This conflict is clearly in evidence in Soviet-type economies (STEs). To make it more transparent, North points out first the modes of rent appropriation in the state sector of the Soviet system. In traditional prerepresentative states the ruling stratum appropriates to its members a larger share of created wealth than they would obtain under a representative government. They simply receive higher salaries, more perquisites and so forth, while their status symbols — articles of conspicuous consumption and/or modern professional equipment — have a priority claim upon the state budget.

In STEs all segments of the ruling stratum — Communist Party *apparatchiks*, bureaucracy, police, the military — benefit in the same way. Their salaries may be relatively higher, their perquisites are relatively more important in a shortage economy, but this mode of wealth distribution appears to be the same as in traditional autocracies.

In the Soviet-type system, however, there is present yet another mode of wealth distribution that maximizes the rent of two of the four segments of the ruling stratum:

1. Douglas C. North, "A Framework for Analyzing the State in Economic History," *Explorations in Economic History* (1979).

party *apparatchiks* and the economic bureaucracy. This mode — unknown in other systems — enables them to draw benefits through protracted interference in the process of wealth creation itself. There are basically two interconnected ways in which they maximize their rent.

The first is through the well-known principle of *nomenklatura*, or the right of the Communist Party apparatus to recommend and approve appointments for all managerial positions. These appointments have always been made primarily on the basis of loyalty rather than competence, and *apparatchiks* have usually appointed themselves and their card-carrying cronies to those well-paid jobs.

The second means of protracted interference is through various kickbacks from managers of enterprises. In a shortage economy these kickbacks are mostly of a nonpecuniary nature. Enterprise managers offer to those who appointed them, and to other superiors and colleagues who may help them in their career, a variety of goods and services. The managers are also given the chance to benefit in the same way themselves. In a shortage economy, a wide variety of goods and services may be bought in this manner at one time or another.

Both ways of protracted interference in the creation of wealth are made possible by the strikingly nonexclusive structure of property rights. Since nominally the means of production are social property, since workers are "the hegemonic class" in a socialist society, and since the Communist Party is "the leading force of the working class," any appointment through the *nomenklatura* procedure, or any other decision for that matter, can be justified on these grounds. Moreover, it does not matter whether or not property rights were originally devised for the purpose of maximizing rent for the said segments of the ruling stratum under communism. What matters is that they serve this purpose very well.

Since loyalty is the foremost concern, enterprise managers, once appointed, continue to be evaluated on the basis of loyalty in fulfilling commands, guidelines, recommendations, and suggestions of their superiors rather than on the basis of efficiency, that is, rather than on the basis of bottom-line results.

Bureaucrats and *apparatchiks* learned long ago that their wealth does not depend primarily upon the creation of wealth but upon interference in the wealth-creation process. Thus loyalty to superiors is important in the struggles between various coteries within the ruling stratum to position themselves so as to extract more benefits from the inefficient economic system.

Inefficient property rights that erode the wealth base of a country create another conflict, however.

The differentiated modes of rent maximization for the ruling stratum are of primary importance for the prospects of reform in the Soviet-type system. For the reasons stated previously, all segments of the ruling stratum prefer the status quo to the alternative of representative government. But two segments only — party *apparatchiks* and economic bureaucrats — have, in addition, a strong incentive to maintain the institutional status quo in the economic sphere as well. Interest in maintaining the status quo is in sharp contrast to the interest of the rulers — or, nowadays, ruling groups — in Soviet-type states. While small but powerful groups at the top need central planning as a necessary ingredient of both their rule and rent extraction, those on whom they depend to maintain that rule live, in fact, off the existing economic system. The ruling group is representative of the ruling stratum, with all the moral, intellectual, and professional consequences of decades of the system-specific negative selection.

But the ruling group is the only group within the ruling stratum for which the generation of wealth—not only its distribution across the ruling stratum—matters. There is nobody else to whom the buck can be passed. It is they who will be blamed for any failure of the competing groups within the ruling stratum. Being interested in real performance, the ruling group is usually more sensitive to falling efficiency and consequently more ready to reform the economy than the average representative of the ruling stratum.

Thus the ruling group finds itself under both transaction-cost and competitive constraints, as described by North.[2] On the one hand, in periods of declining performance the ruling group feels the transaction-cost constraint. Inefficient property rights do not generate additional wealth, a circumstance that threatens the superpower status of the Soviet Union and leads to internal dissatisfaction in all Soviet-type states.

On the other hand, the ruling group pursuing reforms that require significant revisions in the existing property-rights structure runs the risk that important segments of the ruling stratum will turn to an alternative ruling group ready to challenge the present rulers. Thus the ruling group strongly feels the competitive constraint as well.

Also, it is a special feature of the Soviet-type system that even if the competitive constraint on the rulers is lessened and reforms do begin, it is both the party *apparatchiks* and the economic bureaucrats who are entrusted with the implementation of the reforms. If not aborted or weak-

2. Ibid.

ened from the start, changes may then be sabotaged, distorted, or, finally, reversed.

INCENTIVES FOR THE RULING STRATUM TO LIQUIDATE OR KEEP SMALL THE PRIVATE SECTOR

Expansion of the role of the private sector in the production of goods and services may be regarded as a complement to decentralizing, market-oriented reforms in the state sector aimed at increasing the efficiency of the national economy in the Soviet-type state. In practice, attempts at reforms of the state sector have coincided with increased room for expansion for the private sector. Twists and turns of policy toward the private sector, however, have been even more numerous.

The fact that since the imposition of the Soviet-type system the private sector has been only a marginal contributor to economic growth and efficiency—except in agriculture—is invariably ascribed to ideological hostility.

In my opinion, this ideological explanation of the failure to harness private enterprise to the improvement of the performance of persistently disequilibrated and structurally distorted STEs is highly deficient for two reasons. First, ideological fervor has subsided to some—although differing—extent since the imposition of the system. Second, and more important, ideological hostility has to be overcome first and foremost at the top. It is actually the ruling group that has to confess—indirectly—that the state sector cannot do what the private sector is expected to do with the new policy.[3] The question that should be asked is why lower-level bureaucrats or

3. It is not important whether the state sector is unable at all to do it, or unable to do it at a given price, or merely unwilling to do it.

party *apparatchiks*, whose positions depend not on performance but on loyalty, should sabotage the latest twist of the party line.

My argument, following the property-rights approach, suggests that there must be strong disincentives for certain groups to follow that line. Moreover, not surprisingly, such disincentives are not too difficult to find. Let us look at property rights in the private sector.

There are no well-paid posts to be filled by *nomenklatura* appointments in small private enterprises, nor is there a soft budget constraint — unlimited resources obtained from the state — conducive to the variety of rent-maximizing kickbacks mentioned in the preceding section. A shift of activity from state to private sector, therefore reduces the possibilities for party *apparatchiks* and economic bureaucrats to extract rent from the state sector, which would otherwise turn out these products, probably at a loss, in large — expanded or newly built — state enterprises with many new, well-remunerated *nomenklatura*-covered jobs. The hostility toward the private sector is based here not on the actual losses but on gains forgone, which it would have been possible to extract given the existing structure of property rights in the main sector of the economy.

But the story does not end here. A bureaucrat — or even an *apparatchik* who can indirectly influence each decision — may extract rent by taking a bribe for a concession to set up a private industrial firm or to open a restaurant or a repair shop. But this way of extracting benefits goes against the property-rights structure in the private sector — resources are clearly exclusive there — and is consequently much more dangerous; in plain words, it is a criminal act. By contrast, methods of preying on the state sector either are fully legitimized — for example, through *nomenklatura* and the rationing of goods at the center's order — or, like system-specific kickbacks, belong to the gray area between the improper and the criminal.

New developments in some STEs — foremost in Poland and Hungary — with regard to the private sector prove this point. There is a visible shift of many in the ruling stratum toward the private sector, but without their leaving their positions in the state sector and elsewhere in the ruling stratum. As loyalty-based *nomenklatura* nominations and politically motivated resource allocation continue to flourish there, all the wives of party secretaries, ministers' sons, and police colonels' brothers who open private firms rely not on low-cost production or product superiority in their quest for profit but on political linkages that assure them privileged access to scarce inputs from the state sector. The unchanged state sector, with its pseudomarkets, infects the private sector, and the distorted existence of the latter makes it a fertile ground for rent seeking by the ruling stratum.[4]

It is obvious that really competitive private firms, able to put state firms out of business, continue to be a threat to the ruling stratum. Since such firms would curtail the area of the ruling stratum's rent seeking, the ruling stratum will not allow such a threat to materialize.

HOW TO THROTTLE THE CHANGE:
THE OLSONIAN FREE-RIDER
PROBLEM IN REVERSE

The reader has already learned that the relationship of the ruling group and the ruling stratum is crucial for understanding the process of reform, including the abor-

4. For more on this subject, see J. Winiecki, "A Letter from Eastern Europe: The Expansion of the Private Sector," *Economic Affairs*, 8(6) (1988).

tion or reversal of the reforms, in substance if not necessarily in form. Feeling the transaction-cost constraint, a given ruling group decides upon a certain course of reforms to increase efficiency. Both market-type reforms of the state sector and those making room for the expansion of the private sector adversely affect rent-extraction possibilities of bureaucrats and *apparatchiks.* Consequently, those benefiting from the existing arrangements set themselves upon what I call a "counterreformation" course.

Before explaining when and how various counterreformation measures are attempted, additional comments are necessary. Olson stresses that large groups are not always able to act in accordance with their collective interest.[5] This generally valid point is, however, weakened considerably in this particular case. Thus there is a difference between, on the one hand, a large group that finds it difficult to organize in order to bring pressure to bear upon a government and a ruling party to affect certain outcomes and, on the other, a large group that consists for all practical purposes of a government and a ruling political party or of a major part of both. If such a majority decides to thwart reforms outlined by the ruling group with the assistance of their advisers, the organizational capability of the counterreformers is markedly greater than that of outsiders. Their capability of acting efficiently in their collective interest is even greater relative to organized outsiders.

Counterreformers — those hostile to reforms — often coalesce around one or a few top party figures who think that cracking the whip — tightening discipline and increasing control — is enough to solve the

5. Mancur Olson, *The Logic of Collective Action* (Cambridge, MA: Harvard University Press, 1965); idem, *The Rise and Decline of Nations* (New Haven, CT: Yale University Press, 1982).

problem of failing efficiency. Their capability of acting collectively is, as stressed, much greater for the very reason that theirs is a very unusual interest group.

It should also be remembered that their unusual position as an interest group helps them to throw sand into the machinery of reforms even if they do not act collectively but only individually. They are not members of a potentially strong trade union or of a potentially influential professional association. They effectively govern the Soviet-type state. If a minister or a regional party secretary or a city administrator makes a decision, this decision has serious consequences. For example, some decentralizing reforms are twisted and distorted with respect to all state enterprises in a given industry, or private enterprises are not allowed to be established in a given region. This is an Olsonian free-rider problem in reverse: everyone outside the informally organized group of counterreformers brings in his or her valuable contribution to the common course.

Although the effort expended on thwarting economic reforms may be different at different stages, circumstances make it impossible for the interested parties to choose at any given moment the best solution.

Therefore, it is evident that (1) aborting reforms is less costly, in terms of effort expended by the interested parties, than reversing them later, and (2) reversing more inconsistent reforms — with inconsistency consciously built into the system's modifications — is less costly than reversing less inconsistent reforms. Aborting reforms is not construed here to mean that no changes whatsoever are introduced. It means that the actual changes do not threaten the property-rights structure in the state sector that allows party *apparatchiks* and the economic bureaucracy to continue to maximize their rent according to the system-specific mode of wealth distribution. They also do not alter substantially either institutions or procedures of central planning.

The second-best solution is to introduce quasi reforms, that is, reforms that are so inconsistent internally that they are doomed to fail. Such reforms increase somewhat the effort expended by party *apparatchiks* and the economic bureaucracy in controlling economic activity, but that increase is only temporary, since reversal of the reforms is assured by problems arising out of the inevitable contradictions of inconsistently modified systems. In any case, the structure of property rights remains intact.

The worst for the parties concerned are the extreme situations — such as in Poland in the period 1981-82 — when, under popular pressure for reforms combined with the disastrous economic situation, the ruling group has to give in on economic reforms to an extent unacceptable even for the ruling group in order to deflect pressure for political reforms. In Poland the pressure for the latter did not abate, however, and martial law had to be introduced to stave off fundamental change.

IN LIEU OF CONCLUSIONS

The previous considerations should not be construed to mean that the possibilities for market change in the Soviet-type states are nil. They have been made much more difficult than elsewhere in predatory states, given the very specific interface between political and economic spheres. But under certain conditions, like those of the long-term, multifaceted — not only economic! — decline that affects all East European STEs, political changes may positively affect the chances of success for economic changes.

Elsewhere I have described two scenarios of positive change.[6] The first involves the breakdown of consensus within the ruling stratum and the defeat of those interested not just in maintaining political power but also in preserving the existing structure of property rights in the economic sphere, namely, party *apparatchiks* and economic bureaucrats.

A second scenario assumes a gradual withdrawal by the Communist Party, as the decline drags on and the costs of maintaining the existing system become heavier over time in terms of falling absolute wealth and increased effort expended on controlling economic and noneconomic activities. Since the decline of the Soviet-type states is a multifaceted one, combining falling living standards, rapidly increasing pollution, increasing mortality, and so forth, many hard questions will be asked within the ruling groups and the ruling strata in these states. Societies will become more restive as well. Accordingly, the probability that these — and other, even more daring — scenarios will actually occur will increase in the years to come.

6. In particular, J. Winiecki, "Soviet-Type Economies: Considerations for the Future," *Soviet Studies*, 1986, no, 6; idem, *Economic Prospects: East and West* (London: Centre for Research into Communist Economies, 1987).

Computation, Incentives, and Discovery: The Cognitive Function of Markets in Market Socialism

By DON LAVOIE

ABSTRACT: Decisive for the question of the feasibility of various versions of market socialism is the issue of the basic cognitive function markets are expected to provide. Three increasingly comprehensive interpretations of the cognitive function of markets, labeled computation, incentives, and discovery, are described and contrasted. Depending on how the basic cognitive role of markets is interpreted, very different judgments are possible on the feasibility of market socialism. Two types of market socialism are examined in terms of these approaches, and their shortcomings are attributed to their incomplete appreciation of the way knowledge is created, discovered, and conveyed in market processes.

Don Lavoie received a bachelor of science degree in computer science from Worcester Polytechnic Institute in 1973 and a Ph.D. in economics from New York University in 1981. He is currently editor of the scholarly publication Market Process *and an associate professor of economics at George Mason University.*

MARKET socialism is a concept that immediately demands an effort of reconciliation. Traditional interpretations of socialism, under the influence of Karl Marx, were extremely antagonistic to market institutions, so that socialism has had to accommodate itself gradually, in the face of both theoretical and practical considerations, to various elements of markets.[1] The theoretical circumstances involved the attempts in the 1930s to respond to the so-called calculation argument, formulated by Ludwig von Mises and elaborated by his most famous student, F. A. Hayek.[2] This argument could be described in general terms as a claim that the price system provides an indispensable cognitive aid to economic decision making. The early work in response to this challenge by Oskar Lange and others, even though it introduced only very limited elements of markets into socialism, was met with scorn by the purists on both sides. Today, in the age of *perestroika*, we are used to the idea of combining certain conceptions of socialism with certain elements of markets. The issue is no longer whether socialism needs to come to terms with market forms, but how, exactly, it should do so.

The task of this article is to facilitate answering the question of how to combine markets and socialism by asking the more fundamental question of why: Why does socialism need markets in the first place? What exactly is the cognitive function mar-

kets serve for capitalism that socialism needs to retain? Which models of market socialism we consider feasible depends on the way we conceive the function markets are supposed to perform.

WHAT ARE MARKETS FOR?

There is a wide variety of visions of the institutional specifics of systems that could reasonably be called market-socialist. Before we can decisively establish which of these might be feasible we need to clarify what exactly socialism needs to obtain from market institutions.

Economists largely agree that the price system is a vital source of information for decision making. Scarce resources, by which economists mean anything that is not so abundant as to be a free good, need to be allocated in regard to their relative scarcity, and this is at least approximately gauged quantitatively in money prices. Alec Nove, in his well-known study *The Economics of Feasible Socialism,* presents a colorful example to illustrate the basic need for markets.

Suppose that the number of people in Scotland wishing to fish for salmon in the rivers grossly exceeds the number of rivers and salmon available. At present (let us say) payment must be made to a duke for permission to fish, and this helps the said duke to be rich. Suppose one eliminates the duke. This makes no difference either to the desire of the citizens to fish or to the number of rivers and salmon in Scotland. So either the numbers who fish will be limited by a permit system (therefore there will be queues, string-pulling, influence, etc.) or a charge will be made. The charge may even be identical to that levied by the duke. Only now it is a rent which is used to cover social expenditures, not an individual's unearned income.[3]

1. Space will not permit me to take up the empirical issues here, but I would point out that when the theoretical controversy began, it was already tainted by Soviet experience. Mises's original 1920 challenge was shaped by his interpretation of empirical events in Lenin's unsuccessful experiment with "war communism."

2. Elsewhere I have discussed this theoretical debate at more length. See Don Lavoie, *Rivalry and Central Planning* (New York: Cambridge University Press, 1985).

3. Alec Nove, *The Economics of Feasible Socialism* (London: George Allen & Unwin, 1983), pp. 213-14.

Apart from the question of the justice of the practice of paying so-called unearned incomes such as rent and interest, there is the economic fact that these charges serve a vital coordinative function, both locally and globally. Locally, the salmon fishing market clears, and suppliers and demanders of fishing permits come into coordination. Globally, people in related markets — say, tourist agencies and seafood restaurants — can calculate the price of fishing permits into their decisions.

Against the orthodox Marxist, who considers such categories as rent or interest bourgeois and irrelevant to socialism, Nove points out that keeping track of relative prices of scarce resources, whether labor services or any other, is essential for any feasible form of socialism. Markets provide a cognitive aid, in this sense, without which economic activity would be prohibitively inefficient. Where economists disagree is in regard to the precise nature of this cognitive aid.

This article takes up three distinct interpretations of the cognitive function of markets, proceeding from what I consider the most simplistic to the most sophisticated. The three views all contend that the price system is a crucial knowledge medium. They differ over just exactly what the price system involves and what specific kind of cognitive function it serves. Accordingly, they also differ over which conceivable institutional arrangements for market socialism they would suggest are feasible, in the sense of which can reproduce this cognitive function.

The first view, which I shall call the computation approach, takes the cognitive contribution of markets to be a strictly calculative one, equivalent to following a pre-programmed algorithm, step by step. Oskar Lange, the great Polish economist and father of market socialism, is the best-known adherent of this view. The second view, which I shall call the incentives approach, understands the cognitive function as not only a calculative matter but also a matter of psychological motivation, of supplying sufficient rewards to individual agents to get them to exert themselves. Alec Nove is one of the many well-known market socialists who take this approach. The third perspective, the discovery approach, I take from market socialism's greatest living critic, F. A. Hayek.[4] This approach sees the cognitive function of markets as involving the creation, discovery, and communication of knowledge, a social learning process that is akin to verbal conversation. The market, in this view, does involve calculative and motivational aspects. What is crucial to its cognitive function, however, is that it provides a discovery process that by its very nature cannot be centrally directed but depends on a bidirectional communicative interplay between its participants.

COMPUTATION: FROM COMPUTOPIA TO AGORIC SYSTEMS

At root, it is the arithmetic calculation of potential or past profit or loss in terms of money prices that directly provides the cognitive aid to decision makers that socialism requires. The three approaches would agree that there is in this sense an important calculative aspect to the cognitive contribution of markets. We need to calculate with an accurate measure of the relative scarcity of each resource so that we, like the duke, can avoid either over- or underharvesting our salmon. Those non-market forms of socialism that used to

4. F. A. Hayek, "Competition as a Discovery Procedure," in *New Studies in Philosophy, Politics, Economics and the History of Ideas* (Chicago: University of Chicago Press, 1978), pp. 179-90.

argue for the abolition of money needed to be reminded that the cognitive function markets serve requires that profit-loss calculation take place in terms of a common denominator. There can be no systematic comparison of alternative production techniques without cost calculations in money units, and these at base involve matters of simple arithmetic.

What distinguishes what I am calling the computation approach from the others is its reduction of the cognitive problem that market socialism needs to solve to this strictly calculative aspect. The problem is a matter of simple, linear computation, of working out, step by step, an algorithm for solving a system of simultaneous equations.

If simple computation were the sort of cognitive problem that markets are supposed to solve, then a wide variety of market socialisms, many of which are widely considered utopian, should be feasible. If the cognitive function of markets were only computational, then very few elements of capitalistic markets would need to be borrowed to make socialism work. For example, one of the most interesting variants of market socialism, although it appears to have few serious advocates as a practical policy, is what has been derisively labeled computopia, an image of an economy being centrally planned by a massive computer. The idea of computopia is to replace genuine markets completely in the means of production with a single, centralized computer system, which solves a gigantic maximization problem. Even those who consider computopia to be a matter of science fiction would admit that it, like good fiction, raises interesting questions. Of what significance, for example, is the dramatic development, over the past few decades, of the field of computer science? Do the undeniably rapid advances in computer science suggest that even if this computopia is farfetched now, it might become a realistic alternative in the future?

It was the opinion of Oskar Lange that computers offer such a promise. In 1933 it had been proposed by H. D. Dickinson that the cognitive problem facing the central planning board was one that could be dealt with "mathematically."[5] To this F. A. Hayek and his colleague at the London School of Economics, Lionel Robbins, responded that the central planners would face, among other difficulties, an enormous computational problem, a matter of solving a system of hundreds of thousands or millions of simultaneous equations.[6] It was in answer to Hayek and Robbins that Oskar Lange devised his model of what later came to be called market socialism in his famous 1936 essay.[7] In 1967 Lange, reflecting on his original model of market socialism, suggested that computers would have made things much easier for his side in the debate.

Were I to rewrite my essay today, my task would be much simpler. My answer to Hayek and Robbins would be: so what's the trouble? Let us put the simultaneous equations on an electronic computer and we shall obtain the solution in less than a second. The market process with its cumbersome tâtonnements appears old-fashioned. Indeed, it may be considered as a computing device of the pre-electronic age.[8]

5. Henry Douglas Dickinson, "Price Formation in a Socialist Community," *Economic Journal*, 43:242 (1933).

6. F. A. Hayek, "The Present State of the Debate," reprinted in *Individualism and Economic Order* (Chicago: University of Chicago Press, 1948); Lionel Robbins, *The Great Depression* (New York: Macmillan, 1934), pp. 148-59.

7. Oskar Lange, "On the Economic Theory of Socialism," reprinted in *On the Economic Theory of Socialism*, ed. Benjamin E. Lippincott (New York: McGraw-Hill, 1964), pp. 57-143.

8. Oskar Lange, "The Computer and the Market," in *Socialism, Capitalism and Economic Growth:*

Most contemporary market socialists are more skeptical than Lange was of the plausibility, even in the distant future, of implementing a computopian system that could actually solve an economy's cognitive problem. But Lange's conceptualization of the market's cognitive function as essentially a problem of linear computation, albeit perhaps an extremely complicated one, is more widely shared.

The subsequent sections of this article will refer to some crucial aspects of markets that the computation approach leaves out, so there is no need to criticize it here, but there is an interesting ironic twist I would like to add to Lange's quoted comments about computation and the market. Developments that have been taking place in the field of computer science, especially in its subdiscipline, artificial intelligence, argue for precisely the reverse relationship between computers and markets. Markets are not, as Lange thought, primitive precursors to present-day computers, which we can expect to be replaced, eventually, by a centralized computopia. On the contrary, present-day computers can be seen as primitive, central-planning approaches to computation, to be replaced, eventually, by decentralized market approaches.

In the work of B. A. Huberman and his colleagues at the Xerox Palo Alto Research Center, computation is itself being reconsidered, and experimental work is under way to introduce market principles into computational processes. After all, as Lange admitted, "even the most powerful electronic computers have a limited capacity," that is, there are scarce computational resources in need of careful allocation. Especially interesting is the research on agoric systems, named after the Greek word

for "market," by Mark S. Miller and K. Eric Drexler. Basing their analysis directly on Hayek's work on knowledge, they propose to use price information within computers to better allocate the various kinds of resources, such as central-processing-unit time, disc space, and core space, according to their relative scarcities.[9] They contend that whatever degree of intelligence computers have, it is best used not by substituting for, but by integrating with, human markets. Future computer systems, these writers believe, will constitute interactive networks, competitively renting computational services to one another on the basis of freely flexible prices based on current supply and demand conditions. We may one day live in a highly computerized world, but it is likely to be a world at least as dependent on the cognitive contribution of markets as ours is today.

INCENTIVES: SOCIAL OWNERSHIP AND THE PROFIT MOTIVE

The dominant view among contemporary advocates of market socialism is that whatever it is that markets do, it is more than a linear computational task. There is more to the price system than a set of numbers ready for arithmetic operations, just as there is more to profit-loss accounting than accurate addition and subtraction. The incentives approach points out that profit and loss need not only to be calculated; they need to be offered as concrete incentives to decision makers. Whoever offers real services to the economy needs to be induced to do so by, among other possible rewards, flows of money incomes.

Essays Presented to Maurice Dobb, ed. C. H. Feinstein (New York: Cambridge University Press, 1967), p. 158.

9. Mark S. Miller and K. Eric Drexler, "Markets and Computation: Agoric Open Systems," in *The Ecology of Computation*, ed. B. A. Huberman (New York: North-Holland, 1988), pp. 133-76.

This concession to the need for price incentives does not imply a complete retreat to capitalism. The classical socialist opposition to unearned income, that is, income earned from private ownership of the means of production, can still be reconciled with this view of markets as necessary incentive devices. Capital goods are scarce and need to be priced and husbanded accordingly, but, it can be argued, this does not imply that those who are paid this price must be private owners. Many models of market socialism propose a system of social ownership, where the state is the sole or principal owner of the means of production but where it is obliged to rely on prices and price incentives to deploy those means of production intelligently.

In other words, just because some kinds of monetary incentives are needed to call forth socially beneficial efforts, it does not necessarily follow that all the kinds of incentives traditionally offered under capitalism are required. Alec Nove introduced his salmon example to suggest that in fact we should "[eliminate] the duke," that is, stop paying income to people purely by virtue of their ownership. Calculations need to be undertaken that take proper account of the scarcity of nonlabor resources, using such categories as profits, interest, and rent, but nobody needs to be paid in these categories. The state can collect these forms of income, as Nove put it, "to cover social expenditures." To the extent that the duke does something, say, to maintain the river, his efforts can be rewarded with wages, just like anybody else's. But since as an owner, it is argued, he does not actually do anything, he does not need to be induced by a profit motive to put in his noneffort. He should not be able to extort society for the use of his river.

Of course, there is the question of whether agents of the state might not themselves become powerful extortionists. But if we leave such public-choice considerations aside, there seems to be no reason to assume that a market-socialist system could not be arranged to induce significant exertions by most of the labor force. If competitiveness is nothing but a mental attitude that is conducive to productivity, then it can be arranged artificially, as it is in a sporting match. The phrase "profit motive" prompts the idea that the cognitive problem that markets solve is a matter of psychology, a problem of inducing effort, of getting people psyched. Presumably, in the wake of a socialist revolution one could expect psychological motivations to be quite high. If the incentive approach is right, then most models of market socialism other than the computopia variety appear to be feasible in principle.

DISCOVERY: THE MARKET AS A DIALOGICAL LEARNING PROCESS

From the point of view that I am calling the discovery approach, the cognitive function of markets is not exhausted by its calculative and motivational aspects. The problem is a matter neither of mathematics nor of psychology. What the computation and incentive approaches have in common is their focus on the point of view of the single mind, what might be called a monological as opposed to a dialogical approach.[10] Robinson Crusoe would need to calculate in some manner — for example, in labor hours — to husband his scarce resources, even if monetary calculation is not open to him. In addition, he would require psychological incentives to induce him to

10. Richard J. Bernstein uses this distinction between monological and dialogical approaches in the context of the philosophy of science in his *Beyond Objectivism and Relativism: Science, Hermeneutics, and Praxis* (Philadelphia: University of Pennsylvania Press, 1983).

exert himself. If he is lethargic, perhaps the arrival of Friday would encourage a certain competitive spirit, but more or less the same result could be achieved without introducing society, for example, by the use of a stopwatch.

The discovery approach, on the other hand, considers the cognitive function of markets to be, like the process of human discourse in language, an intrinsically social process. Like verbal conversation, the dialogue of the market depends on the specific give-and-take of interaction, a creative process of interplay in which the knowledge that emerges exceeds that of any of the participants. As with conversation, the communicative power of the market is not limited to what is explicitly articulated in words or prices but depends on background understandings shared in a speaking or trading community. Prices carry knowledge by triggering background understandings involving, for example, the value of the monetary unit, the expected marketability of a product, the credit worthiness of a bank's customer, the recognizability of a brand name, and so forth.

Competition is not seen as a psychological attitude but as a creative learning process among minds. My rival does not merely perform a stopwatch function, providing me with a benchmark for my motivation. He may also inform my actions by steering me into more appropriate decisions. Competition is, as Hayek put it, a discovery procedure, where the rivalrous pulls and tugs of the contrary plans of individual participants impart knowledge to the overall social system. This knowledge, as encapsulated in prices, serves in turn to guide the decisions of individual participants. There is thus a bidirectional communicative process that produces a kind of social intelligence that depends on,

but goes beyond, the individual intelligences of the system's participants.[11]

Profit in this view is not so much an inducement to effort as a signal about where opportunities lie. The role of profits is not primarily to motivate people to do the right thing but to find out, through the process of interplay itself, what the right thing to do might be. Price incentives are not tools that the central planner can effectively use to get people to exert themselves; they are our spontaneously grown economic maps. None of us can design the maps, yet they result from our actions and are the only way any of us has of orienting our activities to those of others.

This way of looking at markets raises a challenge to the socialist condemnation of unearned incomes. Incomes from property ownership are information-carrying money flows, just as incomes from labor services are. The question of incentives for exerting effort is not the central issue. The process of competitive interplay between separate owners in a real estate market provides rental price information about the value of alternative uses of the property. "[Eliminating] the duke," that is, replacing the dialogical process of interacting private owners with a single, monological social owner, would only eliminate the very give-and-take process that generates the price information.[12]

Models of market socialism have tended to be made on the basis of an overly narrow formulation of the cognitive prob-

11. I have discussed the idea of social intelligence in my book *National Economic Planning: What Is Left?* (Cambridge, MA: Ballinger, 1985).

12. Of course, this may be taking the idea of social ownership rather too seriously. What happens in practice when ownership is nationalized is not some sort of mysterious unification of interests aimed at applying flows of resources to commonly agreed-upon so-

lem that markets need to solve, implicitly following either the computation or the incentive approach. As a result they have not appreciated the role that competition between private owners of the means of production plays in the market process. The discovery approach suggests that socialism needs to accommodate itself not only to profits as abstract numbers and to profits as psychological incentives for labor services but also to profits as returns to separate, private owners of nonlabor resources.

---

cial expenditures. State ownership does not mean an elimination of the private pursuit of competitive advantage among separate individuals but a rechanneling of competitive struggle from market to political strategies.

Why Is the Plan Incompatible with the Market?

By LARISSA POPKOVA-PIJASHEVA

ABSTRACT: Central administrative command planning and the market system are incompatible due to (1) the ex ante versus ex post method of pricing in the two systems; (2) the antithetical relation of mandatory instructions and economic freedom; and (3) the inability of state capital to compete successfully with private capital. No in-between construct of a socialist market system is viable. It has to be either plan or market.

Larissa Popkova-Pijasheva is candidate of economics and senior researcher at the Institute of World Labor Movement under the USSR Academy of Sciences. She is author of International Economic Theory and Practice of Social Reformism *(1984) and coauthor, with Boris Pinsker, of* Economic Neoconservatism: Theory and International Practice *(1984).*

I do not presume to deny the possibility of planning the activities of a private or a state firm. Any entrepreneur calculates both his expected expenditures and his profits, which enables him to make strategic decisions with regard to investments, updating, rationalization, or production cuts. Neither do I underestimate the part the state plays in regulating economic life, leveling cyclical fluctuations and mitigating the consequences of crises, providing for insurance against unemployment, and other steps it takes that indirectly influence the economic process through a mechanism of credit-monetary, tax, and social policy.

Neither do I claim that the state, under conditions of a market economy, is unable to plan its budget and distribute its revenue according to a plan approved and ratified by the Congress. Nor do I call into question the state's participation in private, mixed, or state-controlled long-term research projects of technological development. Neither do I rule out the possibility of indicative planning, of making up a plan-prognosis based on market analysis.

All these forms of planning and state management coexist in the economic life of the market system and fulfill their stabilizing, regulating, or orienting function.

The present article deals with none of these forms of planning. It postulates that the idea of planning the entire economic process is incompatible either with the market institutions of property and power or with the market mechanism of regulating the economic processes.

INCOMPATIBILITY OF CENTRAL PLANNING AND THE MARKET SYSTEM

The main point is that the five-year plans of economic development — either with monthly, quarterly, or yearly specification or without it — which are sent from the top to the bottom as binding directives, are incompatible with market-economy institutions.

It is either the State Planning Committee, the State Price-Control Committee, and the State Committee for Labor and Social Problems, or it is the stock exchange, the labor and capital markets, the joint-stock company, and so on. The two camps cannot actually coexist within the framework of a single mixed-management mechanism. Neither is it possible to solve specific socioeconomic problems under conditions of the existing centralization, which is treated as a rather abstract conception of society at large. And despite the fact that the planned character of the economy along with all-encompassing centralization have always been regarded as the primary virtues and advantages of socialism by our mainstream theorists, it is precisely the absence of a systematic character in activities, the disproportion in economic life, and the lack of centered effort in confronting such global issues as, for instance, ecology that can be thought of almost as inherent in the socialist system. Wherever environmental problems are put in care of society as a whole, whose noble aim is common well-being, the factory chimneys will emit more smoke and nuclear accidents will be more frequent than in a society of market "anarchy" and individual responsibility, in which there is a person responsible for any smoking chimney or any nuclear incident, a person who would pay for his or her carelessness both financially and juridically.

REASONS FOR PLAN-MARKET INCOMPATIBILITY

There are a number of reasons why the socialist planning system is incompatible with market institutions.

Valuation

The central principle of distribution in a planned system is "according to labor performed": "From each according to his ability, to each according to his work." But the very concept of socially useful[1] labor in a socialist economy is different in principle from that accepted by economic theory in general. Socially useful labor is not that which has been acknowledged by the market and paid for by the consumer, but that which has been performed to fulfill the plan.

In a planned economy, any labor aimed at fulfilling the plan is regarded as socially useful and has to be paid for. The usefulness of a manufactured product is recognized in advance by the very fact of entering it in a plan. Is the mechanism of determining the social usefulness of output beforehand compatible with the market system, which does not acknowledge the result of production until it is sold and paid for by the consumer? It certainly is not. Usefulness can be determined either by the very fact of entering a product in the plan in advance or after the realization of the output, but never in combination.

Why not? Primarily because the planned economy presupposes full employment; it guarantees remuneration of any work performed by anyone employed irrespective of the result of his or her labor, that is, of its social usefulness. If one has fulfilled the plan task, one receives one's wages — in certain cases, even bonuses. If one has not, one receives only wages, which are guaranteed by law.

As soon as the system is restructured and wages are paid after the realization of output, a certain number of workers are inevitably left out of the production process, since the planned economy presup-

poses a good deal of low-quality commodities without demand. As soon as the market mechanism of evolution and selection starts working, all excess labor will be automatically released — this mechanism is only too well known to the Western reader. But this will inevitably run counter to the proclaimed basic principle of full employment and that of every worker's having his or her place of work and minimum wages guaranteed. Where labor is remunerated according to its final results, and thus unprofitable enterprises lose their position on the market through bankruptcy, ruin, merger, and so forth, we inevitably face the problem of some alternative — that is, outside the state sector — uses of labor and capital. That would be tantamount to the elimination of the state's monopoly of property, which has always been regarded as one of the gains of socialism. This would raise the question of transition to some other pattern of property and power, namely, the market, or capitalist, pattern.

Command versus economic freedom

The second reason why the market-economy principle is incompatible with the planned-economy principle is that the directives in the form of plan tasks[2] have to be executed and fulfilled no matter whether they come down in the old way, as plan tasks, or in the new form, as state orders. In both cases they are subject to fulfillment, for in the USSR a plan is a law approved by the Council of Ministers. Besides this, quotas for raw materials, equipment, and machinery are adjusted to and come down together with these plans. The latter practice accounts for the fact that enterprises find it profitable to receive a 100 percent state order. This is so because the absence of an open market of wholesale

---

1. Socially necessary [ed.].

2. Norms, targets [ed.].

trade and the actual impossibility of purchasing the needed raw materials and matériel either on the internal or on the external market, deprive the enterprises of the possibility to make up a portfolio of orders that they find profitable.

No entrepreneur, no firm under the conditions of a market economy, would submit to state planning. No proprietor would obey the directives as regards production and sale or would tolerate being told what range of goods he should manufacture and what their quality should be. The most he would do would be to include the order in his portfolio and avail himself of the advantages the customer would thereby give him. But he would never let any such customer interfere with the firm's financial matters, its commercial strategy, or its relations with other suppliers and customers. The producer reserves the right to turn down any state order if he finds it wasteful or simply unprofitable. The market economy, with its principle of private property, is beyond nationwide state planning, no matter how much the ruling circles wish it were under their control.

This is not the case with the planned economy where there is no private property in the means of production and where enterprises have the right neither to develop a commercial strategy of their own nor to have any commercial secrets, not even to appropriate their own profits. In the socialist economy it is the state that plans the economic process for every five-year period — with annual, quarterly, and monthly quotas — and sends down the binding plan directives to all branches and ministries, which then distribute these directives among individual enterprises. The ministry reserves the right to correct the plan tasks: to raise plan norms for one enterprise and to lower the norms of another, that is, to make some transfers, so to speak, depend-

ing on the specific economic and financial situation. But no enterprise is allowed either to conclude a contract — unless it is sanctioned by the ministry — or to turn down a plan task. The forthcoming reform envisages a certain compromise in this respect. Not until the problem of a wholesale trade market is solved, however, can the problem be really solved.

In the absence of economic freedom — of the right to dispose of one's own earnings, to determine one's own commercial strategy, to make up one's own portfolio of orders, to have a free choice of suppliers and customers, to purchase all that is needed on the domestic or foreign market, and to fix prices according to the state of the market — there can only be such a form of self-supporting management — self-financing — that may be defined in terms of "it would be desirable . . . " or "we should. . . . "

As long as an enterprise that does not have these freedoms — which are inherent in the market economy — is given binding state orders, or plans; as long as all normative indices — the fixing of the wages fund, the rationing of employment and specification of rates of productivity growth, and even regulation of profitability level — are centrally planned; and as long as the domestic wholesale commerce market is not open — which means that enterprises are not allowed to buy raw materials, matériel, equipment, machinery, and all kinds of technological know-how on the foreign market — a switch from plan-based administrative management to economic methods that could replace the former is impossible.

It is either the plan or the market. Just as a plan cannot be a little bit a market plan, a market cannot be a little bit planned or an enterprise a little bit free. Either prices call the tune — that is, credits, taxes and monetary privileges, or sanctions are used by the state as levers of regulation — or the State Planning Committee shapes our economic life according to its science-based conceptions, planning our needs and demands as well as bringing them into correlation with actual possibilities. There is no third way.

The plan is incompatible with the market system because there is no actual possibility of calculating the right prices and of correlating them with a science-based plan.

In the market economy it is pricing that regulates the production process, shapes its structure, and does away with economic disproportions. In the planned economy, instead, the regulating function is performed by a plan, which is supposed to define the necessary proportions and to shape the production structures according to those proportions. What about a kind of mixed economy that would represent a combination of the two principles?

If we mean the degree of market character that is envisaged by the new economic reform, and that presupposes a science-based planning of the right structure of calculated prices, there is actually nothing to talk about. The injection of commodity-money relations that has been suggested up to now will bring about no radical changes. If we raise the question of compatibility of plan and market principles with all seriousness, however, we shall inevitably speak about the use of what V. V. Novozhilov termed a "double regulator of social production,"[3] or, more simply, about a combination of two different management mechanisms. A precondition of a coordinated interaction of the two will be a correlation between plan tasks, on the one hand, and the balance that responds automatically to a supply-demand correlation

on the market in full compliance with the law of value. But in order to calculate the plan task in advance one should know beforehand what the prices will be, that is, the calculated prices are to correspond to market prices in balance. Here lies the primary problem of any planning and administrative management methods, which is the actual impossibility of calculating prices correctly to determine the right proportions, to distribute resources in accordance with those prices, and to ensure the needed rates of growth.

Were it technically possible to calculate all operations in economic life minute by minute and to plan the economic process at least a year ahead — to say nothing of planning for a five-year or a ten-year period — we would not be facing today, as we did yesterday, a badly needed *perestroika*, an all-encompassing economic reform aimed at broadening the sphere of commodity-money relations.

Were it possible to set things straight through planning, the socialist community would not be facing the need for a switch to economic management methods, which it has always faced with the same immutable recurrency.

The experience of all socialist countries that have done their best to put into practice Marx's idea of a planned economy has corroborated only too well the thesis put forward as early as the 1920s by B. D. Brutskus, who held that the economic problem was in principle insoluble under Marxist socialism.[4] His central idea was that economic life cannot be planned in advance, as the very development of the human organism cannot be, nor can that of any evolutionary process in nature itself.

The latter cannot be predicted because the secret wisdom of a human — or any

3. V. V. Novozhilov, *Problems of Development of Socialist Economy* (Moscow: Nauka, 1972), p. 292.

4. B. D. Brutskus, "Problems of National Economy under Socialism," *Economist*, 1922, nos. 1-3.

other living — organism is beyond understanding. This is the case with economics as well, for it is technically impossible to calculate the losses and to bring them into a correlation with the results at all points of the economic system. Besides, the very unit of measurement needed for such calculations is not easy to find.

This problem has been a stumbling block for many a prominent and experienced economist — V. V. Novozhilov, Nemtchinov, and others — who arrived at no positive result; they failed to model a calculated analogy of the market, find a substitute for the system of market pricing, or introduce some new stimuli that could replace competition. A negative result is still a result, as is only too well known. In scientific practice there is such a concept as a blind-alley direction. As soon as it has become obvious that one has come to a blind alley, one stops experimenting and one looks for reasonable alternatives. That was not the case with Marxist political economy. After having discarded the economics — labeled "bourgeois pseudo-science" — it became a theory that does nothing but repeat over and over again its hackneyed ideological formulas. One of the dogmas is the alleged solvability, in principle, of the market problem provided it is replaced by the plan, which supposedly would do away with market anarchy. In today's slightly made-up form, it would look like the possibility of combining plan and market, of introducing some elements of the market system, such as self-financing, self-repayment, and greater economic freedom of enterprises — all this envisaging no change in the system itself, that is, in its property and power institutions.

There is a popular belief in our official circles — including those of experts — that, without any violation of socialist principles — state property, controlled prices, full employment, and so on — we can inject into our economy some elements of market relations as just a working tool that would in no way affect or change the institutional forms of the social system.

The market cannot be a working tool, however, unless the economy is demonopolized. Wherever there is monopoly there can be no market since there is neither competition nor "struggle" for the consumer. The principle is valid for any economic system.

The socialist economy, which has done away with private property and private enterprises or companies, freed all its enterprises from any competition.

Certainly, if we give the situation a strictly scientific analysis, we have to admit that the planned socialist economy may be regarded as a particular case of market economy with underdeveloped institutions of commodity-money exchange, an entirely monopolized structure, a specific — monopolized — market with fixed prices, and a very peculiar fierce socialist competition for state limits,[5] funds, state subsidies, and a characteristic socialist competitiveness of enterprises for diplomas, badges, and titles of shock workers.

This somehow blurs the distinction — a very fundamental one — between the two systems: one that is market liberal — that is, capitalist, in Weber's view of capitalism as a society with free competition and private entrepreneurship — and the other, totally monopolistic — that is, socialist, in Marx's conception of socialism as a society with nationalized ownership, confining more and more the sphere of commodity-money relations, which are supposed to die out in the long run. I do not see any justification for such an identification.

5. Inputs [ed.].

The socialist market may be represented as a mirror image of the capitalist market. In the latter, goods are in search of consumers. In the former, the buyer seeks the goods. On the capitalist market, supply, as a rule, exceeds demand by far. On the socialist market, the very opposite is true: demand nearly always exceeds supply, which accounts for shortages, deficits, long lines, and the black market.

I do not claim that it serves no useful purpose to write treatises on the socialist market. In the larger context of economic theory our state of affairs may be treated as a particular case of economic life held captive by plan-oriented anarchy, hobbled by directives, and nailed to the calculative rates.[6] The title of the treatise might as well be "A Market under Conditions of Planned Prices and in a Monopolistic Structure of Ownership and Power." Whatever the title might be, it would focus on problems such as the shadow economy, the black market, Mafia-like structures, bribery, favoritism, and lines and shortages rather than on traditional economic issues.

In my opinion, free price formation is a sine qua non of any market system. The self-financing system[7] will not be viable if the state reserves the right to fix prices, to dictate them to both producer and consumer, and if it goes out of its way to neutralize the black marketeers who play the part of regulator of what has always been spontaneously regulated on the market. Free pricing is the primary and most fundamental precondition for a switch to a new economy: prices must be determined on the market as a result of the interaction of demand and supply, which reflects any marketing and structural fluctuations in production and responds to any changes in consumer demand. But, clearly, all this

6. Planner-determined prices [ed.].
7. Economic self-accounting [ed.].

runs counter to the interests of the State Planning Committee, which sees its function as the planning of production on the basis of calculated, stable prices. In other words, it is either the market or the State Planning Committee. We cannot get away from this dilemma.

State versus private capital

Another reason why the plan is incompatible with the market is that state capital can in no way successfully compete with private capital. The practice of both capitalist and socialist economies witnesses to the fact that private capital is more profitable and more efficient than state capital. Private capital has these qualities for the simple reason that it is more flexible and more mobile and because it admits of all kinds of risks as regards its investment. State capital and private capital can hardly coexist because the deployment of private entrepreneurship would inevitably exclude any state production from economic life, and a number of people would have not only to forgo their ideological principles but also to leave their cushy jobs in the hierarchical system of administrative power. Under conditions of fair competition — that is, where the state and private investors are on an equal footing — it is private capital that will inevitably call the tune. If we opt for this solution, all our socialist gains will fall into oblivion. Instead we shall have gains of other kinds: shop windows will be crammed with goods, all sorts of services will flourish, and food shortages will be a thing of the past, while our mode of life will become easier and more comfortable. The public health system will be much more adequate, young people will be interested in getting good training because many new channels and ways of social advancement will have been opened for them. But this general progress will have nothing to do with nationalized ownership, or with the socialist law of planned and proportional development, or with free public consumption funds, or even with other so-called achievements proclaimed by the socialist ideologists.

What makes our ideologists, who have always failed to plan the country's economic life, try so hard to develop a model of a mixed economy and thereby solve an extremely complicated economic problem? What makes them want to work out a model of market economy without capitalism; to form a market with no private-property institutions and without a political mechanism that would protect this market, a democratic power system; without its ideology, the spirit of enterprise; and without its main protagonist, the entrepreneur, who works jointly with Schumpeter's innovator; without, that is to say, all the factors that constitute what is termed economic liberalism? Why do we speak about an artificial model of the market economy that would know no economic liberalism but, on the contrary, centralization and dictatorship? G. Popov characterized this new pattern of a mixed economy as "economic centralism." The term is rather apt for it gives a clear picture of what is sought: a market-economy model within the limits of a planned dictatorship. In my opinion, the problem cannot be solved within the framework of traditional economic theory.

What makes the problem of combining plan and market so very urgent? The answer is simple. The plan — the law — is an expression of the omnipotence of our party, which exercises unlimited control over all economic life. Giving up centralized management and the planning system would be tantamount to giving up political power. That is why *perestroika* ideologists go out

of their way to try and make the incompatible compatible: to leave intact the plan-based centralized principle and at the same time to open the market; to introduce freedom of trade, thereby attaining acceleration of rates of development, but not allow the private traders to enrich themselves. They are ready to grant the right of private enterprise and initiative to all, but not to permit any social differentiation or inequality in the distribution of earnings.

What is the main function performed by the market? It is that of distribution. By reflecting in prices supply-demand relations, the market constantly aims at a balance in which all output would meet its consumer and would thus be recognized by society. Under conditions of the planned economy this market function — performed in the market system quite by itself and quite efficiently — is performed by an inflated apparatus whose sole *raison d'être* is to determine consumption norms and allocation quotas. A transition to the market system would entail the liquidation of this bureaucratic administrative apparatus, which distributes both material and spiritual goods according to standards that it considers to be the correct ones.

The plan is backed up by the party *apparat,* which has at its disposal the "common stock"; the market, for its part, plays into the hands of private traders: individuals, cooperators, craftsmen, traders, and entrepreneurs. Peaceful emulation or fair competition between the two is out of the question because the state holds full monopoly and state business has all priority rights, while individual traders and cooperators are in no way protected by any law ensured by the state and are, moreover, deprived of any organizational or political power. A peaceful coexistence of the two is unbelievable: like that of a wolf and a lamb. As the wolf grows hungry it will devour the lamb without a second's hesitation. Thus, once the private trader or cooperator has realized he is an owner, he will claim his right to power, a right that is, anyway, more justified and legal than that usurped by the party elite. The wolf will eat up the lamb. The horns and legs of the poor victim will be displayed as a reminder of the abortive second New Economic Policy — abortive because the plan is incompatible with the market.

Either our society develops along some hypothetical lines devised by the mainstream socialist theorists as planned laws sanctified by socialist ideals even if it means being chronically hungry, cold, and badly organized, or it gives up all plan-oriented ideology and state-minded psychology and makes way for the power of the market, that is, the producer — both economic and political power. For a system in which those who construct are different from the ones who enrich themselves and profit by running the economy is not viable. If the market, which entails economic liberalism and classical bourgeois pluralism as a basis of a democratic social structure, comes to power, there will be no question of calculating another five-year plan and of sending it down to the bottom. No proprietor-entrepreneur would put up with such an infringement of his economic freedom and his commercial initiative, which always presupposes certain individual risks and personal responsibility but which, however, promises profits in the long run.

Viewed in this light, the plan seems to be incompatible with the market. Economic liberalism and planned centralism would never form an intermingling homogeneous whole. Wherever the State Planning Committee is the manager and wherever the Council of Ministers approves the plan, which ipso facto becomes a law, mar-

ket relations — economic liberalism and freedom of enterprise — simply cannot take root.

In this connection I would like to refer to a classical work. A. Menger in his well-known *Right to the Entire Produce of Labor* (1886) writes that in a social system where individual property over land and capital is still preserved, "the formation of prices of goods and personal services by the state . . . would be in permanent conflict with the economic interests of both large and small entrepreneurs in agriculture, industry and commerce."

But it is obvious enough, Menger goes on to say, that a system in which state bodies are entitled to dictate to the entrepreneurs what the latter should sell deprives an individual economy of all freedom and autonomy and has the defects of both private and collective ownership. "It is most likely that both the Roman Empire and France would have made a transition to a purely collective ownership if the relation of social forces in those days had made it possible for this state of affairs to go on."[8]

This century-old simple truth still retains its validity as applied to today's situation in this country.

For more than seventy years we witnessed planned prices bringing unceasing anarchy into the economic process, thereby disturbing all economic proportions, making for a permanent imbalance in practically every link of the economic system, and resulting in an everlasting contradiction between the economic interests of both large and small enterprises in agriculture, industry, and services. Just as Diocletian's edict on prices or the decree on limited prices issued by the French rev-

8. A. Menger, *The Right to the Entire Produce of Labor* (n.p., 1886), pp. 72, 73.

olutionaries resulted in severe punishment, confinement, and the death penalty, so the Soviet decrees on agricultural prices have cost us several million human lives.

That was the case wherever and whenever the state interfered in pricing, thereby forcing some people to sell and coercing other people to consume. For wherever price formation is done by centralization methods, commodity shortages, on the one hand, and overstocking, on the other, are closely associated.

PRIVATE PROPERTY, INITIATIVE, AND COMMAND

Surplus of goods coupled with acute shortage: such a state of affairs never resulted in anything positive. Due to the fact that the "correlation of social forces" in this country has made it possible to go on with what we started in 1917, it is only natural that we have come to a "purely collective ownership," which has been characterized by General Secretary M. Gorbachev as a property that "seems to have become no one's." Steps have been taken to restore to life private ownership and individual handicrafts, to broaden the sphere of small services and build a network of cooperatives that are based on both private ownership and private capital. Emancipation of prices — that is, a switch to market pricing — will be the sine qua non in implementing this program. If not, private commercial activities will be rather short-lived owing to several objective factors:

— lack of freedom to sell raw materials, materials, equipment, and machinery as one thinks best;
— lack of a right to free trade; and
— lack of necessary stimuli and incentives for efficient and productive work owing to the chronic contradic-

tion between prices and economic interests.

How is it possible to inject market competition into the planned economy? How does one make planned price formation compatible with market pricing? How does one realize the social-democratic principle "competition — as far as possible; planning — as far as necessary," which was designed for the market economy based on principles of budget planning introduced into it, an indicative form of planning that is in no way binding for any entrepreneur whatsoever? If, and only if, we give up state planning through directives, denationalize property, organize private enterprises — as cooperatives or joint-stock companies, or firms, or any other form — provided they enjoy complete autonomy and may stake their own real capital. If, and only if, we do away with centralized distribution of funds, the state monopoly over appropriation and distribution of earnings, the system of centralized public investments, and so forth. Until we come to realize that, as F. Hayek has said, "anarchic, separate, uncoordinated efforts of individuals are able to bring about a complicated ramified economic structure in the long run," any reforming steps will take us nowhere. Unless individual energy and initiative cast off the fetters of administrative management, we shall see no raising of economic well-being. We have no other way to ensure growth and solve the food problem.

Are we ripe for action? Private cooperative property, individual labor activity, family contracts, privately owned farms, joint-stock property, and some other items of the *perestroika* program are arguments in favor of the market model. Time will show whether the switch will be radical and consistent enough.

ENVIRONMENTAL PROTECTION
AND ECONOMIC SYSTEMS

In conclusion, there is one more question of paramount importance. Was it absolutely necessary for humankind to proceed along a path on which smoking chimneys and accident-prone nuclear power stations more and more disturb the ecological balance and damage the environment? I do not presume the liberty to judge, but it seems that humanity has had no other way of feeding itself. There is no alternative. We either limit the birthrate by the conditions of natural sustenance or introduce some new, ecologically harmful, self-reproducing technologies. The more complicated and the more ramified the economic process is, the higher are the expenses of reproduction. The planned system is both less efficient and less profitable than the market economy, and thus neither is it so well equipped for environmental protection. The ecological calamities for which our country is responsible cannot but corroborate my central thesis.

ANNALS, *AAPSS*, **507,** January 1990

The Linkage Between Economic and Political Reform in the Socialist Countries: A Supply-Side Explanation

By YU-SHAN WU

ABSTRACT: Political reforms in the socialist countries cannot be understood with the traditional demand-side theories. The property-rights structure is a crucial element in deciding the level of social demand for democracy. But the institutionalization of political pluralism can only be explained by elite strategic thinking. Typically, Leninist elites do not opt for political reforms if they can successfully restructure the economic systems without making political changes. There are two primary reasons for the regime to take steps toward political pluralism: one is to stifle the conservative opponents in the regime who are against economic reform; the other is to strike a social contract with the society to make economic reform acceptable to the population. When the elites are forced to tinker with political reforms, the single-party multicandidate model usually precedes the multiparty solution. Democratization, however, may fail to bring about economic recovery and is vulnerable to the elite's change of mind and the pressure from more orthodox Leninist regimes.

Yu-Shan Wu graduated in political science from National Taiwan University. He received a B.A. degree from National Chengchi University in Taiwan. He is currently a resident fellow at the Brookings Institution (1989-90) and a Ph.D. candidate in political science at the University of California, Berkeley. He has published on politics in Taiwan and the property-rights restructuring in mainland China. His major interest is in comparative economic reform and reform politics in authoritarian regimes.

O NE can safely claim that before 1980, real structural changes of the Leninist systems happened only in the economic realm and only in a minority of countries: Yugoslavia and to a lesser extent Poland in the 1950s, Hungary in the 1960s, and China in the late 1970s. But Solidarity in Poland in the years 1980-81 ushered in a decade of political changes that culminated in *glasnost* and *demokratizatsia* — read for the latter one-party, multicandidate elections — in the Soviet Union, legalization of Solidarity and promise of limited competitive elections in Poland, a pledge of multiparty electoral politics in Hungary, and unprecedented mass demonstrations in China to force the authorities to make democratic reforms. Enough cases have accumulated to warrant at least a tentative theorizing on the economic and political reforms in the socialist countries and their relations.

This article will argue four points. First, the traditional society-centered explanations are insufficient in that they do not take into consideration the property-rights structures and they can only account for aspirations and social demand for democracy, not its institutionalization. It is the elite strategic thinking that has the greatest explanatory power in accounting for the institutionalization of pluralist political reforms. Second, Leninist elites typically do not opt for political reforms if they can successfully restructure the economic system without making political changes. Third, there are two primary reasons for the regime to take steps toward political pluralism: one is to stifle the conservative opponents in the regime; the other is to strike a social contract with the society. Fourth, when the elites are forced to experiment with political reforms, the single-party, multicandidate model usually precedes the multiparty solution.

SOCIETY-CENTERED THEORIES

One can find four major explanations of political reforms in the socialist countries. The first one is an economic argument that asserts that highly concentrated political and economic institutions are needed to collect the scarce and diffuse capital for primitive accumulation.[1] But once a country has been industrialized, the rationale and utility of the totalitarian system are exhausted. The natural tendency is for the system to move toward a pluralistic sociopolitical arrangement.[2] The second explanation applies macrosociological terms to describe an inevitable process of political liberalization. It is emphasized that the high degree of differentiation and specialization characteristic of an industrialized society has created highly complex social interests. The function of the integration of these interests can only be performed by electoral democracy and a plural-party system. Democratic association is thus an evolutionary universal under the pressure of adaptive exigencies of industrialization.[3]

The third theory puts major emphasis on the political legitimacy of the Leninist regimes. It is assumed that the highly educated social audience in an industrialized society will accept no other base of political legitimacy than the consensual principle embodied in democracy.[4] Finally, one

1. Jerry F. Hough and Merle Fainsod, *How the Soviet Union Is Governed* (Cambridge, MA: Harvard University Press, 1979), pp. 136-38; Alexander Gerschenkron, *Economic Backwardness in Historical Perspective* (Cambridge, MA: Harvard University Press, 1966), pp. 5-30.

2. Robert H. McNeal, "Trotskyist Interpretations of Stalinism," in *Stalinism: Essays in Historical Interpretation,* ed. Robert C. Tucker (New York: Norton, 1977), pp. 48-50.

3. Talcott Parsons, "Evolutionary Universals in Society," *American Sociological Review,* 3:338-57 (June 1964).

4. Ibid., p. 356.

can find ad hoc cultural arguments that propose to explain pluralist tendencies in the socialist countries in terms of political culture. The most prominent case is Czechoslovakia. The 1968 Prague Spring is characterized as the reemergence of deeply rooted pluralist patterns cultivated under a series of political arrangements since the 1860s. The First Republic (1918-38) is considered a period when popular orientations realized themselves without the yoke of foreign domination. The later suppression of pluralism in Czechoslovakia only led to the full flowering of demands for democracy in the 1960s, when even influential Communists were affected by the ingrained political culture.[5]

PROPERTY-RIGHTS STRUCTURES AND POLITICAL PLURALISM

The foregoing theories explain the emergence of political pluralism in terms of various kinds of social needs: economic viability, social integration, political stability, and cultural assertion. These social needs presumably spring from the process of industrialization — note that the pluralist cultural tradition developed in Czechoslovakia as the country became one of the most industrialized areas in Central and Eastern Europe. In these theories, no distinction is made between different property-rights structures and their impact on the political outcome of economic development. Industrialization generated by socialist ownership and a command economy is not going to create the same momentum

5. David W. Paul, *The Cultural Limits of Revolutionary Politics: Change and Continuity in Socialist Czechoslovakia* (New York: Columbia University Press, 1979), chap. 5. For a reflection on this approach, see H. Gordon Skilling, "Czechoslovak Political Culture: Pluralism in an International Context," in *Political Culture and Communist Studies,* ed. Archie Brown (Armonk, NY: M. E. Sharpe, 1985), pp. 115-33.

toward democracy as that produced under private ownership and a market system. This is the case because with socialist — that is, state — ownership, no potential opposition group can claim a material base for its actions against the authorities, while the state, based on its monopolist position, can always apply economic deprivation to stifle the dissidents.

Equally consequential is the fact that without a market system there is no social institution to generate the ethos of calculated equal exchange, which is necessary for democracy to emerge. One can understand democracy as a uniquely structured political market that shares important features with an economic market. In a democracy political parties, like enterprises, offer attractive political products — highly advertised candidates and policy packages — with competitive pricing — for example, a promise of low taxes to the targeted groups — and compete on open markets — elections — to court the political consumers — voters — for their votes. In a liberal-capitalist society the market ethos in the economic and political realms reinforce each other. In a socialist country, on the other hand, the hierarchical principle dominates both the economic plan and the political structure. In these two cases the economy and the polity are synchronized. The lack of an economic market in a centrally planned economy thus bodes ill for political democracy. In short, industrialization under Leninism, with its lack of private property and a market system to provide the material base and prevalent ethos for democracy, does not naturally lead to political liberalization. The fact that the most industrialized socialist countries — East Germany and Czechoslovakia — lag behind the less developed Hungary, Poland, and the Soviet Union in pluralization vividly demonstrates this point.

A logical extension of this argument is that once there is a significant deviation from the stringent property-rights structure, one should be able to observe phenomena of political relaxation. It is quite obvious that Hungary, Poland, Yugoslavia, and, before the crackdown in Tiananmen Square on 4 June 1989, China stand out as politically more liberal than other socialist countries, such as East Germany, Czechoslovakia, Bulgaria, and North Korea. If one then takes a look at the property-rights structures of these countries, one finds that Hungary in 1968 introduced the New Economic Mechanism (NEM) and since then has practiced market socialism; Poland since 1956 has had a predominantly private agriculture; Yugoslavia, as the earliest deviant, has both market socialism in the form of the workers' councils and private farming; and China, after the late 1970s, somewhat privatized its agriculture and has been introducing the market-socialist principle into its industry since the early 1980s. These cases clearly suggest that there is a high correlation between property-rights structures and political arrangements.

But property-rights explanations are still society centered and, together with the economic, sociological, political, and cultural arguments, concern primarily the aspirations and demands for democracy in a society rather than its institutionalization. In a Leninist system, social demands are much less important than elite strategic thinking in deciding the degree of the political reform. The democratic movement initiated by the students and joined by other urban residents in China from April through June 1989 vividly demonstrates the momentum toward political pluralism in a society with partially liberated property rights. The crackdown on 4 June, however, even more clearly shows how elite strategic thinking overrides social aspira-

tions for democracy in a Leninist system at critical moments. One thus has to explore the elite's calculations in order to understand the supply side, or the dominant side, of the reform process.

THE NEED FOR ECONOMIC REFORM

The fundamental reason for the structural changes in a Leninist system is the need to improve economic efficiency. One can find four causes, two primary and two auxiliary, of this deep-rooted need. One of the primary causes is the elite's realization that international competition boils down to a productivity contest and that the old economic system is not geared to that contest.[6] *Perestroika* (restructuring of the economy) in the Soviet Union is primarily based on this perception as Mikhail Gorbachev and other like-minded Soviet leaders keenly feel the inadequacies of the centralized system as compared with the West, Japan, and even the East Asian newly industrializing countries. The second primary cause is the elite's desire to save the legitimacy of the regime in the eyes of the population by raising the living standards through an economic reform. The People's Republic of China, after repeated economic fiascoes and political turbulence, radically shifted the regime's legitimacy claim from ideology to material prosperity in the 1970s and made unprecedented structural reforms to reorient the economy.

These two primary cases can be facilitated by two auxiliary conditions: a leadership change and a dominant reforming hegemon.[7] The absence of these two con-

6. Marshall I. Goldman, *Gorbachev's Challenge: Economic Reform in the Age of High Technology* (New York: Norton, 1987), pp. 6-13.

7. David S.G. Goodman, "Communism in East Asia: The Production Imperative, Legitimacy and Re-

ditions, however, may act to thwart the reform momentum based on the primary causes. North Korea is a pertinent case in suggesting that even though a socialist country is under tremendous pressure in international competition — the rise of South Korea — as long as there is no radical change of leadership — the Pyongyang regime is witnessing a hereditary succession of Kim Il Sung by his son Kim Jong Il — and as long as there is no reforming hegemon dictating to the regime — North Korea is a most skillful balancer between Moscow and Beijing — reform will not be forthcoming.[8] Similar situations can be found in Romania, where Nicolae Ceausescu is firmly in power and Bucharest has a track record of independence from the Soviet Union.

PURE ECONOMIC REFORM

If the need for economic reform is recognized and there are no political obstacles that cannot be removed through politburo politics, the regime will change its economic policies without experimenting with political reform. These pure economic reforms are typically based on elite preferences independent of the demands of the larger population. The society plays a highly marginal role in this process.[9]

Two strategies can be taken in the economic reform: perfecting and restructuring.[10] Perfecting refers to reorganization of

the planning system designed to improve economic efficiency. The absolute majority of the reform efforts throughout the socialist countries since the 1950s fall into this category. A typical case is the German Democratic Republic with its introduction of the *kombinate*. Restructuring, on the other hand, refers to reassignment of property rights, the hallmark of which is the state's decision to relinquish its role in physical allocation of materials.[11] In restructuring, even though a significant portion of the control power is transferred to the users of the means of production, ownership — that is, the power to appropriate and dispose of income — is not. Here one can observe a decoupling of the control power from the income power, with the former transferred to the economic agents while the latter is kept in the hands of the state. In short, one has marketization without privatization. The result is market socialism. The purpose of this strategy is to create a market that will presumably bring about competition and efficiency without losing the socialist identity and its positive features. The only three countries qualified for this category are Yugoslavia, where market socialism was introduced in the 1950s; Hungary, where market socialism was introduced in the 1960s; and the People's Republic of China, which introduced market socialism in the 1970s.

If the pure economic reforms can successfully solve the problems that prompted the regime to adopt them, there will be no further structural changes. If, however, the economic situation deteriorates and further changes are required, one can expect a second wave of economic reform, provided the reformers are politically capable of implementing it. If there are political

form," in *Communism and Reform in East Asia,* ed. David S.G. Goodman (London: Frank Cass, 1988), p. 3.

8. Aidan Foster-Carter, "North Korea: The End of the Beginning," in *Communism and Reform,* ed. Goodman, pp. 64-85.

9. Ed A. Hewett, *Reforming the Soviet Economy* (Washington, DC: Brookings Institution, 1988), pp. 20-23.

10. Tamás Bauer, "Perfecting or Reforming the Economic Mechanism," *Eastern European Economics.* 16(1):6 (Winter 1987-88).

11. Tamás Bauer, "The Hungarian Alternative to Soviet-Type Planning," *Journal of Comparative Economics,* 7(3):305 (Sept. 1983).

obstacles blocking the reform path that cannot be removed through intrasystem means, the reformers may experiment with changes of the political system out of desperation.

INSTRUMENTAL POLITICAL REFORMS

Depending on the location of the political obstacles one can find two causes of instrumental political reforms. In one case, the economic reformers may find that their conservative opponents in the regime who are thwarting their plans cannot be removed through politburo politics. There is also the assumption that the society will directly benefit from the economic reform and will support the reformers if it can be emancipated to act in its own interest. It thus makes sense for the reformers to invite social forces to put pressure on the conservatives, to coerce them into silence and acquiescence, or to expel them from the power center.[12] Throughout the whole process, democratization is used in an instrumental way. Hence in the Soviet Union Mikhail Gorbachev did not talk about *demokratizatsia* until September 1986, when he realized the difficulty in launching an economic reform. The retiring of 110 high party cadres from the central organs of the Soviet Communist Party in the aftermath of the lively national election held on 26 March 1989 serves as a good example of how popular pressure can be unleashed from the bottom to force out the opponents to economic reform.[13]

12. The reformers' desire to oust their conservative opponents does not necessarily result in pluralist political reforms. It may lead to a temporary unleashing of social criticism, or even mass rallies, against the conservative incumbents, as happened in China during the Beijing Spring, when Deng Xiaoping manipulated disgruntled masses to denounce Mao's successor, Hua Guofeng, publicly.

13. "Lose Some, Win Some," *Economist*, 29 Apr. 1989, pp. 45-46.

Another locale of political resistance is the society at large. This is the case when the trade-offs inherent in the reform measures — for example, job security versus efficiency — are keenly felt and resisted by large sectors of the society and when the regime has lost its ability to ruthlessly implement its policies over social opposition. Under these circumstances, there is an incentive for the regime to negotiate with the society for its approval of the painful economic reform. Democratization may ensue as a concession made by the regime for the toleration of the negative economic impact associated with reform.

To negotiate a new social contract with the society suggests the existence of identifiable social groups with which the regime can bargain, however. It further suggests that these groups are capable of enforcing the contract among their members once an agreement is reached. Solidarity in Poland, with a membership of 10 million out of a population of 38 million and with a widely respected leader, Lech Walesa, is such a group. But the tens of thousands of Chinese students marching for democracy in Beijing's Tiananmen Square in April and May 1989 did not constitute a group that the regime was willing to bargain with. On the one hand, the students were pressing for democracy and the end of corruption without offering any promise to support the regime's economic plans; hence there was no hope for the Communist leaders to strike a reciprocal agreement with the students. On the other hand, the possibility that the student negotiators could enforce the terms of the agreement, if there was an agreement, among the students and among the population was practically nil. Giving in to the students' demands for democracy would have meant capitulation by the regime under these circumstances. It then makes equal sense for

General Wojciech Jaruzelski to negotiate with Walesa and for Deng Xiaoping to refrain from any significant concessions to the students, since both are exclusively interested in the economic reform.

ONE-PARTY PLURALISM

When a Leninist regime is forced into political reform, it has two strategies to choose from. One is socialist, one-party pluralism. The other one is multiparty democracy. The first one is understandably preferred by the regime. Following the logic of market socialism in the economic realm, the political reformers are first of all interested in creating a political market without losing the party's ultimate claim on the actors. This is done through the Communist Party, or the front organization, offering more than one candidate for each seat in the local and national elections. By letting the voters exercise this limited power of choice, it is expected that the opponents to reform will be voted out and the public will develop a sense of participation that is helpful when the regime later introduces difficult economic changes. The beauty of the hybrid one-party pluralism, quite like market socialism, is its presumed ability to make structural adaptations to the changing environment without shaking the foundation of the rule of the party-state.

Up until mid-1989, Hungary, Poland, and the Soviet Union had instituted and practiced meaningful one-party, multicandidate elections on the national level.[14] In all three cases, there was a national list of candidates who ran unopposed. Top party officials, including, of course, János Kádár, Wojciech Jaruzelski, and Mikhail Gorbachev in their respective countries, were exempt from personal confrontation and perhaps humiliation by having their names on the national list. But outside this small enclave the principles of multicandidacy and electoral competition ruled.

The National Assembly election in Hungary on 8 June 1985, the Sejm election in Poland on 13 October 1985, and the Soviet election of the new Congress of People's Deputies on 26 March 1989 are the three occasions on which the voters in these countries experienced the promise and limits of one-party democracy. The pioneering Hungarian system is arguably the most liberal among the three in terms of the nomination process and the actual ratio between the candidates and parliamentary seats.[15] In the Soviet election, 384 of the 1500 districts witnessed party hacks running unopposed. But there was genuine competition in the multicandidate districts. In both cases the regime could afford to be liberal and make an earnest effort to activate the society because the reformers were confident that popular choice would coincide with their policies and would put pressure on their conservative opponents. This was not the case in Poland, where martial law had added to the coercive image of the regime and the limited democracy was grudgingly adopted by the party in a desperate try to pacify the society. This mentality was reflected in the fact that exactly two candidates were allowed for each Sejm seat and they were selected by the government-controlled electoral commissions. The party also applied many other tactics to ensure that the election did not derail from the official track.[16]

---

14. Werner Hahn, "Electoral Choice in the Soviet Bloc," *Problems of Communism*, 36(2):29 (Mar.-Apr. 1987).

15. "Democratizing Communism through the Ballot Box?" *Radio Free Europe Research*, 2 July 1985.

16. Hahn, "Electoral Choice," p. 35.

Unlike market socialism, which proved to be a workable formula, one-party multi-candidate democracy did not lead to political stability for its early practicers. In both Hungary and Poland in the late 1980s, one witnessed a transition from the multi-candidate formula to a fuller political liberalization in the form of a multiparty system. The Soviet Union, being still at an early stage of one-party multicandidate political reform, has not shown any sign of moving toward the second stage of democratization.

MULTIPARTY DEMOCRACY

As of mid-1989, Hungary and Poland are the only two Leninist regimes aspiring to some version of multiparty democracy. The reformers' desire to liquidate conservative opponents in the party — obstacles found inside the regime — and their hope to incorporate the society politically to facilitate economic reforms in the future — to eliminate obstacles found outside the regime — are factors present in both cases. But the reform wing of the Hungarian Socialist Workers' Party (HSWP) clearly sees a greater danger to their radical reform measures in the conservative part of the party than in the population, hence the urgent call to invite social forces to the political process through democracy. On the other hand, one finds the leadership of the United Polish Workers' Party willing to incorporate the organized opposition only to the minimum necessary to secure Solidarity's promise to keep a lid on popular unrest while the regime tackles the economy. Even though both parties aim at radical economic reforms and resort to democratization to remove political obstacles, the more hostile Polish society sets a natural limit to the regime's maneuvering room. The reform format in Poland is

thus more restricting than its Hungarian counterpart.

THE HUNGARIAN CASE

The story of post-1956 Hungary is the best example for showing how elite strategic thinking and the conflicts between party leaders decide economic and political reforms in that country. Being a regime totally devoid of domestic legitimacy after the suppression of the 1956 revolution and the execution of Imre Nagy, the HSWP leadership under János Kádár took pains to deliberately link its claim to political power with the economic performance of the system. The candid acknowledgments of the tenuous legitimacy of the regime and the explicit linkage between legitimacy and economic performance are without parallel in the Soviet sphere.[17]

Since the mid-1960s, the Hungarian economic policy has been focused on increasing the purchasing power of the population and providing abundant consumer goods on the market, starting with agricultural products.[18] Toward the end of the decade, when the deficiencies of the import-substitution strategy became clear, the balance-of-payments problems in hard-currency trade developed, and the centralized planning system, which was geared to extensive growth, appeared unable to generate productivity increases, the Kádár regime introduced radical economic restructuring in the NEM.[19] Here the decision was

17. Bennett Kovrig, "Hungarian Socialism: The Deceptive Hybrid," *Eastern European Politics and Societies,* 1(1):113-14 (Winter 1987).

18. Wlodzimierz Brus, "Political System and Economic Efficiency: The East European Context," *Journal of Comparative Economics,* 4(1):49 (Mar. 1980).

19. Ellen Comisso and Paul Marer, "The Economics and Politics of Reform in Hungary," *International Organization,* 40(2):424-25 (Spring 1986).

made in the spirit of so-called socialist enlightened absolutism. The elite acted on its own purpose and preferences. The society played a marginal role. This is a pure economic reform, not spilling over to the political realm.[20]

The golden years for the NEM were from 1968 to 1972. Then one witnessed a retrenchment period covering the bulk of the decade, which, however, did not suggest any fundamental changes of Kádárism. The surge of the second wave of reform toward the end of the 1970s testified to the endurance of the NEM. In the 1980s, the regime continued to uphold its commitment to the material well-being of the population while adapting its economic reform to an increasingly stringent environment. Hungary's foreign debt doubled from US$6 billion to US$12 billion between 1981 and 1988, raising the country's per capita debt to the highest level among the socialist states.[21] Austerity brought about high inflation, near zero real growth, cuts in consumer subsidies, and Eastern Europe's first major personal income tax with a top rate of 60 percent. This dire economic picture forced the regime to contemplate another radical restructuring of the economy. But this second economic restructuring was not possible within the old political framework. In order to transform the economy, the reform wing in the HSWP decided to transform the regime first.

Together with a steadily deteriorating economy and bold talk of economic reform, one has found, since the mid-1980s, intensified intraparty struggle, on the one hand, and promises of political pluralization, on the other hand. Three forces were

detectable in the ruling HSWP. The conservatives grouped around the aging and recalcitrant János Kádár, who refused to envision either a radical restructuring of the economy or a political reform deviating from one-party pluralism. Karoly Grosz, the Budapest party leader who then became the prime minister, offered leadership in the realm of economic reform but stuck to the notion of political pluralism under a one-party system. By combining economic flexibility and ideological orthodoxy, Grosz gathered around him a group of political pragmatists. Finally, one could find the radical reformers under the auspices of Imre Pozsgay, general secretary of the National Council of the Patriotic People's Front (PPF). They had a radical economic platform and were willing to amputate a part of the party while democratizing the political system to make the reform irreversible.

From November 1986 to May 1989 there appeared two stages of development of the HSWP politics. First the reformers joined the pragmatists to topple Kádár and replaced him with Grosz. During this stage the anti-Kádár coalition activated the society by unleashing the mass media, enlivening the National Assembly, seeking grassroots support, and courting interest groups as well as critical intellectuals.[22] As a result, the so-called coup of the *apparat* removed Kádár and his entourage from office at the party conference in May 1988. The second stage began when Grosz, after kicking Kádár upstairs to the post of party chairman, found that he and the pragmatists had played into the hands of the reformers. An activated society is the reformers' exclusive asset. With the conservatives in dismay, the reformers now invited social forces to bring the pragmatists into their line. Grosz was compelled to change his

20. Brus, "Political System and Economic Efficiency," p. 50.

21. Georges Schopflin, Rudolf Tokes, and Ivan Volgyes, "Leadership Change and Crisis in Hungary," *Problems of Communism*, 37(5):25 (Sept.-Oct. 1988).

22. Ibid., pp. 32-36.

opinion on the 1956 explosion, considering it no longer a "counterrevolution" but a "popular uprising." His insistence on "a lasting one-party system" also gave way to an endorsement of a multiparty election in 1990 and a promise that if the HSWP loses majority support, it will quietly go into opposition.[23] More than that, the reform wing of the party held a separate workshop in April 1989, without inviting their conservative colleagues to attend, where they talked about splitting the HSWP to liquidate the political obstacles to reform.

Clearly, a desperate attempt to restructure the economy has prompted the reform wing in the HSWP to institutionalize social pressure in the form of multiparty democracy in order to defeat conservative forces in the regime and make reform irreversible. One certainly cannot deny the fact that the society, once activated, developed a pluralist momentum of its own and put pressure on the party, the reform wing included. But the whole process was initiated by the forces within the regime based on its strategic thinking. Yet this line of calculation is rational only when the regime perceives enough social support in the promised elections. Here one can find some favorable factors: the immature and disorganized opposition, the regime's comparatively decent track record, the party's organizational superiority, the residual goodwill of the population, and so on. None of these, however, can be found in Poland.

THE CASE OF POLAND

Economic reform has been on the United Polish Workers' Party's agenda since the 1950s. There was a short honeymoon between the regime and society after Wladyslaw Gomulka took power in

1956 and let the agricultural cooperatives dissolve. But since the 1960s, the elite has found that there was in the society at large a genuine opposition to restructuring the economy. Before the emergence of an organized national opposition — that is Solidarity — in 1980,[24] it was physically impossible for the regime to negotiate with the society for a new social compact in which political liberalization could be exchanged for social tolerance of painful economic reform. By keeping the society without a leader, the regime unwittingly deprived itself of any opportunity to deal with a recognizable social force that could honor a new social compact. The mode of interaction between the state and society was for the regime to implement unpopular measures of economic reform in a blitzkrieg, followed by strong social resistance, the collapse of the incumbent leadership, but no fundamental change of the system.[25] The regime and society basically vetoed each other. Neither got what it wanted. Wladyslaw Gomulka and Edward Gierek were brought down by the society, which in turn got itself General Jaruzelski and his martial law.

It took some social experimenting before Jaruzelski made it clear for himself and for his colleagues that without Solidarity's cooperation, the kind of economic reform needed to save the country from collapse was virtually impossible.[26]

23. "Why It's Stuck," *Economist*, 22 Apr. 1989, p. 47.

24. David S. Mason, "Solidarity as a New Social Movement," *Political Science Quarterly*, 104(1):42-45 (Spring 1989).

25. Neal Ascherson, *The Polish August: The Self-Limiting Revolution* (New York: Viking Press, 1982), pp. 27-29. For a comparison between the Hungarian and the Polish ways of introducing price reforms, see John R. Haberstroh, "The Case of Hungary: Liberal Socialism under Stress," *Journal of Comparative Economics*, 2(2):123 (June 1978).

26. Tad Szulc, "Poland's Path," *Foreign Policy*, (72):212 (Fall 1988).

The government submitted its reform program to a national referendum in November 1987, only to find it flatly rejected by the voters. In the spirit of enlightened authoritarianism, the regime went ahead with a price reform under the program's provision to phase out subsidies in April 1988. Strikes ensued in May and August. As the crisis evolved, Jaruzelski reinforced the liberal wing in the politburo by adding Mieczyslaw Rakowski, Wladyslaw Baka, and Stanislaw Ciosek to that ruling body. In August, the interior minister proposed to talk with Walesa. In January 1989, Jaruzelski threatened to resign unless party conservatives dropped their opposition to talks with Solidarity. The conservatives backed down. The talks began. A new social compact was negotiated and concluded between the government and Solidarity. A freely contested Senate would be created, together with a Sejm where the opposition was guaranteed 35 percent of the seats. Solidarity was legalized and allowed access to the national media. Still the agreement forbade the establishment of new political parties, and the government retained its power to censor the media. For its part, Solidarity promised to help keep a lid on popular unrest while the regime tackled the economy. What makes the timing of the agreement unique is that both parties seemed motivated by the same concern that a young generation of more radical working-class people was emerging that might defy Solidarity and Walesa in the near future. Solidarity may need the agreement as badly as the regime, which desperately wants to reach a new contract with the society before it again becomes leaderless and impossible to deal with.

CONCLUSION

The underlying theme of the political reforms in the socialist countries since the mid-1980s is the regimes' strategic thinking in inviting social forces into the political process to remove the obstacles to economic reforms. These obstacles may be found in the regime or in the society. In the former case, the reformists may choose to unleash social pressure against their conservative opponents through opening up political channels. In the latter case, the regime may try to reach a social compact with the society to exchange political freedoms for tolerance of the costs of economic reforms. But this negotiating process is possible only when there is an identifiable organization that can represent the society and enforce the agreement once it is reached. Two dominant strategies are recognizable: one-party pluralism and multiparty democracy. In the Soviet Union, Gorbachev espoused democracy under the one-party rule to kick the conservatives out of the party. The reform wing of the HSWP first applied socialist pluralism, then multiparty democracy, to amputate the conservative part of the party in order to save the regime. General Jaruzelski in Poland, on the other hand, adopted similar but more restrictive measures of pluralization to reach a new social compact with the organized opposition, namely, Solidarity.

It is doubtful, to say the least, that democratization, particularly its multiparty version, can solve a socialist country's economic problems. A more plausible scenario is for the emerging social groups to veto one another's platform and paralyze a state that has lost its autonomy from the society. The fact that a transition to democracy has not solved the economic problems in Latin American countries and the Philippines is suggestive here. Contrary to the assertions of many East European dissidents, the relationship between democracy and economic efficiency is ambiguous, if not contradictory.[27] Since for the reforming elite there is no inherent interest in democracy but only a manipulative attitude toward it, the unsuccessful experience with political reform in bringing about concrete economic results may touch off a backlash. Unlike Latin American countries, the socialist regimes are equipped with more effective control mechanisms and are capable of reconsolidating their power vis-à-vis

27. Brus, "Political System and Economic Efficiency," p. 47; Richard Lowenthal, "Government in Development Countries," in *Democracy in a Changing Society*, ed. H. Ehrmann (New York: Praeger, 1964), p. 911.

the society after the political reform. These regimes are also operating in a more restricting environment. The concerns of the socialist hegemon — the Soviet Union is still at the stage of one-party pluralism — and the more politically orthodox neighbors are ominous. Thus even though one has seen brave advances toward democracy in Hungary and Poland, the very instrumental motives of the reforming elites, the regime's capacity to reconcentrate political power, and the restricting external environment force one to be more pessimistic than optimistic about the future of democracy in these countries.

ANNALS, *AAPSS*, **507,** January 1990

Reforming the Planned Economy:
The Hungarian Experience

By TAMÁS BAUER

ABSTRACT: Hungary has experienced the longest uninterrupted experiment of reforming a planned economy. A comprehensive reform blueprint was drafted during the mid-1960s with the aim of finding a sound combination of plan and market. The reform of 1968 represented a simultaneous transformation of all aspects of the economic system. The New Economic Mechanism resulting from the reform turned out to be a peculiar transitory economic order substantially different both from the traditional Soviet-type planning system and from a market economy. It brought little actual improvement into the operation of the economy, thus making further reform efforts necessary. The second round of reforms, during the early 1980s, under the constraints of general stagnation in the Soviet bloc, resulted in the first important steps toward privatization. The present, third round of reforms is directed toward a genuine market economy.

Tamás Bauer graduated from the Karl Marx University of Economics in Budapest and received the degree of a candidate in science, the equivalent of a Ph.D., from the Hungarian Academy of Sciences. He is a senior research fellow at the Institute of Economics of the Hungarian Academy of Sciences, Budapest, and professor of economics at the University of Frankfurt, West Germany. His academic interest focuses on comparative economic systems, particularly on reforms and policies of East European centrally planned economies.

T HE aim of this article is to sum up the Hungarian experience in reforming the planned economy. First, the history of the Hungarian economic reform will be briefly outlined. Due to space constraints, the prelude to the reform, namely, the reform blueprints of the mid-1950s, will be completely neglected, despite their importance in terms of reform history. The three phases of the Hungarian reform will, in turn, be analyzed thoroughly and in a comparative way in two senses: compared with each other and compared with reform efforts within other planned economies.[1]

THE CHRONOLOGY OF REFORM STEPS IN HUNGARY

More or less simultaneously with less substantial changes in the economic system in the German Democratic Republic and the Soviet Union and with a very similar economic reform effort in Czechoslovakia, Hungary's leadership undertook an economic reform during the late 1960s. Following the repeated aggravation of economic tensions in the mid-1960s, it was decided to introduce substantial changes in the system of economic planning and management. In the course of two and a half years, a reform blueprint was drafted and translated into detailed measures, most of which were introduced overnight on 1 January 1968 with the intention of a further extension of the reform in the following years.

Despite the relatively smooth implementation of the reform measures, some tensions and conflicts proved to be inevitable. These reinforced resistance to the reform. The external environment of the re-

form, which seemed so favorable in the years 1966-67, turned almost hostile after the invasion of Czechoslovakia in August 1968. At first only the intended extension and deepening of the reform was postponed to a more favorable time, but a few years later, during the early 1970s, the reformers found it appropriate to retreat in many respects.

Under the conditions of détente, Hungary could maintain reasonable growth rates and welfare without moving ahead on the reform course but at the cost of foreign indebtedness. That process had reached its limits by the end of the 1970s. Due to the fact that the rest of the bloc, which explicitly abandoned the course of reforms by the late sixties, suffered from similar — often stronger — economic tensions, the Hungarian leadership responded with reform-minded measures again in the early 1980s. Although the idea of a second comprehensive reform of the entire system was rejected, numerous important partial reforms were undertaken during the early and mid-1980s.

The half-heartedness of the measures and the serious mistakes in short-term growth policy resulted again in an aggravation of economic tensions in the years 1986-87. This time, the economic difficulties were combined with a deep political crisis at a time when a reform-minded policy was developed by the Soviet leadership. The response has been a third round of economic reform, which is still in process at the time of writing.

WHY REFORMS?

The idea of reforming the economic system was generated by dissatisfaction with the system's operation and performance. Economic officials both in central control agencies and in firms as well as

---

1. This article relies strongly on earlier publications of the author's on the same topic where space constraints were less rigid. References are, therefore, mostly omitted herein.

academics had become disappointed by the operation of the economic system, by the numerous irrationalities caused by it, and also by the deteriorating performance of the economy that could well be explained by, among other things, the malfunctioning of the planning and management system. All that might seem obvious to bourgeois economists who have always held that planning cannot work. The economic control agencies and the ruling posts in firms were, however, manned predominantly by communists and socialists deeply convinced that planning is superior to spontaneous market forces. During the 1950s and 1960s most of them maintained this view and, therefore, did not simply opt for abandoning socialist planning and returning to a capitalist market economy. At the same time, however, they felt deeply disappointed by the poor functioning of planning and searched intensively for a model that maintained some key features of planning and still allowed for money, market, flexible prices, and local initiative. This is what economic reform, as a third way between preserving and abandoning socialist planning, meant in Eastern Europe in general and in Hungary in particular.

THE NEW ECONOMIC MECHANISM
OF 1968

Hungary's New Economic Mechanism of 1968 has been the most ambitious and well-conceived reform effort in the Soviet bloc up to now. It took more than two years of intensive preparatory work until a reform blueprint with a clear and consistent general concept and also successful translation into detailed measures emerged. This was mainly due to the close cooperation between academic economists and officials from party and state administration, including enterprise managers. The point

was to find a sound combination of planning and market.

It was clear that planning as a conscious state activity that governs the actions of the state administration regarding economic issues should be preserved, and that macrostructural and technological policies of the government should fit into that framework. Thus five-year plans with a focus on technology policy and annual plans with a focus on macroeconomic proportions were to be drafted and approved. These plans, however, would concern the government only; enterprises had to set up their own plans autonomously. They were assumed to consider government plans as part of the economic environment, but not to derive their plans mechanically from government plans by means of breaking them down, as had been the case before. While in other reform endeavors mandatory plan targets and quotas were reduced in number, or some targets were replaced by other ones, mandatory targets and quotas were fully abolished according to the Hungarian reform blueprint of the mid-1960s. Correspondingly, centralized resource allocation was to be abolished and replaced by free trade in material inputs.

Enterprises and cooperatives, freed from the constraints of mandatory plan targets and supply quotas, were supposed to decide autonomously on purchasing, production, and sales activities. Their decisions were to be guided primarily by the criterion of profitability. A comprehensive price reform, liberalization of price formation, and the introduction of uniform taxation as prerequisites to such managerial behavior were also to be introduced. A considerable part of decision making on investment was to be decentralized and transferred to enterprises, with self-financing and bank credits as the main source of finance instead of the budget allotments that had been the rule in the past.

The 1968 reform blueprint did not envisage any significant increase in the role of private initiative in the economy. It was assumed that the desired changes could be attained on the basis of state and cooperative ownership. In addition to that, and unlike economic reforms in neighboring Yugoslavia and — at least in the 1968-69 version of the reform — in Czechoslovakia, the character of state ownership was not affected at all: top managers of state enterprises continued to be officials of the state, appointed and dismissed by the ministries or local authorities. The powers — formal and informal — of party administration over economic organizations were also maintained. Thus Hungary was an example of a technocratic or managerial version of market-oriented economic reform, as compared to the syndicalist or self-management version in Yugoslavia and, to a certain degree, even the model adopted in Czechoslovakia in 1968-69. This feature of the reform appeared also in the form of income distribution and taxation of enterprises: while in Czechoslovakia and Yugoslavia the net income of enterprises was considered to be the main success indicator of firms, in Hungary profits were.

The managerial character of the Hungarian reform was reinforced by the most important concession the reformers made in 1968. Though aware of the fact that a sound operation of the profit motive is subject to the presence of a sufficient number of market agents creating a competitive environment, they postponed deconcentration of industry and trade to avoid forceful resistance on behalf of managers of big firms. This concession, feasible at the time of introduction, proved to be perilous for the reform during its implementation. Given the very limited number of firms, ministries and managers found it easy to retain direct links and to manipulate all monetary categories to their mutual advantage at the cost of the consumer and of efficiency in general. In the absence of competition, the profit motive could not result in anything else but pressure to increase prices. In addition to that, trade with countries of the Council for Mutual Economic Assistance (Comecon) subject to bilateral government agreements continued to be a considerable part of output. All in all, instead of a market economy Hungary arrived at a state where economic activities were governed neither by traditional mandatory planning nor by market forces but rather by a peculiar coordination system in which mutual courtesy and permanent bargaining over rules and exceptions from them prevailed.

The main achievement of the reform was that while the principal components of the traditional system were removed, the economy did not disintegrate. On the other hand, in the absence of market forces, very few of the expected positive changes did occur. Moreover, the new behavioral rules emerging from the peculiar interplay between state administration and large enterprises have been consolidated during the last two decades, and the system has been capable of integrating numerous partial changes — such as, among others, modernization of taxation and the "world market simulating" pricing rules — and of paralyzing their expected positive impact on the behavior of agents.

Still, something had changed. The counterincentives so characteristic of the traditional system like the rachet principle and the hiding of resources were substantially weakened if not eliminated. Enterprises started to make calculations on the basis of prices, interest, and exchange rates and to consider opportunity costs. Enter-

prise managers became much better informed about external market conditions.
Small and medium-sized enterprises and
cooperatives obtained a certain degree of
independence from the state administration.

All this implies that while no formal
change was introduced into ownership relations, property rights were, in fact, to
some extent transferred from sectoral ministries[2] to enterprises. Within the enterprises, the holder of this portion of property
rights was neither the whole of the staff, as
under workers' self-management, nor the
managing director alone but rather a small
group of managers and party officials
within the enterprise. Decisions such as
those concerning the appointment of top
executives, large investments, and mergers
could essentially be made by this group in
cooperation with the supervising ministry
staff and the local party administration.

The main achievement of the 1968 reform was that the economy, free of mandatory planning and centralized resource allocation, operated without any serious
disturbance. The expected substantial improvement in efficiency and adjustment,
however, was not attained either. Things
did not turn worse, but they did not turn
considerably better. Some improvement
was achieved due to the changes previously described, but this was far from
sufficient to enable the economy to cope
with the new requirements of the late 1970s
and early 1980s, of the new era following
the crucial changes in the external economic environment. Moreover, the
Hungarian government responded to the
first minor tensions that emerged in the
course of reform implementation by halt-
ing the reform procedure during the early
1970s. The adaptability of the economic
system to external changes was rather

2. Branch ministries [ed.].

weakened, at the very time when a
strengthening would have been absolutely
necessary. As a result, external and internal
tensions were growing again by the early
1980s, and the government returned to the
course of reforms.

THE SECOND ROUND
OF REFORMS

What made the reform blueprint of the
mid-1960s acceptable to the party leadership? At that time, a certain reform naiveté
prevailed in Eastern Europe: the reforms
suggested by experts, being limited in
scope in general and avoiding explicit references to ownership in particular, seemed
easily compatible with the existing forms
of state and cooperative ownership, one-
party rule, and adherence to the Soviet
bloc.

This reform naiveté, surviving up to
now in the Soviet Union, vanished in Eastern Europe in the course of the 1970s. At
first the developments in Czechoslovakia
had shown that the logic of economic reform required more fundamental changes
in ownership and in the political superstructure than had been assumed by
Hungarian reformers and party rulers. On
the other hand, the Hungarian experience
of the 1960s and 1970s made it clear that
the economic system itself should be reformed more substantially if considerable
improvements in performance were to be
achieved: dependency of managers on the
state administration needed to be eliminated, excessive concentration of social
capital in a limited number of large state
firms and cooperatives had to be overcome, a capital market should be added to
the market for commodities and labor, involvement of party organs in economic
management had to end, and so on. Academic economists formulated such ideas

during the early 1980s, without any illusion that their suggestions might be accepted by the leadership.

Actually, the Kádár leadership was much less receptive to such ideas than 15 years earlier. After all, this was the late Brezhnev period of stagnation in the Soviet Union, whose approval of any reform effort had been indispensable since the invasion of Czechoslovakia. The idea of a second reform was explicitly rejected by the party leadership. A comprehensive new reform was out of the question. At the same time, however, the need for further changes was obvious.

Such constraints induced the reformers to make suggestions that promised improvement without questioning the character of the system that had prevailed since 1968.

The new private sector

Hungary has some tradition of concessions at the periphery when reforms in the center seem impossible. After the suppression of the 1956 uprising, when a comprehensive economic reform in the state sector proved to be impossible, the government made concessions concerning the extension of semilegal private initiative, particularly in agriculture and housing. These concessions contributed substantially to the post-1956 consolidation of the regime. Again, during the early 1980s, the government was ready for further concessions with respect to private initiative. By that time, government experts had realized how serious an impact on the general performance of the economy the lack of small and medium-scale enterprises had. It was decided to allow people to set up small private business units—"economic partnerships"—of two to thirty people engaged in any trade or industry, except agriculture.

If more than thirty people wished to establish a new business unit, they could set up a "petty cooperative."

Under the conditions of stagnating real wages, many people employed in the state and cooperative sectors were ready to work beyond the usual eight hours per working day to add to their earnings from there. In fact, many people had had additional illegal incomes for a long time already, and the idea was to make that situation legal. The establishment of "intra-enterprise contract groups" was also a suitable solution for the labor shortages prevailing in most sectors and regions in Hungary. It meant that employees of an enterprise undertook certain tasks for their own employer during their free time not as employees but jointly, as business partners. Their incomes were subject to taxation but exempt from wage regulation, which made this solution particularly attractive for both sides.

The country where all social capital used to be concentrated in a few hundred state enterprises and large cooperatives now experienced a boom in small-scale business. Several tens of thousands of new business units were established with several hundreds of thousands of employees. For most of them, this activity compensated for the income losses on the first job, but at the cost of increasing self-exploitation. Somewhat contrary to expectations, the intra-enterprise contract groups proved to be nothing else than a new form of overtime work, with some autonomy in work organization. The economic partnerships and the petty cooperatives, in turn, proved to be genuine autonomous business units whose survival or failure depended exclusively on their market performance. Mostly they did not offer the same kind of products as the state and cooperative enterprises but products and services that were simply unavailable on the Hungarian market. As a result of their establishment, the market supply was marginally improved and the operation of the economy became a little bit more flexible than it had been before.

As a result of this new development, the ownership structure of the Hungarian economy underwent some significant, although not substantial, change. Up until the early 1980s, social ownership dominated absolutely. In 1980, the legal private sector contributed only 3 percent of the gross domestic product. Even if we add the only one important semiprivate sector, the household plots in agriculture, the two sectors together did not reach 10 percent. About 90 percent of the gross domestic product was produced by the state sector and the so-called cooperative sector, which, however, mostly represented large agricultural and industrial enterprises being called cooperatives but, in fact, with very little say of the members in management and great influence of regional or local party and state authorities on management.

By the late 1980s, the share of both the legal private sector and household plots had roughly doubled. The extension of the private sector resulted mainly from the expansion of the economic partnerships while private handicrafts grew only to a limited degree. Under the title of "cooperative ownership," the petty cooperatives represented a new form of ownership, with less dependence on the authorities and somewhat more dependence on their members.

New management forms in state enterprises

The other innovation of the mid-1980s was the effort to overcome the mutual dependence of state administration and enterprise management. In Hungary, as mentioned earlier, state enterprises continued to be subordinated to branch ministries or — in the case of small state enterprises, particularly in retail trade and communal services — to local authorities. It was these authorities who were exclusively entitled to establish a new state enterprise, to merge it with another one, or to split it into several ones. It was these authorities who appointed and dismissed the top managers of the state enterprises and also set their salaries and bonuses. In exceptional cases, they were also entitled to issue orders to them concerning their production and sales activities. It was also their job to form a judgment on the performance of the state enterprises.

That, however, was all. While under the traditional system they had to issue orders regularly and govern the activity of enterprises in a comprehensive way, under the conditions of reform they were assumed to avoid interventions, with very limited exceptions. It is worthwhile noting that, under the traditional system, the ministries had their own output plans and other plans summed up from the plans of the enterprises and they were responsible for fulfilling their plans. Thus their plan fulfillment was absolutely dependent on plan fulfillment of enterprises subordinate to them. The Hungarian reform eliminated plans at the ministry level and, by that means, the dependence of ministries on fulfillment of enterprise plans.

Thus ministries were to set up the enterprises and appoint their top management and then refrain from intervening in their autonomous operation. Provided production and sales of goods were carried on under the conditions of a perfect market, flexibly moving prices, and a continuous supply of all necessary inputs, such a system might work. This, however, had not been the case. The economy continued to be characterized by local shortages. The supply of inputs was far from satisfactory. Prices were only partly liberalized. Thus the emerging conflicts could not be solved by the price mechanism. After two years of balanced development, tensions in the balance of payment reappeared, resulting in a need to promote exports.

In addition to that, the withdrawal of the state administration and the freedom of enterprises did not relate to trade with Comecon countries. The Hungarian branch ministries were the only adequate partners for the branch ministries of the other countries. Such Comecon deliveries continued to be obligatory for enterprises.

Under these conditions the ministries, after a short pause in 1968-69, made frequent use of their powers concerning the appointment, dismissal, and remuneration of top managers. Despite having the right to do so, they hardly ever issued formal orders but frequently "informed" the enterprises about their "wishes" or "expectations" concerning the activities of the latter. And, as soon as enterprises acted according to such wishes and expectations, they lost their responsibility for performance and felt entitled to claim favorable priority treatment in matters of taxation, subsidies, or government price controls. It was in this way that bargaining about the plan was replaced by bargaining about "regulators," for example, about pricing rules, taxation, and subsidies.

The first effort to counter this mechanism was the price reform of 1980. The inventors of this reform assumed that independence of enterprises required reliable prices independent of manipulation by both enterprises and authorities. Domestic wholesale prices were to be deduced from prices on the world market. The intention was to make prices exogenous both to the enterprises and to the authorities. This effort failed primarily due to the fact that

prices that neglect interrelations between supply and demand on the domestic market cannot operate there; consequently, frequent exceptions from the rule had to be made, and this gradually destroyed the system.

The next approach was an institutionalist one. During the early 1980s, it was assumed that the mutual dependence between authorities and enterprises was the primary cause of the distortion of prices and of the preservation of subsidies. Thus emphasis was put on the emancipation of state enterprises. As a first step, the three branch ministries operating in industry were abolished and replaced with one single ministry of industry. This ministry was deprived of any power concerning interenterprise commodity flows and price setting. The second step was the party resolution of April 1984, the intention of which was to make enterprise managers independent of the ministries or local authorities. State enterprises were grouped into three classes. For those operating in mining and energy generation, armament production, and some other areas, subordination to the ministries was preserved. The majority of enterprises — by number of enterprises, not by number of employees or capital size — were freed from the control of the ministries. The smaller ones were transformed into self-managed enterprises in which the management was to be elected and the plan approved by a general meeting of the staff. The bigger ones were to be controlled by an enterprise council half the members of which were to be appointed by the director — or become a member ex officio according to a new statute of the enterprise — and the other half elected by the staff. This council, in turn, was to elect — or, at the beginning, to confirm — the director, make any decisions concerning mergers or splitting the enterprise, and approve long-term plans.

This reform was drafted before Gorbachev's takeover, during the very last months of the period of "stagnation" in the Soviet Union. The way in which it was presented to the public was extremely defensive: it was said not to affect ownership relations at all; the enterprise councils and even the general meetings of the staffs were exercising their powers "on behalf of the state" as the owner. In fact, however, it represented a substantial change in ownership relations: a move from traditional Soviet-type state ownership to a hybrid between a managerial and a self-management version. Anyway, a significant portion of property rights was to be transferred from the authorities to the enterprises. The powers to merge or split an enterprise, to appoint or dismiss the director, to set the director's salary—all this was now within the power of the enterprise council or the general meeting of the staff.

In fact, the experiment with enterprise councils failed. Formally, it represented a move in the direction of self-management. Since, however, the measures were drafted and introduced exclusively from above, they actually resulted in a strengthening of the role of that managerial group as holder of property rights, a role that that group had already shared with the state and party authorities during the 1970s. The main problem, however, was different. At the very time when the "new forms of enterprise management" were introduced, Hungary experienced serious tensions in its foreign trade. During the international debt crisis of 1982, the country hardly avoided rescheduling. Import controls, essentially nonexistent since 1968, were reintroduced and the practice of export contracts between the government and enterprises emerged. Government organs including the new ministry of industry again obtained substantial powers vis-à-vis

the enterprises not as holders of property rights but as holders of control functions, together with the ministries of finances and of foreign trade. Despite their greater legal or formal independence, Hungarian state enterprises were more dependent on bargaining with state authorities by the mid-1980s than they had been 10-15 years earlier.

TOWARD A MARKET ECONOMY

That hybrid state of the economic system that I characterized as "neither plan nor market" some years ago László Antal described as "indirectly centralized" in his important book on the Hungarian reform experience.[3] In this way he distinguished the system both from the traditional Soviet-type system called directly centralized and from the desirable market economy called decentralized. He stressed that, under the reformed Hungarian system, economic processes continue to be governed by the authorities. The change that occurred was that direct means of governing the economy were replaced with indirect ones. It is still the authorities who intervene in all details of economic turnover, and market self-regulation is missing. The message of this type of analysis is that a further step toward a decentralized market system with self-regulation or competition is desired.

The third round of Hungarian economic reforms represents this very course. It was made possible by three factors, all closely connected. First, economists and officials understood by the late 1980s that indirect centralization may harm almost as much as direct centralization: motives to improve efficiency were also missing in this system,

3. László Antal, *Gazdaságirányítási és pénzügyi rendszerünk a reform útján* [The Hungarian economic control and financial system reformed] (Budapest: Közgazdasági és Jogi Könyvkiadó, 1982).

and voluntarism[4] was not prevented here either. Second, the deep political crisis resulted in a reconsideration of social values and objectives. The belief in the supremacy of planning had disappeared, and the conviction that a genuine market is indispensable prevailed. Instead of the "organic combination of planning and market," the idea of a "socialist market economy" or even "market economy without any attribute" gained ground. Third, the external conditions were favorable for such a shift: *perestroika* in the Soviet Union removed ideological constraints from the Hungarian process of rethinking.

So far, the first steps in this direction have been taken. In the course of the banking reform of 1987 the formal single National Bank, being simultaneously a central bank and the only business bank, was replaced by a separate central bank and several business banks between the services of which enterprises have a free choice. Bonds as a form of capital investment both for enterprises and for individuals were introduced. They are subject to free purchase and sale. A new company law was passed that reintroduces joint-stock companies and other company forms in Hungary. A separate transformation law allows existing state enterprises to transform into joint-stock companies. The upper employment limit for privately owned companies is 500 employees, which, in fact, means removal of any limitation on private initiative. In addition to that, the government intends to launch a comprehensive privatization program, particularly with respect to retail trade and services.

The emergence of a strong private sector in small-scale business is very likely now. More open remains the question of what new forms of ownership will replace state ownership in large-scale industry. Let us wait and see.

---

4. Willfulness [ed.].

ANNALS, *AAPSS*, **507**, January 1990

Economic Reform of Socialism:
The Dengist Course in China

By JAN S. PRYBYLA

ABSTRACT: After the death of Mao Zedong it became clear that the Chinese economy needed to be reformed. The need arose from the economy's serious quality problems: chronic shortages, waste, low factor productivity, and technological backwardness. By 1979 it had been decided that reform must be structural and consist of decentralization of decision making that involves marketization of transactions and privatization of property rights. For the centrally planned system's quality problems to be solved successfully, reform must be comprehensive, that is, systemwide, not partial and selective. China, however, opted for the latter. By mid-1988 it was clear that incomplete reform did not do the quality-improvement job expected of it and that it produced some additional problems. There were distinct signs of regression as the reform momentum fizzled out.

Jan S. Prybyla is professor of economics at the Pennsylvania State University. He is the author of The Political Economy of Communist China *(1970);* The Chinese Economy: Problems and Policies *(1978, 1981);* Issues in Socialist Economic Modernization *(1980); and* Market and Plan under Socialism: The Bird in the Cage *(1987), as well as numerous articles in scholarly journals and periodicals. He is a contributing editor of* Current History *and member of the board of editors of* Comparative Strategy.

AFTER the death of Mao Zedong, in September 1976, and two years of domestic political housecleaning — the campaign against the Gang of Four and the progressive political neutering of Mao's allegedly hand-picked successor, Hua Guofeng — the Chinese Communist leadership under Deng Xiaoping got down to the business of reviving and revitalizing the country's economy. The signs of morbidity revealed by that economy were many, among them: chronic shortages of wanted goods; huge resource misallocations — waste; breakdown of the incentive system — low factor productivity; and technological backwardness. These signs were similar to those shown by other qualitatively deficient centrally planned economies of the Soviet type. Reviving and revitalizing the economy, which began in earnest in 1979, was given the shorthand name of "Four Modernizations," referring to the four areas — agriculture, industry, science and technology, and national defense — to be modernized. By 1980, having made what may turn out to have been a fatal mistake by crushing popular demands for a fifth modernization, democracy, the majority of the leadership had concluded that modernization required more than old-fashioned rectification of the party's erroneous style of work and that all-embracing shortage, waste, apathy, and technological retardation were due to more fundamental causes than policy mistakes. What was needed was a reexamination of the economic system itself, of its principles and institutional arrangements, followed by a restructuring of both. There was need for reform.

WHAT REFORM?

For a Communist leadership to acknowledge, however reluctantly, that central planning is responsible for chronic shortages, waste, ossified enthusiasm for production, and lack of innovation is in itself a remarkable achievement. In the Soviet Union it took the best part of seventy years to arrive at that conclusion, and not everyone in the party concurs. In China the process took only thirty years, and there, too, there is still no unanimity on the subject within the leadership. Important as is this discovery, it represents only the first step on a long and tortuous road. Once it is agreed that there has to be reform, the question that naturally arises is, What reform? What system is to replace the existing one? How does one get there from here? What is the minimum critical mass of reform measures that has to be introduced for the changes to be successful in eliminating shortages, reducing waste, improving incentives, and stimulating innovation? Can the political traffic bear the minimum mass of indispensable economic changes?

When it becomes clear that under the scrutiny of the four qualitative criteria of abundance, static efficiency, motivation, and innovation — hence, dynamic efficiency — administrative command planning does not work, there are only two systemic remedies. The first is perfect electronic centralization of allocative decisions — computopia; the second is decentralization of such decisions, which means transition to a workably competitive market system. Computopia, or perfect dictatorship, involving mathematical models, behavioral engineering, and electronic gadgetry, is technically impracticable at present and ethically repugnant always. It cannot solve, now or in the future, the socialist system's inability to supply people efficiently with increasing quantities and qualities of goods that the people want at prices they are willing and able to pay, which is what any self-respecting economic system must reasonably be expected to do. Therefore the only available alternative is economic decentralization, or economic freedom, which is synonymous with the market system. This was understood in China by the end of the 1970s and in Russia by the mid-1980s. But, as we shall see, it was not fully understood by those at the top who were going to bring the reform about. Nor is it fully comprehended by them to this day.

MARKET SYSTEM

It is important to make the point that the necessary transition — necessary to deal successfully with the planning system's four qualitative defects — is to the market system, not to individual markets. A system is an organic whole of internally consistent, interrelated, and interacting parts combined to form a regular relationship for the attainment of given purposes. The given purpose of an economic system is the optimal allocation of relatively scarce resources among competing and changing alternative uses. Each system has an inexorable internal logic that requires that its interdependent parts work harmoniously together, that is, that they be compatible and not work at cross-purposes. The parts comprise institutions — socially agreed-on and legally sanctioned ways of doing things — and ideas — positive theories and ethical norms of conduct.

The market means voluntary, contractual, competitive, horizontal transactions carried out by individual, autonomous, property-owning buyers and sellers who consult spontaneously generated price signals for utility- and profit-maximizing purposes. They generate the price signals by disbursing money votes to reveal their preferences for the alternatives facing them. The market system is the internally consistent and allocatively optimal web of all this higgling and bargaining. Indispensable to the market system are the principles of individual autonomy — the individual person's inherent right to make decisions and the personal responsibility for those decisions; voluntariness, or freedom from externally imposed choice; competition, or the presence of alternatives; and private property, or the socially sanctioned and legally protected right of individuals and freely constituted associations of individuals to the use of, transfer of, and income from things, including goods, services, and factors.

Moreover, the market system, because it is not foolproof or crookproof and because it is subject to dislocations and breakdowns like any other man-made mechanism, requires for its proper operation not only a system of laws but the rule of law, that is, adherence to an external absolute system of morality that recognizes the inherent, natural dignity of the individual person and of personal rights, including the right to own property, that do not derive from any human agency, the government included. The presence of government in the market system has never been contested. But the functions of government must be limited, and government, like everyone else, must be subject to legal order. "Justice," says Adam Smith in the The Theory of Moral Sentiments (1759), "is the main pillar that upholds the whole edifice. If it is removed, the great, the immense fabric of human society . . . must in a moment crumble into dust."[1]

1. Adam Smith, *The Theory of Moral Sentiments*, ed. D. D. Raphael and A. L. Macfie (New York: Oxford University Press, Clarendon Press, 1976), p. 96.

OBSTACLES TO REFORM

China's long march to economic reform quickly, perhaps from the outset, ran into two roadblocks. The first was the unwillingness to go all the way to the market system but instead to use individual, quite imperfect, and unintegrated markets to infuse life into the arthritic plan. Whereas economic freedom is indivisible, in China selective and disjointed marketizing and privatizing was used — in the sense of being exploited — for purposes of allegedly perfecting the plan. "One of the major goals of China's program of reform is the creation of an economic system in which 'the state regulates the market, the market guides the enterprise.'"[2] That is a sure prescription for nonreform, failure, and regression, for stagflation with Chinese characteristics, or for the Chinese equivalent of Brezhnevite and Gorbachevite stagnation. It is so because markets cannot work efficiently if they are not integrated into a system. Their functioning is impaired and their allocative outcomes are distorted when they are mixed with instrumentalities and principles that belong to a different, in fact, opposite and incompatible system of administrative command. What results is not a mixed system but a mix-up. It is not possible to have a price mechanism that is at one and the same time flexible — responsive to changing utility and cost conditions — and administratively fixed. Markets cannot perform their efficiency function if they are free for, say, rice but do not exist for the land, labor, and capital that produce the rice. Allocatively rational market prices must be explained by an allocatively meaningful price theory, not by

2. Wang Jiye, "The State, the Market and the Enterprise," *Beijing Review*, 10-16 Apr. 1989, p. 20. Wang is director of the State Planning Commission's Economic Research Institute.

a political scientology of labor exploitation by means of surplus value. For government intervention in the workings of markets to be effective through, say, monetary policy, the banking system cannot be the administrative appendage of the government, and there have to be free financial markets.

There is no such thing as market socialism or a socialist market. There is a market system or there is a system of central planning. The market system must be unequivocally conditioned by the principles and practice of individual autonomy, voluntariness of transactions, competition, and private-property rights, that is, by economic freedom and limited government intervention in behalf of that freedom, for example, to assure equal opportunity for everyone at the start, protect contracts, correct market failures as, for instance, in the provision of public goods. The in-between construct of neither market nor plan, half of this and half of the other, produces in practice the kind of mercantilism that Adam Smith inveighed against more than two centuries ago but that persists to this day in most underdeveloped countries — that are wrongly labeled capitalist — and in those socialist ones — China included — that have grafted disjointed and imperfect markets and limited private-property rights onto the body of a partly decomposed plan. In such a nonsystem, neither markets nor planning works. Markets are corrupted by the monopoly Communist Party's inserting itself into the economic process through the plan — political bargaining or exchanges of favors — and the plan is corrupted by the money-making opportunities provided by politicized markets to officials in positions of bureaucratic power.

To sum up: to be successful in providing increasing quantities and qualities of goods and services that people want at prices they are willing and able to pay, and to do this efficiently at a point in time and over time, the market system must fulfill the following general conditions:

1. All markets, for goods as well as factors, must be free. There must be free entry and exit for buyers and sellers, no rationing of inputs or outputs, and voluntariness of transactions.

2. Prices must reflect relative costs to producers and utilities to users, and they must be the principal source of information, coordination, and incentive in the system.

3. There must be workable competition, that is, the presence of alternatives. This implies — with strictly circumscribed exceptions — the absence of monopolies private and public, central and regional.

4. There must be maximizing — rational — behavior by sellers and buyers. Sellers must want to make profits by responding to buyer demands expressed in competitive prices, and buyers must want to maximize their satisfactions.

5. Private-property rights must be dominant. Such rights carry with them the obligation of personal responsibility for decisions freely made.

6. Macroeconomic — monetary and fiscal — instrumentalities of indicative government intervention in the market process must be in place, as must institutionalized arrangements, such as social security and unemployment insurance, to deal with market disturbances and structural market failures.[3]

The second roadblock to reform in China has been the absence of the rule of law. The situation is better than it was in Mao's time, for at least there are now laws on the books whereas formerly there was next to nothing — a void praised by some Western legal scholars for being a manifes-

tation of social cohesiveness and maturity. But lawlessness can exist when there are many laws, as demonstrated by Stalin's and post-Stalin Russia. Even had there been the political will to go all the way on the road of economic democratization, once arrived at the market, the system could not have worked in the absence of a legal order.

COMPONENTS OF ECONOMIC REFORM

Sectorally, reform-tending changes in China began in agriculture (1979-84) and then proceeded to industry (1984-88). Beginning in mid-1988 the reformist movement in both sectors slowed significantly and by mid-1989 there had been intimations of retreat.

The reformist movement tackled two problems: marketization of the price system, and privatization of property rights. In both instances the movement was carried less than half way, resulting by the end of the decade in a two-track arrangement: part plan, part market; part socialized, part private property. This malformed offspring of plan and market magnified the defects of both parents and proved resistant to attempts at disciplining it either through market-type macroeconomic fiscal and monetary interventions — these being at an infantile stage of development and ineffective because of the unintegrated nature and imperfection of markets for individual goods — or through concurrently used administrative orders. The symptoms of the systemic disorder included repeated bouts of industrial overheating, inflation, unemployment, large and growing income and wealth disparities, and rampant corruption.

Agriculture

Agriculture was quite simply decollectivized. But the decollectivization was

3. Jan S. Prybyla, "China's Economic Experiment: Back from the Market?" *Problems of Communism,* Jan.-Feb. 1989, p. 9.

incomplete. Collective land was distributed to peasant families according to either the number of people or the number of able-bodied workers in the household, sometimes equally. The land was divided into strips for equity's sake: each family received some good land and some bad, some irrigated and some not, some near a road and some far away. The average size of the family farm worked out to about three-quarters of an acre, smaller even than in minimalist Bangladesh. Although land could be consolidated, ceilings were placed both on the size of farm and on the number of laborers, other than family members, who could be hired for wages.

Legally, the land remained social property and could be sold by the family only with the collective's permission. In other words, transfer rights were not privatized. The land was, in essence, leased to the peasants for periods of up to 15 years, longer for orchards and woods. Only fairly extensive, but not complete, use rights were privatized. Collective farming was transformed into family tenant farming, the state being the landlord. Moreover, the principle of voluntariness was not observed. In exchange for the right to use the land allotted to it, the peasant family was obliged to sign a contract with the local state authorities to deliver to the state specified amounts and assortments of produce at state-set prices, which were normally below, often well below, the going market price. If the family did not sign a contract, it could not use the land. Anything above the contracted delivery quotas could be consumed or sold by the peasants on the free market at market prices. This means that income rights from property were only partly privatized. The peasants' profits from using land were affected by the peasants' contractual obligations that had

to be fulfilled at nonmarket, allocatively irrational prices.

An important requirement of marketization, the rule of horizontality of transactions, was violated since the state party to the contract was clearly in a dominant position that it used to the full by extracting from the peasants, in addition to contractual deliveries, all manner of taxes, levies, and fees, nominally for the upkeep of collective infrastructures — for example, roads, schools, clinics, irrigation and drainage facilities — but not infrequently for less socially minded purposes. Horizontality of transactions was also absent on the input side. The state remained the only supplier of indispensable inputs — chemical fertilizer, pesticides, plastics, farm equipment — which it sold to the peasants at prices of its own making and on its own conditions. For example, chemical fertilizer and deliveries of hand tractors were made conditional on the peasants' growing what the state wanted them to grow — usually grain — even against the dictates of market price signals, thus distorting the peasant's maximizing behavior.

Contracts, hence land, were also tied to the peasant families' observance of the state's birth-control policy. If there was one child over the permitted quota, the contract could be revoked — or, more simply, the roof of the offending peasant's house would be removed by birth-control cadres.

In times of cash shortage, such as 1988-89, the state resorted to paying the farmers with IOUs instead of money, in violation of both laws and the rule of law.

The produce acquired from the peasants under the contract was sold in urban areas by the state at subsidized government-fixed prices that were lower than free-market prices and the contractual prices paid for the produce to the peasants. The result is that China has a dual agricultural price system of flexible pseudomarket prices — although these are interfered with by local authorities whenever they exceed what the officials consider to be just levels — and state-fixed prices that bear little or no relation to supply and demand. There are, therefore, some quasi-free markets for goods but practically no markets, free or otherwise, for land, labor, and capital. Labor can move to rural towns but not to the larger cities, although it does so, massively and illegally, adding to urban food shortages by buying up unrationed but subsidized foods in government shops. Agricultural capital such as small and medium-sized tractors, livestock, draft animals, carts, and trucks are legally owned by the peasants, but most farm capital of industrial origin has to be bought from the state monopolist or acquired on a few markets for surplus equipment. Some agricultural commodities — mostly staples such as grain, vegetable oil, and pork — continue to be rationed on and off but are also available on the free market. Some nonstaples — for example, eggs, vegetables, aquatic products — can be purchased on the free market either for money or, sometimes, for grain coupons, which the peasant sellers use to purchase grain at low subsidized prices in the state outlets to feed to their livestock.

The long and the short of it is that all the conditions of a successful market system are to various degrees violated in China's rural economy. Hence changes in supply and demand are not accurately or promptly or even at all translated into reallocation of resources. The result is systemic near chaos. The absence of legally sanctioned private-property rights in land and labor — so long as labor mobility is legally obstructed, the laborer does not own his or her labor — has a negative effect on motivation.

"'Farmers,'" says one Chinese economist, "'must feel that they have control over the land. Nowadays farmers use their lands carelessly and make little effort to improve soil fertility. They act as if they don't expect to live off the land too long.'"[4] Perhaps most important of all, there is no popular trust. The peasants do not trust the government. They look at the white slips — the IOUs — with which they have been paid for produce delivered to the government at below-market prices — 20 percent of the grain crop in 1988 was paid for with white slips, most of which remained unredeemed in mid-1989 — and they refuse to hand over any more goods. The government responds with veiled threats of recollectivization, squeezes by local cadres, and other harassments. But it is not just a matter of white slips; it is also one of the continued absence of the rule of law and the very imperfect and incomplete institutionalization of the economic reform at a time when personalized power is insecure and held in popular disrespect.

By 1985 the initial, one-time boost to farm production and productivity due to the freeing of the peasants from the shackles of the collective and from the forced egalitarianism of the Mao era had worn off. The production of grain, cotton, and other basic products stagnated. The excessive parcelization of land, neglect by the state of infrastructural investments in the countryside — resulting in what appears to be net disinvestment — persistent uncertainty and insecurity of tenure experienced by farm families, the unfavorable terms of trade between official prices that the farmers received for their contractual deliveries to the

4. Li Yining, professor of economic management, Beijing University, quoted by Adi Ignatius, "Chinese Policies Run at Cross Purposes in Fumbled Attempt to End Farm Crisis," *Wall Street Journal,* 1 Feb. 1989.

state and the prices they had to pay for modern inputs such as chemical fertilizer, pesticides, and machinery weakened the initial positive effects of the incentives of the earlier property reforms. Per capita output of basic foods stagnated. The hand of those in the leadership who had opposed reform from the beginning was strengthened, and warnings of the dire social consequences of grain shortages became increasingly common and strident in high quarters.

Urban industry

The record agricultural production of 1984, which has not been equaled since then, encouraged the reformist leadership faction to push ahead with similar, but not identical, partial privatization and marketization of industry in order to bring the two major segments of the economy into institutional harmony. Unlike agriculture, which had been subject since 1956 to the collective regime, the greater part of urban industry — commerce included — was in the much more bureaucratized, financially coddled, supply-favored, and reform-resistant state sector. While the desocialization of property rights — that is, the incomplete privatization of use and income rights to land — in agriculture had been to the level of a truly private unit, the family, in industry matters were different.

Although much has been written about the phenomenal expansion of private business, such progress has to be kept in perspective. The growth was from zero and even at its peak did not represent more than a very small fraction — 4-5 percent — of industrial output value and the urban labor force. Private enterprise was, and continues to be, concentrated in retail trade, consumer services, and construction. While useful in absorbing unemployed workers

and consumer welfare intensive, it remains a small feature of China's urban-industrial property landscape even though its real share — if unregistered transactions were properly counted — is probably larger than the official figures allow.

More quantitatively important has been the denationalization of some medium-sized state firms and the transfer of these firms to the relatively more autonomous, less planned, and bureaucrat-ridden cooperative sector. In the decade 1978-87, the share of state enterprises in the gross output value of industry declined from 80 to 60 percent, while the share of cooperative industry rose from 19 to 27 percent. Mixed forms of property — state-cooperative, cooperative, private, state-foreign private — have also emerged or reemerged, as have leasing and subcontracting arrangements. Wholly owned foreign firms have been established. Still, the key raw-materials, energy, metallurgical, machine-tool, chemical, transportation, and telecommunications industries and the bulk of wholesale trade remain the property of the state at various levels — central, provincial, municipal, local.

An attempt was made — but it did not get very far — to transform state and cooperative firms into stock companies held by workers in those firms and even by the public at large. Ideological opposition to such quasi privatization of public property was countered by the argument that issuing shares of stock to workers was merely "reestablishing the individual rights of workers," and since everyone in China is now by definition a worker, issuance of such stock to the general public was doctrinally correct and perfectly socialist. Because it is not easy to sell multimillion-yuan enterprises to either workers or the public at large in a country where the per capita income is equivalent to around $300 a year and financial markets are primitive, ingenious theoretical schemes have been hatched by reformist economists to overcome these difficulties, but so far with little practical application.[5] The stock markets located in a few of China's larger cities — for example, Shanghai — are pathetic backroom affairs and most of the stock resembles bonds.

The conclusion that emerges is that privatization of China's industry has fallen far short of even the partial and unfinished privatization of agriculture. Moreover, like Liu Shaoqi, who in 1958 was made to publicly advocate Great Leap policies with which he profoundly disagreed, party head Zhao Ziyang, the reputed leader of the reformist leadership faction, found it politically expedient in 1988 to pledge publicly — before the Central Committee of the Communist Party — that "China's state-owned enterprises will never be privatized."

Industrial marketization, as measured by the growth of a free industrial price system comprising goods and factors, has similarly been piecemeal, hesitant, contradictory, and modest. Although there has been a reduction in the number of mandatory output targets issued by the planners to industrial enterprises and in centrally determined input rationing, compulsory norms have not been totally abolished nor have the irrational administratively set prices attached to the physically controlled outputs and inputs. By and large, the industrial price system remains allocatively irrational, seriously distorting information conveyed to planners and firms alike. It makes nonsense of the marginally greater autonomy granted to firms for the sake of reducing allocative waste and improving incentives to managers and workers. As in agriculture, there is a two-track price arrangement: some prices — the more pervasive ones of energy, materials, and producer goods — are set administratively by the planners and bear as much resemblance to relative costs and utilities as Leninism does to Jeffersonian democracy. Parallel to these are so-called free-market prices — so-called because whenever the authorities do not like them, they freeze them or compensate with subsidies those who claim to incur losses because of them, provided the plaintiffs have good personal political connections cemented by bribes and services rendered.

Schizophrenic prices apply to goods as well as factors. For example, most industrial capital is allocated administratively to producers, but above-plan capital goods can be bought and sold on residual producer-goods markets in some cities. Most labor is allocated physically by labor bureaus and is paid under the old Soviet-type basic job grade wage and bonus system, the relationship of which to marginal revenue product is purely coincidental. Most of this labor is permanently attached to its work unit (*danwei*), and this attachment extends in some cases to the children of retired workers. Some labor is hired — and, one is told, can even be fired — nowadays under a contract system with the wage rate being determined by the enterprise. Few firms go bankrupt, especially large state enterprises, no matter how deep in the red they are.

"'We're living in the worst of two worlds,'" says an official of the State Council, "'where central directives are no longer effective and the free market is distorted by all sorts of restrictions.'"[6]

---

5. "Privatising China," *Economist* (London), 11 Feb. 1989, p. 36.

6. Quoted by Julia Leung, "Energy Crisis Shuts Factories in China: Fast Growth, Policy Confusion Blamed," *Wall Street Journal*, 6 Jan. 1989.

CONCLUSION

While it is true that China's economy confronts on a daily basis objective problems of unparalleled magnitude — for example, a net addition of 26 people every minute, people who have to be fed, clothed, housed, educated, kept in good health, and eventually employed — and that policy mistakes add to these problems, the fundamental obstacle to China's modernization is the inadequacy of the economic system. That the Soviet-type system is the prime cause of China's economic problems, as it is of Russia's, is recognized in China by most people, many leaders included.

What China's post-Mao attempt to solve these problems clearly shows is how difficult it is to restructure a system completely. Economic reform, the total replacement of a system at both the theoretical and the institutional levels, calls for an act of prodigious political courage and will, readiness to risk the pain of transition, and willingness to liquidate oneself as the exclusive retainer of power. Because of the dimensions of what is required to bring about economic reform and the strength of special interests that are sure to be adversely affected by the change, the temptation is to compromise, postpone, and draw back when trouble strikes. The tendency is to mix selected elements of incompatible systems, passing them off as remedies under an attractive name — for example, "socialism with Chinese characteristics" — while in reality they lack cohesion and substance. Although the last word has not been spoken, the signs since 1988 are that the Chinese experiment, like the Soviet one before it, will go pfut unless spontaneous forces from below become strong and resolute enough to take over the half reform from the discredited and economically irresolute party and guide it to its only effective and viable modernizing conclusion in a full market system.

ANNALS, *AAPSS,* **507,** January 1990

A Property-Rights Analysis
of the Yugoslav Miracle

By SVETOZAR PEJOVICH

ABSTRACT: The Yugoslav experiment with labor participation in the management of business firms captured worldwide attention. The critics of capitalism seemed confident that the labor-managed economy would provide a long-sought alternative to the accomplishments of capitalism. Instead, the labor-managed economy has produced a crisis of enormous proportion in Yugoslavia. The article argues that the economic crisis in Yugoslavia is a predictable consequence of the system of labor participation in the management of business firms. It demonstrates that inherent in the structure of property rights of the labor-managed economy are some positive transaction costs and negative incentives that are specific to its institutional structure. Those transaction costs and disincentives are responsible for inflation, unemployment, declining income, and other economic problems in Yugoslavia. The conclusion is that the labor-managed economy is not a viable institutional arrangement.

Svetozar Pejovich is Jeff Montgomery Professor of Economics and director of the Center for Free Enterprise at Texas A&M University. He received a law degree at the University of Belgrade, Yugoslavia, and a Ph.D. in economics at Georgetown University, Washington, D.C. He has written and edited over ten books and numerous scholarly articles and is included in the second edition of Who's Who in Economics.

NOTE: The Lynde and Harry Bradley Foundation has provided financial assistance in support of my research for this article.

T HE Yugoslav experiment with labor participation in the management of business firms — hereafter called the "labor-managed economy" — captured worldwide attention in the 1950s and 1960s. Starting with a system that was a carbon copy of the Soviet economy, the Yugoslav leaders, driven by their own survival requirements in the aftermath of the Tito-Stalin rift, embarked on a series of institutional changes that aimed at approximating the production efficiency of capitalism while preserving the socialist character of the economy. Business firms were given some limited independence, horizontal relations — contracts — slowly replaced vertical relations — administrative orders — among economic agents, and new property rights were beginning to emerge.

By the early 1970s, the Yugoslav economic experiment was pretty much in place. It set the Yugoslav economy apart from the free-market, private-property economies in the West and centrally planned economies in the East. Perhaps the most important difference between the institutional structure in Yugoslavia and elsewhere was in the mode of entry into decision making. In the West, the mode of entry into decision making is the prerogative of ownership, either directly or through hired managers. In the East, the mode of entry into decision making is the prerogative of the ruling group. In Yugoslavia, the mode of entry into decision making is the prerogative of the working collective subject to the formal and informal limits imposed by the ruling group. The critics of capitalism seemed confident that the labor-managed economy would provide a long-sought socialist alternative to the accomplishments of capitalism. Horvat asserted that self-management by workers would accelerate the growth of output and technical progress

beyond anything known before,[1] Vanek became its major marketing agent in the West, while many European economists linked the idea of codetermination with the Yugoslav economic experiment.

At about the same time, a series of property-rights models of the labor-managed type of economy were developed. Those models demonstrated that the involuntary labor-managed economy is not a viable institutional arrangement[2] because inherent in its institutional structure are incentives and transaction costs that tend to produce unemployment, inflation, low growth, and liquidity problems. Looking back on the performance of the Yugoslav economy, it is clear that the property-rights analysis of the Yugoslav firm has passed the test of time.

The objective of this article is to explain why the involuntary labor participation in the management of business firms is not a viable alternative to a free-market, private-property economy. To accomplish this objective, the article describes basic institutional features of the Yugoslav system of

1. Alexander Bajt, "The Economic Growth of Yugoslavia" (Paper delivered at the CESES Conference, Florence, 1983).

2. Alexander Bajt, "Property in Capital and the Means of Production in Socialist Economies," *Journal of Law and Economics*, 11:1-4 (Apr. 1988); Armen Alchian and Harold Demsetz, "Production, Information Costs, and Economic Organization," *American Economic Review*, 62:777-95 (Dec. 1972); Svetozar Pejovich, "The Firm, Monetary Policy and Property Rights in a Planned Economy," *Western Economic Journal*, 7:193-200 (Mar. 1969); Eirik Furubotn and Svetozar Pejovich, "Property Rights and the Behavior of the Firm in a Socialist State: The Example of Yugoslavia," in *The Economics of Property Rights*, ed. E. Furubotn and S. Pejovich (Cambridge, MA: Ballinger, 1974), pp. 227-52; Svetozar Pejovich, "Freedom, Property Rights and Innovation in Socialism," *Kyklos*, 40(4):461-75 (1987); Michael Jensen and William Meckling, "Rights and Production Functions," *Journal of Business*, 52:469-506 (1979).

involuntary self-management, discusses their effects on transaction costs and incentives, and offers an explanation for the ruling group's decision in the late 1980s to announce a new round of institutional changes.

THE DEVELOPMENT OF THE YUGOSLAV ECONOMIC SYSTEM, 1950-70

The turning point for the Yugoslav economy's deviation from the Soviet model was the Law on Management of Enterprises by Workers' Collectives of 1950. This law stated a few general principles about the labor-managed firm, established the workers' council as the highest governing body of the Yugoslav firm, and, in effect, promised to transfer some property rights in the firm to its employees.

Once the employees were promised the right of managing their firm, the government had to clarify the problem of handling the firm's fixed assets. The Law on the Management of Fixed Assets by Enterprises of 1951 set a few basic criteria for the subsequent legal and administrative decisions concerning the firm's rights in capital goods. The law gave the workers' council a sui generis property right over the firm's capital: the right of use. The firm was allowed to sell its assets to other firms, to buy capital goods from other firms, and to change the composition of its assets. The right of use, however, is a narrower property right than the right of ownership because the firm must maintain the book value of its assets. This requirement, which asserts the state's right of ownership, is satisfied via obligatory reinvestment of depreciation allowances and the proceeds from the sale of capital goods.

As new property rights were introduced into the Yugoslav economy, horizontal relations between economic agents—contracts—began to replace vertical relationships—economic planning. The Law on Banks of 1961 started a long and perhaps the most difficult process in the development of the Yugoslav system of self-management: a search for the method of allocating investment funds in an environment in which the ruling group has the right of ownership in capital goods while the working collective has the right to appropriate the flow of returns from those assets. The investment behavior of the Yugoslav firm is perhaps the most critical issue in evaluating the behavior of the labor-managed firm.

The last phase in the development of the Yugoslav system occurred in the early 1970s and was institutionalized in the Constitution of 1974 and the Law on Associated Labor of 1976. They said that if and when the results of the joint labor of a group of employees could be measured in terms of value in either the market or within the firm, the group should be encouraged to form its own plant, such as for shipping and receiving in a manufacturing firm, and elect its own workers' council. When the firm had more than one plant, the firm's workers' council consisted of representatives from each plant. The purpose of this change was to dilute decision-making powers of Yugoslav managers.

The five legal acts that have been described defined de jure principles of the Yugoslav economic system. The subsequent laws and regulations determined de facto development of the system. The former are the ruling group's declarations of intention, while the latter are their actual translation into real life. In general, the divergence between de jure and de facto institutional changes has two causes. First, major legal acts have unintended and unexpected consequences that force the lawmakers to modify them or to redefine them or even to change them as time goes by. Second, the translation of major legislative acts into specific actions is in the hands of various implementing agencies that often have their own interpretations of the lawmakers' intentions.

By the mid-1970s, major institutional features of the Yugoslav economy were (1) the state ownership of capital goods, (2) the employees' ownership of the returns from capital goods held by the firm, (3) the employees' right to govern the firm, (4) the substitution of bank credit for the system of administrative distribution of investable funds, and (5) the system of quasi-contractual agreements between firms, institutions, and various agencies. The term "quasi" means here that contracts were not voluntary. They were mandated by law and many contractual terms were stipulated in advance. This institutional framework defined the bundle of property rights in the firm in Yugoslavia as follows: (1) the employees own the residual, (2) the employees have the right to fire and hire the firm's management, including the director, and (3) the employees can neither sell the rights just specified nor continue to enjoy them when they leave the firm. Moreover, the right to capture the residual was contingent on the association of one's live labor with the firm's physical assets.

De facto development of the labor-managed economy was cyclical, with ups and downs that reflected internal and external political conditions in Yugoslavia. Yet, over a period of twenty years, the ruling group developed a unique system that was supposed to end the alienation of labor, ensure industrial democracy at the firm's level, provide incentives for the collective to seek the best allocation of resources, and encourage the flow of innovation.

Instead, the labor-managed economy has produced a crisis of enormous propor-

tions in Yugoslavia. Inflation has already destroyed the dinar; the value of the dollar increased from 4500 dinars in December 1988 to 36,000 dinars in October 1989. The rate of unemployment is well into two digits. The rate of growth has been negative in the late 1980s. Personal incomes are declining. Most enterprises are not liquid, and a sizable number are being subsidized. Finally, commercial banks have yet to develop sound economic criteria for long-term investment decisions. Clearly, the cause or causes of the economic crisis in Yugoslavia constitute an important analytical issue.

One explanation for the crisis is that the government has failed to develop and implement good economic policies. In mid-1988, Branko Horvat, a Yugoslav economist, claimed that he could put together a team of economists that would quickly turn the economy around. This type of attitude toward economic problems considers government as an active agent, justifies its action-oriented approach over a range of specific issues, and seeks economic remedies in the relation between policy instruments that are available to government and goals expressed by a social-welfare function that is constructed by social engineers. It reflects a social engineer's conviction that there must exist a set of discretionary public policies that will stabilize the economy, neutralize exogenous shocks, and enhance growth.

This approach to economic problems is consistent with both the objective of preserving the prevailing institutional structure as well as the traditional wisdom of political philosophy that says that better leaders make better government, that better scholars make better policies, and that better policies lead to better outcomes. The interventionist approach assumes that policymakers, politicians, and bureaucrats know the social-welfare function, that they are unselfishly guided by it, and, most critical, that they know the responses of interacting economic agents to their policies.

The fallacy of this argument arises from two conditions. First, the policymakers could not possibly have full and reliable information about the economy's dynamic response structure. Thus the implementation of economic policies contributes, with substantial probability, to the opposite of the desired objectives. Second, the interventionist economic policy implicitly assumes a public-interest theory of government. The characterization of policymakers as optimizers of a social-welfare function expressing a social consensus is, however, remarkably irrelevant.[3] Nobel laureate Stigler wrote that "the state is a potential threat to every industry in the society. With its power to prohibit or compel, to take or give money, the state can and does selectively help or hurt a vast number of industries."[4]

The property-rights analysis is another method for evaluating current economic problems in Yugoslavia. It rejects the interventionist presumption that a group of people is somehow empowered to mold the world for others and endowed with sufficient knowledge to do it. The property-rights analysis is about the rules of the game. In the context of this approach, economic analysis means an examination of the effects of alternative institutional structures on the economy. Institutions are defined here as the legal, administrative, and customary rules that structure repeated human interactions.

3. Karl Brunner, "The Limits of Economic Policy," in *Socialism: Institutional, Philosophical and Economic Issues*, ed. S. Pejovich (Dordrecht, Holland: Kluwer Academic, 1987), pp. 48-49.

4. George Stigler, "The Theory of Government Regulation," *Bell Journal of Economics and Management Science*, 2:3 (1971).

THE INVOLUNTARY LABOR-MANAGED ECONOMY AND THE SOCIAL-OPPORTUNITY SET

The involuntary labor-managed economy creates a set of specific incentives and transaction costs that affect the social-opportunity set. It is through their own system of incentives and varying transaction costs that institutions affect the behavior of economic agents in ways that are both specific and predictable. The behavior of economic agents, in turn, determines economic outcomes. For the analysis of the comparative efficiency of alternative institutions, it is then important to establish the effects of incentives and transaction costs on the social-opportunity set.

Transaction costs and the social-opportunity set

The total costs of a business activity include production costs and transaction costs. The former are the costs of all the resources, including entrepreneurial skills, required to change inputs into outputs. The standard neoclassical production function is about those costs. The latter are the costs of all the resources, including entrepreneurial skill, required to transfer property rights from one economic agent to another. Transaction costs include the costs of making an exchange — for example, monitoring production, marketing output — and the costs of protecting the institutional structure, for example, by the judiciary or the police. Transaction costs depend critically on the institutional structure.[5] Examples of transaction costs that are specific to the

5. Douglas North and John Wallis, "Measuring the Transaction Sector in the American Economy," in *Long-Term Factors in American Economic Growth*, ed. S. Engerman and R. Gallman (Chicago: University of Chicago Press, 1987), pp. 95-159.

labor-managed economy of Yugoslavia are found in the choice of organization, in the bureaucracy, and in the location of decision making within the labor-managed firm.

The choice of organization. In a free-market, private-property-rights economy, we observe a variety of organizational structures such as small proprietorship, multinationals, not-for-profit firms, and labor-managed firms. All those different types of firms have emerged through voluntary contractual negotiations and have survived competition from other types of firms in their respective lines of activity. In fact, capitalism generates a selection process among various types of firms that is consistent with economic efficiency. It is a survival requirement for the owner or owners of resources to seek the most efficient form of business organization in the owner's or owners' specific line of activity.

In Yugoslavia, the choice is mandated by law. The labor-managed firm has not emerged voluntarily in Yugoslavia; it has not survived by demonstrating its superiority over competing types of firms. The very fact that the ruling group had to mandate the labor-managed firm and protect it from competition means that the transaction costs of maintaining and enforcing the prevailing institutional structure in Yugoslavia must be higher than in a private-property, free-market economy. Analytically, it means a contraction of the social-opportunity set.

The bureaucracy. The ruling group's mandate that business organizations must be labor-managed precludes the choice of other institutional forms, while the state ownership of capital goods precludes the capitalization of the expected future benefits of a current decision into their present market value. It means that labor participation in management and state ownership creates a divergence between the alloca-

tion and use of resources by the labor-managed economy and the valuation of resources by the individual persons in the society. Thus it must be costly to monitor the labor-managed firm.

It follows that the institutional structure in Yugoslavia produces two kinds of governmental control over business firms. Those controls could be called the system-specific controls and the political controls. The system-specific controls are those whose primary purpose is to maintain the labor-managed character of the system. For example, the Agency for Social Bookkeeping has to check every single receipt and approve every single payment made by every single firm, and Self-Managing Communities of Interest have developed huge bureaucracies to supervise social compacts in the areas of health, retirement, and welfare.

Political controls are rules, regulations, and behaviors whose primary objective is to preserve the ruling group's political monopoly within the framework of the labor-managed economy. Examples of political controls are social compacts, price controls, and so-called informal controls through the party channels. Social compacts are contractual agreements between firms, trade unions, local governments, welfare agencies, and chambers of commerce in a region. They specify criteria for the distribution of income by business firms and other institutions, price policy, the pooling of resources for joint projects, and other economic issues. Those contracts are required by law and the basic terms are stipulated in advance.[6] Political and economic analysts who argue that a reduction in the size of the bureaucracy could improve the performance of the Yugoslav

6. Svetozar Pejovich, "The Incentive to Innovate under Alternative Property Rights," *Cato Journal,* 4:427-46 (Fall 1984).

firm are missing an important point: the labor-managed firm needs the bureaucracy to protect it from competing institutional forms.

According to *Danas,* an influential weekly magazine, the number of nonproduction employees in 1988 stood at about 40 percent of total employment in Yugoslavia.[7]

The location of decision making in the labor-managed firm. The following quote from McManus describes one of the most crucial issues in the labor-managed economy.

On the Yangtze River in China, there is a section of fast water over which boats are pulled upstream by a team of coolies prodded by an overseer using a whip. On one such passage an American lady, horrified at the sight of the overseer whipping the men as they strained at their harness, demanded that something be done about the brutality. She was quickly informed by the captain that nothing could be done: "those men own the right to draw boats over this stretch of water and they have hired the overseer and given him his duties." [8]

The story is analogous to the classic paper by Alchian and Demsetz, which said that the employees have incentives to shirk.[9] Shirking workers capture all the benefits of their action for themselves and shift the cost to other resources. Thus the extent of shirking in a firm depends on (1) the cost of monitoring workers, (2) the monitor's incentives, and (3) the monitor's power to hire and fire members of the team.

The story makes an important point. Those who support the labor-managed firm have confused participatory democracy within the firm with the specialized knowledge required to run it. The right of all

7. *Danas,* 14 Feb. 1989, p. 10.

8. John McManus, "The Cost of Alternative Economic Organizations," *Canadian Journal of Economics,* 8:335 (Fall 1975).

9. Alchian and Demsetz, "Production, Information Costs and Economic Organization," pp. 777-95.

workers to participate in running the firm rules out the right of any individual to make key decisions. Thus decision making in Yugoslavia is a time-consuming process carried out by resources that do not have the specialized knowledge required to identify and evaluate business decisions.

Moreover, the collective — that is, the workers' council — hires and fires the manager and approves hiring and firing of workers. It means that the manager of a Yugoslav firm, who is supposedly hired because of his or her specialized knowledge of business, has strong incentives to substitute policies that are consistent with his or her perception of the collective's preference for those that would maximize the value of the firm. The result is an increase in transaction costs and, consequently, a contraction in the social-opportunity set. To make the labor-managed firm more efficient it would be necessary (1) to transfer to the manager a broad range of property rights, the most important being the right to hire and fire workers and the right to be independent from the collective's preference; and (2) to design a new penalty-reward system for the manager that would give him or her incentives to seek and pursue policies that maximize value. The problem is that if those changes in property rights were made, they would de facto, if not de jure, do away with labor participation in the management of business firms.

Incentives and the social-opportunity set

The prevailing institutional structure in Yugoslavia affects the social-opportunity set via the employment problem, the allocation of risk, the demand for investment, and the flow of innovation.

The employment problem. Employees of the Yugoslav firm have the right to appropriate the residual, determine its allocation among the wage fund, the investment fund, and other legal uses, decide on the distribution of the wage fund, and approve the firm's employment policy. With workers given such decision-making powers, Professor Ward demonstrated that the level of employment in a labor-managed firm is determined by the equality between the average product and the marginal product of labor. It is clearly a restrictive and inefficient solution to the problem of employment.[10] Furubotn suggested that the employment policy of business enterprises in Yugoslavia is even more restrictive.[11] Evidence supports their respective findings that the labor-managed economy creates strong incentives for business firms not to hire new workers.

The rate of unemployment in Yugoslavia is difficult to estimate for at least two reasons. First, most blue-collar workers react to unemployment by either staying in or returning to their villages. Second, more than 1 million Yugoslavs are working in the West. Leaving those two groups of workers out, total employment in the labor-managed sector — including government — increased by only 4.6 percent from 1980 to 1987, while the rate of unemployment increased from 12 percent to 14 percent. During the same period, total employment in the private sector of the economy increased by 39 percent.[12]

The allocation of risk. The nontransferability of the workers' right of ownership in the firm's earnings means that the

10. Benjamin Ward, "The Firm in Illyria: Market Syndicalism," *American Economic Review,* 48:566-89 (Sept. 1958).

11. Eirik Furubotn, "The Long-Run Analysis of the Labor-Managed Firm," *American Economic Review,* 66:104-23 (1976).

12. *Statisticki godisnjak* (Belgrade: Statisticki zavod, 1988) pp. 134, 150.

labor-managed economy provides no room for specialization in risk bearing across individuals with different degrees of risk aversion. Moreover, the workers are forced in the aggregate to bear risks that are in fact insurable by diversification.[13] Thus the labor-managed economy does not provide incentives for risk takers and risk averters to engage in transactions that move resources to more highly valued use.

Investment decisions. The employee of a labor-managed firm has the right of ownership in the firm's earnings but not in its assets. When workers leave the firm, they lose all their claims to the future returns from investment decisions that were made during their tenure. Thus the employees have incentives to choose investment alternatives that promise to maximize cash flow during their expected employment with that firm. Moreover, the collective has strong incentives to seek long-term loans for either short-lived investments or for investments that promise a larger cash flow in the initial period following investment. In general, the labor-managed firm creates incentives for the collective to choose investments that shift the flow of income forward and postpone costs — to be borne by the next generation of workers.

Incentives to innovate. Given the prevailing property rights in the labor-managed sector of the Yugoslav economy, the pool of those who have the right to innovate is restricted to the working collective. The term "working collective" is important here. Individual employees can neither acquire productive assets nor determine their uses. Only the working collective as a whole can, through its workers' council. An employee who perceives an opportu-

13. Jensen and Meckling, "Rights and Production Functions," pp. 469-506.

nity to innovate must sell his or her idea to the workers' council, a group of people who have diverse attitudes toward risk, limited business experience, inadequate understanding of production techniques and market processes, and different time horizons. This process impedes the flow of innovation.

Moreover, the prevailing property rights in the labor-managed economy preclude the capitalization of the future benefits of successful innovations into their present value. The absence of the right to capture the future consequences of current innovation in one lump sum means that the collective has incentives to seek primarily those innovations that increase the near-term cash flow.

NEW INSTITUTIONAL CHANGES IN YUGOSLAVIA

This section of the article evaluates reasons for economic reforms in Yugoslavia and in Eastern Europe in general. It would clearly be beyond the scope of this article to address the content of the reforms.

In evaluating reasons for economic reforms at any particular time, it is necessary to distinguish between the institutional structure that defines the total relationship (hereafter called the "contract") between the ruling group and the people, on the one hand, and changes at the margin, on the other. Economic reforms are obviously changes at the margin. The ruling group would never voluntarily make reforms that would change the contract itself. Economic reforms are then a vehicle through which the ruling group modifies the terms of the contract between itself and the people. They represent the ruling group's response to changes in the opportunity costs of the people.

The ruling group's announcements of institutional changes should best be ignored until they are actually implemented, for the actual implementation of institutional changes is what affects the economy. The major objective of the ruling group in Yugoslavia is to maintain its political monopoly; however, the circumstances that determine the costs of the ruling group's trade-offs might and, indeed, do change. In that sense, economic reforms that are implemented carry a powerful message. They tell us that the circumstances that affect the opportunity costs of the people have changed.

Two circumstances have raised the opportunity costs of the Yugoslav people. The first is common to all East European countries: the death of Marxism means that the ruling elite cannot continue to hide its desire for political monopoly behind a facade of words about the historical inevitability of socialism. The end of the theory of history means that the present value of future benefits of socialism has fallen relative to the cost of building it today. Since it cannot continue to justify its political monopoly by claiming to be the "torch" of history, the ruling group must substitute some real results for a hazy vision of things to come. The accomplishments of capitalism then become the strongest case against socialism. Economic reforms in Yugoslavia, and in Eastern Europe, then reflect the search for institutional forms that could improve the economy and, at the same time, preserve the ruling group's political monopoly.

The second circumstance is specific to Yugoslavia. Marshal Tito was a charismatic, strong, capable, and decisive autocrat who was able to secure a good contract for the ruling group. His death created a power vacuum within the ruling group in Yugoslavia. The absence of a strong leader tends to increase the opportunity costs of the people.

An important point is that it is wrong to think of economic reforms in Yugoslavia, and Eastern Europe, as a choice that the current ruling group, more enlightened and caring than the previous one, has chosen to make. The evidence is that the circumstances that affect the cost of the ruling group's political and economic power have changed. The very survival of the ruling group depends on its willingness to identify new trade-offs and to respond to them. Economic reforms are then a specific and predictable outcome of a set of objective circumstances.

Given its imperfect knowledge about the world in which we all live, the ruling group might easily either overreact or underreact to its new trade-offs. The latter could lead to an upheaval that could change the very nature of the contract between the rulers and their subjects. The former might lead to a slow evolution of Yugoslavia into a private-property, free-market economy.

CONCLUDING REMARKS

The property-rights analysis indicates that the labor-managed economy creates some positive transaction costs and negative incentives that are specific to its institutional structure. They contribute to a contraction in the social-opportunity set. Lack of incentives to innovate also limits the expansion of the social-opportunity set in response to new technical opportunities.

The conclusion is that the labor-managed economy is not a viable institutional arrangement. Recent economic reforms in Yugoslavia support this conclusion. The entire package of reforms reflects both the ruling group's recognition that the labor-managed economy has failed and its awareness of the efficiency of private-property, free-market institutions. The package attempts to save the basic outline of the labor-managed economy while making institutional changes in the direction of a private-property, free-market economy. The former is essential for preserving the ruling group's political power. The latter is necessary for making the system work.

ANNALS, *AAPSS*, **507**, January 1990

East German Traditional Centralism:
An Alternative Route to
Economic Reconstruction

By PHILLIP J. BRYSON

ABSTRACT: This article is a response to the question of why the German Democratic Republic (GDR) has not demonstrated any inclination to adopt economic reforms, although most socialist countries have. Since the early 1980s, the GDR has made extensive efforts to refine its planning organization and techniques. Continual changes, less dramatic than those announced by the Soviet Union and some other socialist countries, were long considered plan perfecting rather than economic reform. This article reviews some highlights of the East German plan amelioration effort and attempts to show how the success achieved by *Planvervollkommnung* has been at least partially responsible for the GDR's reluctance to embrace *glasnost* and *perestroika*. The prospects for change in the current GDR position are discussed. The East German determination to avoid fundamental, systemic change persists, and there is as yet no acknowledged willingness to adopt market-oriented economic reform or pursue dramatic changes in property rights. One should observe, however, that the GDR has since the beginning retained a private handicrafts sector and private ownership of land.

Phillip J. Bryson is professor of managerial economics in the Marriott School of Management, Brigham Young University. His writings address the domestic and international economic problems of the German Democratic Republic and the Soviet Union.

THE worldwide retreat from traditional central planning may be the most interesting social phenomenon of our time. But it has not yet become apparent whether a country can in fact extricate itself from the planning institutions of Marxist-Leninist-Stalinist socialism. If such a country can so extricate itself, would it still be a socialist country?

The German Democratic Republic (GDR) is still asking these questions and wondering whether a reform path leads anywhere at all, or if it should be taken, given where it might lead. East Germany is the most affluent and economically successful of the countries of the Soviet-dominated Council for Mutual Economic Assistance (CMEA), and while other countries of Eastern Europe have joined China in an attempted flight from central planning, the GDR remains firmly in that tradition.

East Germany did not escape the harsher planning environment that afflicted Eastern Europe after the energy crises of the 1970s. The deterioration of the international terms of trade of the socialist countries resulted in borrowing and a credit crisis for the GDR by 1980. The response was an export drive, a tightening of imports, and a diminution of funds flowing into domestic investment. Within a short time the GDR had overcome the credit crisis and in doing so had maintained its economic growth.

Not only were the CMEA countries severely challenged by the world economy in this period; they were also being forced to recognize that the central planning system itself was a major problem. The Soviet Union and other CMEA countries continued to drift toward stagnation, awaiting the arrival of Gorbachev and the green light for economic reforms. By 1970 the East Germans had already experienced and become disillusioned with reform; they believed they had found the answer to their problems in economic reorganization and in planning innovations. These processes, some of which had been inspired by Soviet experiments, were referred to by the GDR and the Soviets as plan "perfecting" (*Planvervollkommnung* and *sovershenstvovanie*, respectively, but according to the context they can be translated more modestly as plan "improving").

By 1985, the GDR was not only the most affluent of the socialist countries but also the bloc's leading economic performer, the only CMEA country in which the growth rate of net material product was greater for the 1980-85 plan period than for the period 1975-80.[1] This formidable success in the early 1980s can be attributed in part to the favorable access that country enjoyed to West German and European Community markets, as well as to the sizable transfers of various sorts the GDR received from the Federal Republic of Germany.[2]

But most observers agree that part of the credit should go to the extensive efforts of the GDR in the early 1980s to refine its planning organization and techniques. The next section of this article will review some of the highlights of that effort. The third section will show how the success achieved by *Planvervollkommnung* has

1. See Jan Vanous, "The GDR within CMEA," in *Symposium on the German Democratic Republic*, ed. Irwin Collier, *Comparative Economic Studies*, 29(2):1 (1987). Klaus Steinitz, "Probleme des Wirtschaftswachstums in der oekonomischen Strategie," *Sitzungsberichte der Akademie der Wissenschaften der DDR* (East Berlin: Akademie Verlag, 1987), p. 7, indicates that for the last three quinquennial plans (1971-75, 1976-80, 1981-85) the growth of national income was 5.4 percent, 4.1 percent, and 4.6 percent, respectively. The growth of labor productivity for the three periods was 5.3 percent, 3.7 percent, and 4.3 percent, respectively.

2. See Jan Prybyla, "The GDR in COMECON: Does the GDR Economy Demonstrate that Orthodox

made the GDR reluctant to embrace *glasnost* and *perestroika*. The fourth section will discuss the prospects for change in the current GDR position. At the time of writing, East German determination to avoid fundamental, systemic change — including any kind of market-oriented economic reform or changes in property rights — appeared to persist.

Although the GDR has as yet shown no inclination to embark on a reform program modeled after *perestroika*, one can expect that further change will be forthcoming. By 1987, difficulties had begun to appear. Aggregate growth declined to 3.6 percent that year, the second lowest increase for this decade. The feat was duplicated the following year with an even more modest 2.7 percent increase.[3] Two bad winters in this period adversely affected, through sectoral interdependencies, the economy's general performance. Nevertheless, these and other problems certainly were not sufficient to induce any inclination to restructure along the lines of a Yugoslavian, Hungarian, or Soviet model.

GLANCING BACK AT
PLAN PERFECTING

In the review of plan perfecting that follows, the focus is on two aspects: organization and planning refinements.

Organizational change

By 1980, the GDR had begun to dismantle its industrial associations, the organizational link between ministries and individual enterprises. They were replaced by industrial combines (*Kombinate*), which represent a major vertical and horizontal integration of enterprises. These large production units were intended to enhance industrial communication and coordination and to reduce growing conflicts of planning jurisdiction. The planners also hoped to achieve scale economies through increased industrial concentration and the consolidation of decision functions — especially those of production, research and development (R&D), and both domestic and foreign marketing — in the hands of a single decision maker, the combine's director general (DG).[4] Combine formation strengthened the middle level of the planning hierarchy, which in a sense represents organizational devolution from the center. The enhancement of combine decision authority, however, was at the expense of the enterprise, which received no additional decision-making prerogatives.

The DG exercises both planning and management powers. The material balancing of certain goods, structural investment planning, and certain international transactions were delegated to that officer. An-

Central Planning Is Viable and Has a Future?" *Comparative Strategy,* 7:39-49 (1988). Prybyla puts the yield of the special economic relationship the East Germans have with the Federal Republic at about DM1.5 billion a year, coming through loans, interest-free swing credits on inter-German trade, duty-free access to West Germany and hence the European Community, and West German payments for transit fees, sewage removal, purchases of exit approval for GDR citizens, visiting fees, and so on.

3. For reviews of these developments, see Doris Cornelsen, "Die Lage der DDR-Wirtschaft zur Jahreswende 1987/88," *DIW Wochenbericht,* 4 Feb.

1988, p. 59; idem, "Die Lage der DDR-Wirtschaft zur Jahreswende 1988/89," ibid., 2 Feb. 1989, pp. 53-61.

4. For a more detailed treatment of other benefits that GDR planners anticipated from combine organization, see Phillip J. Bryson and Manfred Melzer, "Planning Refinements and Combine Formation in East German Economic 'Intensification,'" (Carl Beck Papers in Russian and East European Studies, University of Pittsburgh, 1986), 508:19-23. By the mid-1980s combine formation had been completed. The 133 combines in centrally directed industry employed an average of about 25,000 workers associated with 20 to 40 individual enterprises. In regionally directed industry there were 93 combines of smaller size.

swering for all aspects of industrial production, the DG's primary responsibilities include directing the industry's R&D program; acquiring capital equipment; producing in-house facilities and equipment (*Rationalisierungsmittelbau*) required to develop innovations; producing intermediate goods; producing final goods; and marketing the commodity both within and beyond national borders.[5]

The parent enterprise and the director general

Combines were originally organized in various ways, but the form featuring the parent enterprise (*Stammbetrieb*) was soon established as the standard.[6] Enterprises were united under the leadership of the most visible and effective firm, the so-called parent in the industry. The DG was to manage not only the combine itself but also that parent enterprise.

GDR economic leaders are convinced that this dual leadership role forces the DG, through his or her enterprise, to confront real prices prevailing in the industry, that is, to become acquainted with information available to other enterprise managers: real opportunity costs, production possibilities and constraints, and so forth. Combine formation can thus be viewed as an attempt to address the information problem arising from the divergent objectives of center and

periphery[7] as the *Kombinat*'s DG gains access to and provides previously unavailable production-level information to the center.

Under the former organizational structure, directors of the industrial associations were perceived by enterprise managers as being removed from actual managerial practice and problems. Directors no longer seemed to be colleagues, and enterprise managers were not willing recipients of their recommendations, directives, wishful thinking, or so-called petty tutelage. The DGs, more readily perceived as managerial colleagues, are taken more seriously.

In spite of combine formation, effectively managing and planning industry remains a challenge. The redesigning of East German industry has even created some new difficulties,[8] and the combine era has been characterized by extensive experimentation and an ongoing effort to refine economic organization.

Planning refinements

GDR plan perfecting (*Planvervollkommnung*) has featured, in addition to these reorganizational efforts, a large number of new regulations and directives. The aim is

---

5. Helmut Richter, "Zu Aspekten der Entwicklung leistungsfaehiger Kombinate in der Industrie der DDR," in *Zu Grundfragen der Betriebswirtschaft in der DDR und in Japan*, ed. E. Sachse (East Berlin: Hochschule fuer Oekonomie "Bruno Leuschner," 1981.

6. See Guenter Mittag, "Theoretische Verallgemeinerung der Erfahrungen der Entwicklung der Kombinate fuer die Leistungssteigerung in der Volkswirtschaft, insbesondere bei der Nutzung der qualitativen Faktoren des Wachstums," *Wirtschaftswissenschaft*, 32(1):5-60 (1984).

7. Manfred Melzer and Kurt Erdmann, "Probleme der Kombinatsbildung in der DDR — volkswirtschaftliche und betriebswirtschaftliche Aspekte," *FS Analysen, Die Kombinatsbildung der DDR in Theorie und Praxis*, no. 8, pp. 27-104 (1979); Hannelore Hamel, "Sozialistische Unternehmenskonzentration und Managerverhalten. Die Kombinatsbildung in der DDR als Effizienzproblem," in *Anreiz-und Kontrollmechanismen in Wirtschaftssystemen*, ed. G. Hedtkamp, (West Berlin: Duncker & Humblot, 1981), 1:67 ff.

8. For a more extensive treatment of some of these, see Phillip J. Bryson and Manfred Melzer, "The *Kombinat* in GDR Economic Organization," in *The East German Economy*, ed. I. B. Jeffries and M. Melzer (London: Croom Helm, 1987), pp. 51-68.

to overcome planning insufficiencies and strengthen cost-benefit thinking on the part of managers. The new regulations focus on (1) industrial cost reduction through greater cost discipline, (2) control mechanisms on the use of investment funds to secure more consistent and expansive technical progress, (3) credits to promote the improvement of enterprise management and finance, and (4) the use of indirect instruments — for example, so-called profitability and the use of retained earnings — to stimulate the so-called intensification of production.

The abandonment of the gross output target — industrial commodity production — was a significant attempt to improve planning effectiveness. Since 1984, the main coefficients by which enterprises are evaluated have been net production, net profit, production of commodities and services for the populace, and production for export. Numerous new norms target reduced consumption of raw materials and energy in production.

Indirect planning levers include (1) new financial mechanisms to stimulate plan fulfillment and (2) an extension of the application of economic accounting (*wirtschaftliche Rechnungsfuehrung*), inspired, of course, by Soviet *khozraschet*. Profitability has become the measurement criterion of rational resource use in production.[9]

Various levies extracted from production units are designed to provide the state with revenues, of course, but also to encourage more prompt implementation of planned investment projects. Combines and enterprises have access to several types of funds that encourage innovation and risk

taking, especially for import-substitution purposes, and reward cost savings.

In spite of *Planvervollkommnung*, organizational and planning problems remain. These include, for example, the following: (1) continued intervention into enterprise affairs by ministries and combines — so-called petty tutelage; (2) parent enterprises' claiming favorable production specialization tasks and delegating less favorable ones; (3) imperfect communication and competition between and within combines — witness the poor quality of intermediate goods supplied by enterprises not confronted by more contested domestic and foreign final-goods markets; (4) the sometimes inadequate internal cooperation and coordination of R&D agendas within combines; (5) the ongoing lack of reserves and flexibility in production; and, at the core of numerous other problems, (6) the nonscarcity prices that distort outcomes and prohibit efficiency.

The GDR still places hope for its economic future in organizational improvements, greater cost savings in production, and better use of investment resources. The continuation of economic growth is offered by them as evidence that plan perfecting can continue to drive economic performance.

Production units, international trade, and technology

The combines have substantial new opportunities and responsibilities in the area of international trade and socialist economic integration, being empowered to participate directly in those activities. The combine's second officer in command, the deputy DG (*Stellvertretender Direktor*), is usually responsible for export. The deputy answers not only to the DG but also to the foreign trade ministry and encourages the DG not to avoid or shortchange his or her

9. *Gesetzblatt der DDR*, "Anordnung ueber die Planung und Zufuehrung des staatlichen Erloeszuschlags," Teil I, pp. 164 ff (1983).

international trade obligations. The new arrangements are designed to cause producers to respond to the quality, assortment, and product service demands of the world market. Nearly all combines are now expected to export some share of their output.

Before reorganization, R&D activities were the responsibility of a separate ministry; work desired by an industrial association or large enterprise was contracted out to specialized agencies detached from the practical needs of production and marketing. In many instances, R&D organizations have been moved directly into combines, and they are now more vitally interested in effective resolution of industrial technological problems.

Plan perfecting without privatization

Ideological change is becoming possible in Eastern Europe as a reverential attitude toward Marxism-Leninism is no longer a sine qua non of economic discussion. Questions of ownership arise when the exigencies of Soviet *perestroika* prompt a legalization of small, family-type handicraft and service industries. Property-rights issues are integral to the question of new roles for the cooperative[10] and of the proposed rights of individuals to lease lands for extended periods for private farming.

In the GDR, however, there has been no discussion of privatization of industry nor of any basic change in ownership of the means of production, except to disavow it. Two East German writers find that in spite of *perestroika* and *glasnost* there remains a "universal" socialist consensus that the ap-

propriate, systemically inalienable dominance of social ownership of the means of production is "one of the great advantages of socialism."[11] Nor has there been in the GDR any tendency as yet to discuss increased possibilities for collectives, as in the USSR. An important feature of GDR socialism, however, is the private handicraft sector. Of significant size, it has been an important element of GDR economic success since 1948.[12] Currently, the GDR also intends to expand the opportunities for rural and city dwellers to farm their own private plots.

EAST GERMAN SUCCESS AND THE GDR ROAD TO SOCIALISM

Around 1985, especially at the quinquennial party congress, the GDR was making the claim that it had successfully mastered the fundamentals of central planning. In a milieu of stagnation and malaise, it had been able to maintain respectable economic growth rates. Although the GDR's Socialist Unity Party (SED) has no inclination to criticize Soviet-style reform, it feels no necessity to adopt it. Erich Honecker, the general secretary of the SED, assumed leadership when the abrasiveness of his predecessor, Walter Ulbricht, proved excessive for Soviet tastes.

10. See Abel Aganbegyan, *The Economic Challenge of Perestroika* (Bloomington: Indiana University Press, 1988), pp. 25-30.

11. H.-G. Haupt and K. Hoevelmans, "Zu ausgewaehlten Entwicklungsproblemen des sozialistischen Weltsystems," *Wirtschaftswissenschaft*, 36(7):961-77 (1988).

12. After imposing rigorous restrictions on the handicrafts, the GDR decided in 1976 to promote them, and they have remained an important source of supply for services, construction, repairs, and so forth. Since 1972 there has been an increasing attempt to include this sector in the national planning effort. See Maria Haendcke-Hoppe, "Struktureffekte der SED-Handwerkspolitik seit 1976," *FS Analysen* (West Berlin: Forschungsstelle fuer Gesamtdeutsche Wirtschaftliche und Soziale Fragen, 1988).

He is unlikely to become a strident critic of Soviet policies.

To embrace *perestroika* prematurely could in fact be very risky. Should it fail in the Soviet Union, the effort could prove devoid of positive effect. More important, *perestroika*-inspired changes could represent a political liability if Soviet reform — either of the current or some later variant — fails.[13] It would seem prudent for the SED to give the appearance of pursuing or at least contemplating policies that suggest openness and economic reconstruction.

The East Germans do in fact have reason to continue their planning "reform" — the word "reform" is now back in fashion even in the GDR. Persisting problems provide the incentive.

PROSPECTS FOR CHANGE IN SED STONEWALLING

To proceed slowly with systemic change would seem to be sensible strategy from the East German perspective. It is important to avoid potential embarrassment to Honecker and/or the party as accommodation is made to the changing rules of the socialist planning game and to world economic conditions. Problems arising from the search for an optimal sequencing of reform measures can also be minimized by proceeding cautiously.[14] The designers of change can gain instructive experience

from observing how implementation problems are best avoided in sister systems undergoing economic reform.

Prospects and
persisting planning problems

The GDR economy continues to be the most successful and prosperous of the economies of the socialist countries, but persisting systemic deficiencies make the future uncertain. Pricing inadequacies, organizational shortcomings, and other problems have already been mentioned. An additional significant problem is the capital-goods deficit that developed in the period of the credit crisis and continued thereafter. In order to sustain the export drive of that period without cutting too deeply into consumer-goods supplies, investments were scaled back sharply. That left the capital stock in severe need of augmentation and modernization; it also made continuous and costly repairs essential. Labor, energy, and raw-material shortages can also be overcome only through substantial investments.

After 1985, investment became an area of emphasis in GDR planning. First, the tempo increased. Rates of growth ranged from 5 to 8 percent through 1988, but the level was at nearly 20 percent of national income in 1989. Second, an enterprise self-finance measure from the New Economic System of the 1960s was recycled in 1987, giving managers the opportunity to fund their own investments both from retained earnings and through credits. This innovation was coupled with an experiment in which 16 combines — employing 18 percent of the GDR industrial labor force — will have significantly increased powers of

---

13. Many who consider Gorbachev unlikely to succeed believe, nevertheless, that some kind of reform effort must continue in the USSR with or without the current leadership.

14. A most serious problem for the GDR in sequencing reform changes arises from granting greater responsibility to the combines for cost accounting and self-financing before introducing needed price reform. The latter would make evident whether a production unit's performance was worthy of praise or censure. Without adequate prices, profitability may accompany poor performance and losses may accompany what would otherwise be commendable achieve-

ment. Additionally, *khozraschet* and self-financing would logically precede appropriate changes in the system of centrally directed supply.

self-management and self-finance, including the use of up to 25 percent of export earnings for discretionary factor imports. Participation increased to 52 combines in 1989.[15]

Another problem is that the horizontal and vertical concentration of industries in the combine system results in a low technical and qualitative level of many input deliveries, which negatively affects production costs.[16] The GDR's response to this problem has been to encourage in-house production (*Eigenproduktion*) of important industrial inputs, which tends to decrease specialization and labor division, reducing East German competitiveness in world markets.

Promoting key technologies

The GDR is currently attempting to provide new momentum to growth and to increase labor productivity through the promotion of particularly important sectors.[17] An information-system infrastructure is perceived as the necessary basis for thoroughly automated and technical production processes.

To strengthen the *Kombinat* in its technological role, East German strategists believe, need not imply a downgrading of the role of the party or of central planning. The GDR can make a contribution "to a modern model of the socialist economy" by integrating "the results of the scientific and technological revolution with production."[18]

The social contract: "The unity of social and economic policy"

In hopes of maintaining worker motivation—which is low in comparison with Western Europe but high in comparison with Eastern Europe—the Honecker regime is still intent on honoring the social contract embodied in the "unity of social and economic policy," which implies that if the workers are willing to supply their labor, they will be rewarded directly at retail sales outlets. As with Gorbachev, the human factor was an immediate concern for Honecker when he came to power. Since that time the SED has performed well—by socialist standards—in that area.[19]

In the first half of 1988, industrial combines increased consumer-goods output, but there were some gaps later in the year. The campaign to promote the production of consumer goods, even in combines primarily engaged in manufacturing producer goods, was continued with determination. Housing targets were again overfulfilled as the GDR moved to the end of a long campaign to provide adequate housing for all citizens.

Whither tends the GDR?

How will economic development proceed? What structural changes are forth-

15. See Cornelsen, "Jahreswende 1988/89," pp. 55-56.

16. Doris Cornelsen, "DDR-Wirtschaft im ersten Halbjahr 1988," *DIW Wochenbericht*, 55:379-85 (July 1988).

17. Key technology industries are listed by Garbe as: microelectronics; information technologies; computer-aided construction, design, and production; flexible, automated production systems; new processing technologies for materials; biotechnology; nuclear energy; and laser technologies. See E. Garbe, "Theoretische und praktische Aufgaben bei der weiteren Entwicklung der sozialistischen Betriebswirtschaft in den Kombinaten der DDR," *Wirtschaftswissenschaft*, 36:805 (June 1988).

18. Wolfgang Heinrichs, "Comments," in *Symposium on the German Democratic Republic*, ed. Irwin Collier, p. 50.

19. See P. J. Bryson, "GDR Economic Planning and Social Policy in the 1980's," *Comparative Economic Studies*, 28(2):19-38 (1987); idem, *The Consumer under Socialist Planning: The East German Case* (New York: Praeger, 1984).

coming once the current period of uncertainty ends and the highest echelons of GDR leadership initiate a new course of action? Will such a course be based on the model of *perestroika*? Even before then, one may expect the East Germans to address their most significant problems, although it is not certain that they will do so with sufficient boldness. Certainly the example of the Soviets should provide some courage.

Some elements of change seem clear. Subsidies for basic goods will have to be reduced or eliminated — many GDR economists have hoped that this would have been accomplished already. Prices will have to be revised, and, more significant, pricing processes themselves will require reform. The power of state-constructed monopoly, as manifest in the combine structure, will have to be countered, if not broken. One would predict that the German response here would be for continued central regulation of monopoly power, which could have negative characteristics similar to those of central planning. The system of central supply planning should be dismantled as the system of contracts and decentralized interindustrial relations is permitted to blossom. Investments will have to be greatly increased and the effectiveness of investing will as well. The investments would likely involve foreign credits but will also require some reconsideration of domestic priorities.

These tasks have already been under discussion for some time, and many recognize that they will have to be undertaken. All these accomplishments may not be necessary to guarantee the short-term survival of the GDR, but if *perestroika* prevails, the East German people will ultimately demand economic success that will require no less.

Book Department

INTERNATIONAL RELATIONS AND POLITICS

GOLAN, GALIA. *The Soviet Union and National Liberation Movements in the Third World.* Pp. ix, 374. Winchester, MA: Unwin Hyman, 1988. $49.95.

As the processes of *glasnost* and *perestroika* unfold, the world wonders to what extent the Soviet Union will change radically its global policies and behaviors. The book under review, by Professor Galia Golan of Hebrew University, is a useful analysis of Soviet intentions and behaviors in a most significant international area that has threatened confrontation between the United States and the USSR in Afghanistan, the Middle East, Africa, and elsewhere. Golan's thorough and perceptive presentation makes clear that even during the cold war Soviet responses were far from foregone conclusions depending upon the situation. Her scholarly and balanced treatment of a complex and difficult subject well informs our understanding. I have a minor complaint, however: over 25 acronyms for the names of movements are used without a list spelling them out.

This comprehensive and detailed study, utilizing extensive authoritative sources, focuses on the postwar period. It divides the topic into two parts: Soviet national liberation theory, for two-thirds of the book, and Soviet policy and behaviors toward national liberation movements. The Canary Island, Micronesian, and New Caledonian movements are not covered. The movements that are covered are typed: anticolonial, secessionist-separatist, and idiosyncratic — for example, the Palestine Liberation Organization and Polisario. Both theoretical and behavioral patterns are analyzed within these categories, and degrees of Soviet control are assessed.

The theoretical analysis draws upon Soviet scholars', journalists', and leaders' writings and statements. No one consistent theory on liberation movements emerges. Rather, there is an orthodox/conservative theory and several fragmented theories, more realistic and sophisticated. For the first group, class was the key factor, in orthodox Marxist fashion; the other views were more wide-ranging, considering national, cultural, and psychological factors. The leadership position was neither monolithic nor consistent.

As to the pattern of Soviet behaviors, these are well analyzed. Several tables summarize the degree of support (from virtually never to most of the time); the degree of support by type (anticolonial, separatist); the nature and instruments of Soviet behavior (a continuum from military force against to no role to intervention); and indicators of political support before statehood. Golan concludes that "where the theory, the rhetoric, and the behavior coincide, beginning in the early 1980s, if not earlier, is their generally pragmatic, relatively cautious tactical approach. . . . " One wonders if Soviet theoretical rejection of separatist-secessionist movements reflects fear of such movements in the multinational USSR.

CHARLES HOFFMANN

State University of New York
Stony Brook

HEALY, DAVID. *Drive to Hegemony: The United States in the Caribbean 1898-1917.* Pp. xi, 370. Madison: University of Wisconsin Press, 1988. $27.50.

Drive to Hegemony is a comprehensive, nuanced, and constantly thoughtful account of the process by which the United States achieved overwhelming predominance in the Caribbean and Central America by the end of World War I. The quickening pace of American interest in the region was spearheaded by individual entrepreneurs, soon followed by security concerns over European competition, along with the Spanish-American War and the creation of Panama as a separate state and of the Panama Canal Zone with American rights "as if sovereign" and "in perpetuity." And if Europeans were not permitted to police this turbulent region now deemed essential to national security, then the United States had to perform that task. Furthermore, many Americans came to believe that the United States, with its superior technology, capital, culture, and racial characteristics, had the obligation to lead the natives toward the full realization of the Caribbean's potential.

Without stability, neither American security nor Caribbean development could be achieved. To bring about stability, different means were tried. First was financial control. When this

proved insufficient, the deployment of American troops became essential.

President Woodrow Wilson added a measure of idealism to American purposes: to spread democracy and to make the international behavior of the United States a model for the rest of the world to emulate. While Wilson was quickly overwhelmed by the refusal of the Latin Americans to behave in an approved fashion, Healy points out that the president also accepted much of the American establishment's prior consensus on the region: that stable governments were necessary in order to achieve liberty and freedom, economic development, and any significant progress in social goals such as health and education; conversely, that revolution was the principal barrier to progress in the Caribbean.

American troops were to intrude, for varying lengths of time, in Cuba, after formal independence; Haiti; the Dominican Republic; Panama; Nicaragua; and Mexico. All but Mexico became clear protectorates under the civilizing supervision of the North — as did Honduras. Along the way, Puerto Rico was annexed and the Danish West Indies purchased.

After Wilson, the promotion of democracy was jettisoned as a vital goal. But how was the United State to disengage from direct, recurrent, and domestically unpopular intervention? "Apolitical" constabularies were created and trained in three of the states, with well-known but unforeseen political consequences whose effects are still felt.

There is far more to this judicious book than a history of the expansion of American power. For example, the impact of U.S. intervention in Cuba is finely analyzed, while competing explanations of continuing Caribbean want and dependency are carefully weighed. Healy also makes clear that important sectors of the Caribbean elites welcomed, if not publicly, American intervention and came to exploit it for their own sectoral or personal purposes.

U.S. economic and political hegemony has been in place for three generations. Healy, with his eyes on lessons for the present and graciously conceding the good intentions of past policymakers, raises fundamental questions that should still be central to policy debate: what kinds of intervention produce what kinds of outcomes; to what ends should stability be used; and is stability, with a narrow political definition, of benefit to the peoples of either the North or the South? It is also noteworthy that the American people and Congress were then, as now, skeptical of the executive's actions in the Caribbean: they would accept intervention, but only within limits and when fully convinced of its need and real purposes.

DONALD HINDLEY

Brandeis University
Waltham
Massachusetts

HUTH, PAUL K. *Extended Deterrence and the Prevention of War.* Pp. xi, 227. New Haven, CT: Yale University Press, 1988. $25.00.

This is an important and timely addition to the literature on extended deterrence. Applying probit analysis to 58 cases of attempted extended-immediate deterrence, Huth concludes that "short-term military and diplomatic actions do have a strong impact on crisis outcomes." This conclusion — with which many readers will already be familiar as a result of articles by Huth and Bruce M. Russett — takes up the challenge posed by the research of Richard Ned Lebow and Janice Gross Stein. Applying cognitive analysis to a series of cases studies, Lebow and Stein — following Robert Jervis — doubt that crisis bargaining is of any value.

The dispute involves a number of issues including the manner in which historical data should be used, the interpretation of specific cases, the utility of aggregate data and the inductive treatment of such data, and the appropriateness of rational-choice assumptions in foreign-policy analysis. This dispute is not merely a matter of intellectual preference but has fundamental policy implications. Lebow et al. doubt that deterrence strategies can be devised that enhance crisis stability yet produce credibility, and they argue that such strategies tend to increase the probability of conflict. By

contrast, Huth concludes that "tit for tat military escalation," and "firm-but-flexible diplomacy" by a defender contribute to the successful management of acute international crises.

Extended Deterrence does not resolve these issues, and Huth shows that some of the putatively divergent claims of the two approaches need not be incompatible. The volume is, however, a meticulous, clear, and thorough presentation of the rational-choice approach. The data have been gathered with painstaking care and treated with suitable caution, and Huth shows imagination in the selection of indicators for key variables like "military balance" and "bargaining behavior." They reflect, moreover, his acquaintance with substance as well as method. Two chapters are devoted to illustrating the analysis by examining selected cases of deterrence success and failure. Although not intended as definitive studies, the cases are chosen to illustrate the applicability of Huth's conclusions under differing conditions and in different temporal and geographic arenas. They serve their purpose well.

In sum, *Extended Deterrence* is a model of clever and thorough quantitative research in international politics. It will prove especially useful in the training of graduate students and makes a significant contribution in its own right to our understanding of deterrence and crisis.

RICHARD W. MANSBACH

Iowa State University
Ames

WINHAM, GILBERT R., ed. *New Issues in International Crisis Management.* Pp. x, 258. Boulder, CO: Westview Press, 1988. $36.00.

The 44-year nuclear dimension in foreign affairs has impelled the closest scrutiny of successive global crises, given their catastrophic potential. Thus the subject of the present volume draws instant attention, confirmed by the group of known authors and their informative articles.

Before commenting upon textual substance a note on semantics is relevant. "Crisis management" as a phrase is a typically American oxymoron connoting that everything is under control. The then industrial engineer Robert McNamara asserts in 1962 hyperbole: "There is no longer any such thing as strategy, only crisis management." Some scholars and practitioners venture to differ, and happily James Richardson claims that "crisis coping" would be a more appropriate term. In concurring, some officials use the figure that in crises they are riding a surfboard beneath an overhanging wave.

In the articles, contemporary issues are given varied treatment, both historically descriptive and operationally prescriptive. Richard Lebow describes loss of control in crises, with examples from the Kissinger era. The actions that occurred then make plausible why the man can expect no further top appointment, while being able to capitalize as a consultant.

Alexander George examines the U.S.-Soviet global rivalry with such insight as to make his contribution exceptional. After describing types of understandings and competitive gaming, he details six game structures: high- and low-interest symmetries, interest symmetries successively favoring the United States and USSR, and the dangerous dual disputed and uncertain interest symmetries. In these last, the threat of one superpower's intervention, notably in the Mideast, forces the other to curb its client state. As George shows, the superpowers have major unsolved problems in determining the scope of their interests and communicating this to the adversary. A remedy, he concludes, would be to establish a mechanism between them for detailed and regular talks on regional problems so as to narrow and possibly resolve disagreements. A case-by-case approach thus is his current tactical proposal.

It is most helpful to have a succinct and readable story on the arms-control negotiations. Karen MacGillivray and Gilbert Winham lucidly assess their problems, such as the vulnerability of command structures. They fault recent arms-control proposals as indiscriminate rather than focusing on priorities. These contributors assert that it is more useful to continue talks on a broad range than to seek major, but elusive, arms-control agreements.

How can the risk of nuclear war be reduced? Here Joseph Nye and William Ury give varied and inventive proposals, such as the early cabinet briefings President Bush adopted. Still there is a caution, for their suggested bilateral risk-reduction centers involve problems of critical disinformation, intelligence leaks, added bureaucracy, and foreign misunderstanding.

A thoughtful selection by Charles Hermann emphasizes the overlooked current aspect of crises, that of increasing instability. He believes that changes in force structure and doctrine have contributed to this, as have shifts in the character of strategic weapons, of strategic alerts, of command and control, and of strategic plans. To ease the flight-time threat, he would concur in Lebow's suggestion of keeping missiles at a considerable launching distance from targets, despite the obvious issue of verification.

In examining the dual nuclear rivalry, some contributors are attracted to an international monitoring concept. Yet this would oblige the United States and the USSR to relinquish their own judgment in an area of vital national concern.

World security is fragile, given the scope and complexities of command and of nuclear types and numbers. The observations in the collected articles give a valuable perspective on the fundamental international-security issue of our time and are instructive reading. Still there is one stark, clinching fact unmentioned but asserted elsewhere: with the thousands of posed missiles on each side, only some fifty, it is reputably claimed, would suffice to disrupt completely all American communications.

ROY M. MELBOURNE

Chapel Hill
North Carolina

*AFRICA, ASIA, AND
LATIN AMERICA*

BARSHAY, ANDREW E. *State and Intellectual in Imperial Japan: The Public Man in Crisis.* Pp. xx, 315. Berkeley: University of California Press, 1988. No price.

ROBERTSON, MYLES L.C. *Soviet Policy towards Japan: An Analysis of Trends in the 1970s and 1980s.* Pp. xvii, 234. New York: Cambridge University Press, 1988. No price.

In a world that seems flooded with books about the Japanese private sector and Japanese foreign trade, it is a pleasure to see the emergence of substantial works dealing with the nature and role of the Japanese government. Andrew Barshay scrutinizes the dilemma faced by Japanese intellectuals during the imperial period prior to World War II, when the Japanese state was moving deliberately toward confrontation and conflict in the name of a "new order." Intellectuals in almost every country have faced the dilemma of how to influence the course of government from the outside. What seems particularly relevant in the Japanese experience is the fact that their cultural sense of national community became powerful leverage for the government to call upon the loyalty and cooperation of all elements of the Japanese public in supporting public policy, even when there were strong misgivings about it.

Many intellectuals therefore elected to remain inside the circles of power to attempt to modulate state courses of action, but these moderating voices were overpowered by "the consensus among the nation's leadership to make a forced march to national strength."

While this view is now seen in retrospect as both tragically wrong and intellectually illegitimate, it did appeal to some real sense among Japanese that they are destined for world greatness. It can be argued that this national view still persists — now cast in the form of an economic development that many suspect goes well beyond a natural desire for the health and economic well-being of the nation toward a new form of world economic domination. It is this modern trend that Barshay's deep understanding of Japanese history and his wonderfully articulate perceptions of political and cultural forces in Japan make far more comprehensible.

If one follows the more enthusiastic assessments of modern-day Japanese economic success, it would be easy to conclude that the combination of Japan's government and private sector has succeeded in forging an unfailingly successful master plan for the national future. It is therefore strangely reassuring to read Myles Robertson's comprehensive assessment of the interplay of Soviet policy with Japan and the Japanese reactions at various levels. The book is divided into four parts, dealing with ideological issues and differences, economic relationships, military postures and strategies, and the arena of global political influence. In each of these arenas, the Soviet-Japanese relationship seems to have been muddled and indistinct, based more on propagandistic posturing than on insightful strategy. The sense of Robertson's analysis is that the Soviets had little to offer beyond their own preoccupation with military strength, and they persistently piddled away economic opportunities by ineptitude and their own incurably doctrinaire political and bureaucratic stubbornness. The Japanese in turn seemed to lose interest in the Soviet connection, in large part because there were so many other linkages in the world that proved of greater interest and value. Thus this book seems somehow frustrating because it describes the dissipation of prospects rather than their realization, but it stands as the first really comprehensive analysis of this important world-class relationship.

CHARLES F. BINGMAN

George Washington University
Washington, D.C.

BENNOUNE, MAHFOUD. *The Making of Contemporary Algeria, 1830-1987: Colonial Upheavals and Post-Independence Development.* Pp. xii, 323. New York: Cambridge University Press, 1988. No price.

After a colonial era that was in many respects traumatic even by African standards and a bitter and protracted war of independence, Algeria has emerged as a relatively stable and prosperous nation. Since independence, it has been governed by only three rulers, and it is clearly a middle-income country in terms of per capita gross domestic product. It stands apart from other African countries because of its significant reserves of oil and natural gas. Nevertheless, debates over what strategies are most appropriate for the country's economic and political development have resembled those that have swirled elsewhere on the African continent concerning countries far less fortunate than Algeria. Two of these issues have been the relative priority to be given to industrial — as distinct from agricultural — development and the nature and degree of governmental direction required to stimulate and focus development. For the past decade, in the wake of persistent economic stagnation and in the context of heavy pressure from the World Bank and the International Monetary Fund, many African countries have opted for a restricted governmental role and for greater emphasis upon the agricultural sector.

The Making of Contemporary Algeria is a history of Algeria's political economy. Based on that history, Bennoune contends that substantial public management of the economy and an emphasis upon industrial development are necessary for Algeria's continued and enhanced economic development.

After a brief review of pre-1830 Algeria, Bennoune traces the uneven development of Algeria under colonialism. He centers on the dissolution of traditional social structures, the impact of the alienation of more than 3 million hectares of agricultural land by French settlers, and the crystallization of a class structure in which the settlers constituted the dominant and most favored class.

Bennoune's analysis of the history of Algeria's political economy since independence looks kindly upon the Ben Bella and Boumedienne regimes because of their commitment to "Algerian socialism." Under Ben Bella workers' self-management committees formed as an important element of the "subjective populism" by which Ben Bella struggled to reactivate all sectors of the economy in the wake of the costly war of national independence. Bennoune credits Boumedienne with sustaining the popular basis of economic reconstruction and development even though he did so in authoritarian fashion and relied upon some very conservative people in his administration.

By contrast, Bennoune is sharply critical of the Benjedid regime for exacerbating rather than correcting the drift away from socialism that began under Boumedienne. He argues that in arresting the development of the public sector, Benjedid compromised "the economic viability of society and hence the political independence of the new nation." Rather than foster a modern industrial sector, Bennoune argues that Benjedid has permitted Algerian industrialization to be dominated by "a pre-existing mercantile speculative logic." Bennoune concludes that Algerian development has suffered for lack of an "enterprising industrial bourgeoisie," "a dynamic middle class," and a "powerful, skilled and experienced working class."

As a history of Algeria's political economy, *The Making of Contemporary Algeria* provides a useful overview supported by pertinent data. It is also a welcome contrast to the decade-long predominance of neoclassical liberal analyses of African political economies. Bennoune's theoretical orientation is omnipresent in the work, however, without ever being clearly specified and contrasted with alternative readings of the country's development. Because Bennoune does not contrast his perspective to other very different ones, he does not help the reader to weigh the merits of these alternative approaches in general or in the particular case of Algeria. A nonspecialist on Algeria will find it difficult to determine the worth of Bennoune's interpretations.

JOHN W. HARBESON

City University of New York

DUPUY, ALEX. *Haiti in the World Economy: Class, Race, and Underdevelopment since 1700.* Pp. viii, 245. Boulder, CO: Westview Press, 1988. $42.50.

The bitter irony of Haiti's modern history is that Haiti was once the most productive and one of the wealthiest of all the Caribbean slave colonies and yet today is the poorest and most underdeveloped country in the Western Hemisphere. By comparison with other Caribbean and Latin American nations, Haiti currently has the lowest per capita income, the highest rate of infant mortality, the lowest life expectancy, the highest rate of illiteracy, and one of the highest rates of unemployment. Since the end of the eighteenth century, when Haitians waged the only successful slave revolution in modern history and subsequently became the second independent nation in the New World—after the United States—things have somehow gone terribly wrong.

Alex Dupuy takes upon himself the task of explaining what has occurred and why. He works from a theoretical perspective that conceives of underdevelopment as caused by the dialectical interaction of external and internal social relations and forces. His starting point is the incorporation of Haiti into the capitalist world economy as a peripheral economy specializing first in the production of agricultural crops for export and later in a limited range of manufactured goods for export. This specialization constituted the "general determinant" of the nation's underdevelopment. But Dupuy makes clear that this needs to be understood in conjunction with specific class, racial/color, and political relations and structures, forged within Haiti by local actors, not merely determined by the logic of capital accumulation at each stage of its development. The search for social and economic advancement by members of the Haitian bourgeoisie and middle class and the endless conflicts surrounding the capture of state power that this generates thus constitute the detail of Dupuy's historical and political analysis. The story is taken from the period of French colonialism via the Duvalier eras to the brief five-month history of the presidency of Leslie Manigat in 1988. His salutary conclusion is that Duvalierism remains in power with the present military dictatorship and that the Namphy regime's prospects of consolidating its hold on power by fashioning a new modus operandi with the domestic bourgeoisie and foreign capital are, sadly, quite good.

In sum, Dupuy has written an excellent and informative account of Haiti's relationship with the world economy over nearly three centuries. The analysis is scholarly, the writing clear, and the appendages, such as the bibliography, very comprehensive.

ANTHONY J. PAYNE

University of Sheffield
England

FASS, SIMON M. *Political Economy of Haiti: The Drama of Survival.* Pp. xxxi, 369. New Brunswick, NJ: Transaction Books, 1988. $34.95.

Haiti's tragic experience makes it an easy prey for sociohistorical tracts masquerading as scholarship. In *Political Economy of Haiti,* Simon Fass does something worthy of note: he weaves together what the book jacket correctly characterizes as an "extraordinary assemblage of facts" and paints a vivid picture of Haiti's desperate environment—and he does that without jargon or political science abstractions. This is actually a vignette—the focus is on two urban communities—but the political and economic assessment Fass draws from it is of broader relevance.

Although the subtitle of this book is "the drama of survival," Fass successfully avoids the virtuous and quaint commentary that can be found in studies of Haiti's admittedly catastrophic situation. The only place where the book falters a bit is in its conclusion, "The Devil's Hand"; in a mildly emotional tone, Fass struggles to bridge the gap between the national desperation that the book describes so well and the sense of hope that individual Haitians may bring to achieve progress. In the way it is written, this is an unconvincing conclusion to an otherwise solid work.

Fass attaches full blame for the severe conditions of the ordinary class to those who wield political and economic power. He attacks Haiti's elite for their purely self-interested motivations and their ensuing failure in attempting to alleviate the nation's problems. Chapter by chapter, Fass delves into topics of politics and economics, employment, food, water, shelter, schooling, and credit. Two appendixes address the entrepreneurial capabilities of individuals or small subcommunities. Such capabilities underscore the life of an underground economy that exists in the midst of adversity and political and administrative limitations, a theme that Hernando de Soto, writing about Peru, has recently popularized with *The Other Path.*

Ignorance, which Fass ascribes to the governing political class, results in this class's attempts to understand the impoverished situation of the nation. This becomes evident as he reveals failed government policies and programs, which have, in some cases, caused more harm than good. Interestingly, it is therefore, according to Fass, this ignorance, and not some particular form of government, that separates the two classes. Poverty has ostracized ordinary people so much that even if the nation's leaders do want to listen to the voice of the poor, none of their policies or programs seem to heal their pain. As Haiti goes through a number of post-Duvalier political transitions, this is an intriguing theme. With governmental programs discredited, Fass places his faith in the Haitian people.

GEORGES FAURIOL

Center for Strategic and
International Studies
Washington, D.C.

HARBESON, JOHN W. *The Ethiopian Transformation: The Quest for the Post-Imperial State.* Pp. xii, 230. Boulder, CO: Westview Press, 1988. $32.50.

The Ethiopian Transformation is a provocative analysis of the process of change that has been unfolding in Ethiopia since the early 1970s. The book joins several recent works attempting to comprehend the nature and implications of this process of transformation. What is unusual about the analysis is that Harbeson eschews the application of the term "revolution" to the process in favor of what he feels is the more "appropriate" concept, "transformation," because it has "dual meaning" and is "relatively

neutral." He argues that since we cannot be sure of how far the changes that have occurred in Ethiopia since 1974 will go, we cannot really say that there has been or will be a real revolution. He identifies, over the period 1974-88, three "revolutionary movements"—military-led socialism, civilian socialism, and separatist nationalism—but no revolution! The primary thesis of the book is that the constitution of 1987 represents a "milestone" not of revolutionary consolidation but of "the entrenchment of a once transitional regime."

Harbeson describes in rich detail the transformation of the Ethiopian government from imperial rule to transitional reformist military rule and then to a consolidated military regime. He chooses to focus on the military quality of the new regime rather than the content of its ideology or the uniqueness of the organizational forms it has created. The strength of the book is the insights it provides into the events leading up to the overthrow of the ancien régime, but this is not followed with a convincing argument in support of the idea that for the past decade and a half, Ethiopia has not been experiencing a revolution.

Harbeson does not begin his analysis with a clear articulation of what is or is not a revolution, but he seems to believe that revolution is evident when, in addition to institutional and ideological transformation, there also has occurred in society a radical social transformation. The weakness of the book is its fundamental premise that "transformation" is a more appropriate representation of the process of change in Ethiopia than "revolution." In fact, Harbeson contradicts himself throughout the book, using such phrases as: "a genuine Ethiopian revolution"; "the Mengistu regime [impinges] fundamentally on the lives of its subjects to a degree greatly exceeding anything the emperors ever attempted." Indeed, he presents evidence that revolutionary changes have occurred in Ethiopia since 1974.

Revolution is a process, not an event. It is complex and usually proceeds at an erratic pace. Some revolutions never move beyond the stage of being an ideal. Some are hijacked before they can reach fruition. Others are not recognizable until after the fact. But the existence of a revolutionary ideal and the consequent emergence of a revolutionary movement can allow us to pass judgment on the success or failure of a revolution. We cannot ignore revolutionary intent, especially in the case of Ethiopia, where there has been a systematic attempt to radically reorder society in both structural and ideological terms.

By focusing on the military nature of the new regime and ignoring the importance of the Marxist-Leninist ideology and modes of social, political, and economic organization, Harbeson never really grasps the true essence of the Ethiopian transformation. To be sure, the new regime is as autocratic as the one that preceded it. Yet it is different in terms of the content of its ideology and the character of its political organization. Harbeson fails to realize that all Communist-inspired regimes, in terms of their emphasis on top-down authority patterns and on strict discipline among cadres, look very much like military organizations. But, for Communist leaders, political objectives are paramount rather than military ones. The new regime in Ethiopia has been attracted to the Soviet model of political organization because of the organizational power it promises, and this power is primarily used to pursue political objectives. Ideology is important not in and of itself, but because it seeks to legitimize the rule of an oligarchic ruling class and the right of that class to define the new normative order. Harbeson seems to ignore the fact that military regimes can also be revolutionary.

The Mengistu regime is far from consolidating and legitimating its brand of revolution. It may fail. It may be overthrown by yet another revolutionary movement; but revolutionary change has been taking place in Ethiopia.

Despite conceptual problems, *The Ethiopian Transformation* represents a useful contribution to the debate over the nature and implication of the changes that have occurred in Ethiopia since 1974.

EDMOND J. KELLER

University of California
Santa Barbara

MILLER, JOSEPH C. *Way of Death: Merchant Capitalism and the Angolan Slave Trade, 1730-1830.* Pp. xxvii, 770. Madison: University of Wisconsin Press, 1988. $35.00.

Miller presents a comprehensive study of the Portuguese slave trade in the South Atlantic. He describes the geography, economy, culture, and politics of all participants in overwhelming detail. Proceeding systematically from the west-central Africans through the mulatto, Portuguese, and Brazilian traders at Luanda to the merchants and shippers based in Portugal and Brazil, Miller offers a thorough view of each step along the slave trail. The study concentrates on the capture, sale, and shipping of Africans and does not extend to the use of slaves in America or to slavery's effect on European economies. The central theme is how slave mortality shaped the structure of the slave trade from African village to the pens in Luanda to debarkation in Brazil. Secondary themes include how Portuguese efforts to dominate the trade through mercantilist regulations proved futile and how capital scarcity necessitated costly credit arrangements. This study not only complements recent scholarship, which has concentrated more on the British, French, and Dutch slave trades of the North Atlantic, but also contributes to the general understanding of African slaving, particularly with regard to African and mulatto involvement. The book could have been shortened by a third without loss, however, and Miller's inferences about what slaves and merchants actually believed and felt tempts the line between historiography and historical fiction.

The theoretical analysis is less satisfying. A mixture of anthropological, economic, Marxian, and Polanyian theory is used to analyze West African society. This eclectic approach leads more to chaos than to enlightenment. The behavior of merchants in Luanda, Brazil, and Portugal is analyzed with ersatz economic reasoning that frequently produces dubious and inconsistent conclusions. For example, Miller argues that merchants along the slave trail tried to avoid owning slaves because of their high mortality. He concludes that the mulatto merchants in Luanda, who owned the slaves during the Atlantic crossing, must have been forced into this position because they had less economic and political power than European or Brazilian merchants. But if information on slave health could be determined during the sale, then slave prices would adjust to compensate for expected mortality losses and ownership would not matter. If information on slave health was imperfect, then Miller's evidence on slave mortality would be consistent with mulatto merchants' having a cost advantage in slave ownership during the Atlantic crossing. This advantage would imply efficiency and reduced slave mortality compared with alternative ownership arrangements. Other applications of economic reasoning, such as the determinants of tight packing on slave ships, should not be accepted uncritically.

FARLEY GRUBB

University of Delaware
Newark

NAFZIGER, E. WAYNE. *Inequality in Africa: Political Elites, Proletariat, Peasants and the Poor.* Pp. xii, 204. New York: Cambridge University Press, 1988. Paperbound, no price.

OJO, OLUSOLA. *Africa and Israel: Relations in Perspective.* Pp. xiv, 181. Boulder, CO: Westview Press, 1988. Paperbound, $23.50.

An important link between these different studies is their contention that so-called black Africans have mismanaged their affairs. The masses suffer because elites give priority to the maintenance of their power and political leaders make poor choices of friends in the international arena.

Nafziger focuses on urban-rural, income, and educational inequality in black Africa. Utilizing comparative data for least developed countries, the highly respected economist reinforces the morose image of a region in continual decline. During the last two decades the area — excluding Nigeria and South Africa — has suffered almost zero economic growth. It is burdened with poverty and fertility rates that are among the highest, the lowest physical-quality-of-life index, the lowest life expectancy, no industrial surplus, and a declining percentage of self-sufficiency in food. These conditions are unrelated to capitalist or socialist — really, statist — development, as is often argued. African countries have little with which to become capitalists, and they lack sufficient ethnic and class solidarity and administrative skills to build socialist states.

Nafziger indicts Africa's rulers. While colonialism reinforced social inequalities and is responsible for some economic problems — including the drought — African leaders of the post-1960s deserve the blame for most of their countries' present misfortunes. After independence the "bureaucratic bourgeoisie" monopolized the decision-making apparatuses and severely limited income distribution and access of nonelites and females to education. Primary "free education" is often ill-affordable for poor parents who must provide school necessities and transport. Higher education, which is rarely attained, does not always guarantee material comfort. The "managerial bourgeoisie" are primarily responsible for the plight of farmers, who have little access to credit, seldom control land use, and receive unfair returns from produce.

Agreeing with the World Bank's criticisms of African economic policies, for which he may be censured, Nafziger offers several remedies. These include elite-initiated "patron-client relationships" with the poor, and investments in educational, agricultural, and health programs. *Inequality in Africa* will illuminate economists and noneconomists, scholars and officials.

Ojo, a Nigerian political scientist, presents a chronology of African-Israeli relations during the 1960s and 1970s. In a slightly biased manner, he discusses African independence, the two "Middle East" wars of 1967 and 1973, and their effects on African-Israeli relations.

African-Israeli relations are competitively connected with African-Arab relations. Israel, a single country, competes with many Asian and African Arabic-speaking states for good relations with an even greater number of non-Arabic-speaking African states. Given its numerical disadvantage, its economic limitations, and its lack of traditional ties to Africa, which is not the case with "Arab states," contrary to Ojo's contention, Israel has performed remarkably well. American Jews and the U.S. government have helped Israel; the Soviet Union, its allies, and China have aided the Arabs.

Israel has been able to maintain, though sporadically, useful diplomatic, economic, political, and military relations with various African countries. Israeli offers of aid to independent Africa were quick and generous, and, where accepted, the aid was effective. Israel's occupation of Arab land in 1967 negatively affected its relations with African countries, but the real decline followed the 1973 Egyptian offensive. The analogy between Israeli occupation of Egyptian African territory and South Africa's policies in southern Africa, along with friendly South African-Israeli relations, led to mass African severance of diplomatic and other ties with Israel.

To Ojo, Africans behaved unconventionally and compromised their sovereignty and integrity, for they received too little from their Arab allies. African leaders who continue to insist on Palestinian self-determination as a precondition for normalization of relations jeopardize Africa's place in world affairs and hurt their peoples. Ojo may be criticized for not presenting broader African and Arab views and for overreliance on Israeli sources.

AKBAR MUHAMMAD
State University of New York
Binghamton

PATTERSON, WAYNE. *The Korean Frontier in America: Immigration to Hawaii, 1896-1910.* Pp. xii, 274. Honolulu: University of Hawaii Press, 1988. $30.00.

From 1903 to 1905 some 7500 Koreans arrived in Hawaii to work on sugarcane plantations. This subject may not appear to warrant a 274-page treatise, yet Wayne Patterson manages to tell a story that gets at the interstices of the triangular relationship between Japan, Korea, and the United States while portraying the interface between race relations and domestic politics within Hawaii and the United States in the early part of the twentieth century.

Patterson's attention to detail causes the book to get off to a slow start. When theoretical issues concerning the push-pull theory of immigration are presented later on, however, the narrative comes alive. We are treated to a story where the imperatives of Hawaiian plantation capitalism required the illegal importation of field laborers from Japan, who in turn either left for better-paying jobs in California or engaged in strikes to obtain higher wages in Hawaii. Korean urbanites, displaced by rapid social change in the last days of the Yi dynasty and recent converts to Christianity, were then recruited essentially as strikebreakers until Japan established hegemony over Korea as a quid pro quo arranged at the highest levels of government in Tokyo and Washington for leaving the Philippines in the U.S. imperialist sphere of influence.

The book can be criticized for being too factual, even redundant in a few places, for giving credit to Captain Cook rather than Galeano as Hawaii's Western discoverer, for generalizing about elite public opinion from statements made by an occasional editorial writer, for claiming that European immigration was "spontaneous," and for failing to recognize that the evidence supports a world-system analysis of immigration policy as a replacement for push-pull analysis. An unanswered question is why the sugarcane planters in Hawaii were illegally importing Japanese and Koreans at a time when Filipinos could have come legally instead. Patterson is, doubtlessly, unhappy with the press over the placement of many important substantive footnotes in the rear of the book rather than at the bottom of the page, and a map on page 10 clearly belongs on page 52.

Nevertheless, Patterson has carefully assembled information from a variety of documentary sources. Footnotes and bibliography occupy about 50 pages, with a fascinating 23-page appendix of statements by Korean immigrants and a useful 7-page glossary of names and terms.

The book is an important addition to our understanding of many themes of national and world politics, while serving to explain more about the politicoeconomic role of Koreans in Hawaii than perhaps any other source to date.

MICHAEL HAAS

University of Hawaii at Manoa
Honolulu

ROSEBERRY, J. ROYAL, III. *Imperial Rule in Punjab: The Conquest and Administration of Multan, 1818-1881.* Pp. 285. Riverdale, MD: Riverdale, 1987. $34.00.

The prospective reader of this book should pay attention to its subtitle, *The Conquest and Administration of Multan, 1818-1881.* Roseberry provides a carefully crafted, tightly focused study of one small part of the Indian subcontinent, the area in the southwestern Punjab — now in Pakistan — encompassing the city of Multan and the surrounding district. The book is primarily narrative in form. Roseberry largely eschews consideration of imperialism as a theoretical or an analytical construct. The book therefore makes no explicit contribution to the wider study of the nature and consequences of imperial rule in the Punjab, India, or elsewhere in the nineteenth-century world. Readers will find, however, further confirmation of some well-established themes in the historiography of British India.

What the book does provide is an interesting reconstruction of some aspects of the administrative and political history of Multan albeit based heavily on official, British Indian sources. Roseberry sets the stage in an initial couple of chapters, where the social and physical geography of the region is described and the administration of the area under Sikh rule reconstructed. A subsequent series of short chapters gloss over British involvement in the Punjab, ending with its annexation to British India in March 1849. The annexation was a process in which Multan figured prominently. The final half of the book describes in chronological order certain aspects of British administration of the Multan area up to 1881. These aspects include Multan in the Mutiny, the post-Mutiny political adjustments, judicial and revenue administration in the Multan district, economic growth and social dislocation, and the increased presence of hostility between Muslims and Hindus that culminated in a communal riot in Multan in September 1881.

The central theme of the book is that the authorities in Multan, both under the Sikhs and under the British, had to govern in cooperation with the local elites. The British, however, in ways they only partially understood, altered the nature of the authority exercised by those elites, and thus the British did not understand well the nature of the accommodations the imperial power had to make in order to sustain low-cost, effective administration.

The history of Multan is important within the context of Punjab history. Students of the Punjab will probably want to read this book. Others, however, are unlikely to place this book high on their reading list. Within his self-imposed limits, Roseberry has given us a careful and readable history but those same limits have given us a book of limited vision and narrow focus.

IAN J. KERR

University of Manitoba
Winnipeg
Canada

EUROPE

FERRIS, JOHN ROBERT. *Men, Money and Diplomacy: The Evolution of British Strategic Foreign Policy, 1919-1926.* Pp. xiii, 235. Ithaca, NY: Cornell University Press, 1988. $24.95.

Ferris has undertaken a careful analysis of the evolution of British strategic policies during the interwar period. He argues that much of the existing literature on the subject is flawed for several reasons: first, because scholars have more often than not been concerned with aspects of such policies only as they relate to the actions of particular government departments, such as the Foreign Office, the Admiralty, or the Treasury; second, because they have misunderstood the importance for policy formulation of the ten-year rule for war planning and thus misjudged the power that the Treasury is assumed to have exercised over the process by means of that rule; and, third, because they have divided the interwar years so as to misinterpret "the 1920s as a time of arms limitation and the 1930s as one of rearmament."

The consequence of these flawed approaches, according to Ferris, has been a widely held view that from 1919 to 1931 Britain had no coherent strategic design to ensure its national security and imperial defense; that financial imperatives dominated military planning and fixed the requirements of foreign policy; and that the country's precarious strategic position in the 1930s resulted from the muddle of the preceding decade. To demonstrate the inadequacy of these interpretations, Ferris has made a detailed study of the official records of the departments and private papers of the men involved. By focusing on the dynamics of the relationship among the men and agencies responsible for financial, foreign, and military policies, he has attempted to discern who and what issues shaped the strategic policies of the British government between 1919 and 1926.

With careful attention to the details of shifting domestic and international requirements, Ferris notes the links between the strategic principles adopted in August 1919 and the elements of strategic policy until 1926. He demonstrates that until 1925, Whitehall pursued not one but several policies that reflected the decision makers' efforts to balance foreign policy goals, military means, and economic constraints. But in 1925, a Cabinet decision to cut military service budgets led to a new look at the principles of August 1919 and resulted in the formulation of a strategic policy based on Treasury control and the ten-year rule. This meant, Ferris writes, that "for the first time . . . finance was a more important component of power than military strength." The government also considered Britain a status quo power, posited a stable world for the foreseeable future, and assumed

"that at any given date there will be no major war for ten years." Thus, from 1926 to 1932, British strategic policy entailed the characteristics conventionally ascribed to it for the entire 1920s.

Carefully researched and comprehensive in its treatment of the dynamic interrelationship among foreign, military, and financial policymakers and issues, Ferris's work calls for a reassessment of some conventional interpretations concerning Britain's interwar national and imperial security policies. His arguments are sustained by detailed comparative analyses of service budget requests and allocations, the interservice rivalries over these allocations, and the rationale that decided such struggles at the Cabinet level. Unavoidably, the text is thus laden with facts and figures that will be of interest to the specialists but make difficult reading even for the well-informed general reader.

J. H. HOFFMAN

Creighton University
Omaha
Nebraska

HOBSON, CHRISTOPHER Z. and RONALD D. TABOR. *Trotskyism and the Dilemma of Socialism.* Pp. xvii, 551. Westport, CT: Greenwood Press, 1988. No price.

The authors of this complex monograph have set themselves extremely ambitious goals. Within the confines of a single volume, Hobson and Tabor attempt to combine a history of Trotskyism — both as a tendency within the Communist Party of the Soviet Union in the 1920s and as an important strand in the radical movements in Europe, Asia, and the United States after Trotsky's exile — with a critique of his conception of the USSR and with their own detailed analysis of the USSR as a sociopolitical system. In the process, they successfully demonstrate that there was an integral connection between the shortcomings of Trotsky's own analysis of the USSR throughout his career, on the one hand, and the weaknesses that plagued the Trotskyist movement throughout the world, on the other. They criticize Trotsky's overweening faith in the Bolshevik party, his authoritarianism, and his apparent unwillingness to support direct working-class control over the means of production during the first decade of Bolshevik rule. They also demonstrate that Trotsky's subsequent definition of the USSR as a "degenerated workers' state" blinded him and his followers to the most significant distortions of the Bolshevik program of 1917 made by Lenin and Stalin and his successors. Hobson and Tabor argue that while Trotsky and his followers were vigorous and well-informed critics of Stalinist repression, they failed to realize that genuine workers' control over the means of production through local soviets, factory committees, and other institutions was essential for the creation of a genuine socialist system. The discussion in this book of the immense ideological confusion within the Trotskyist movement caused in part by its founder's own rigid definitions is particularly revealing and interesting.

Rejecting the definition of the USSR as a "degenerated workers' state," Hobson and Tabor provide an effective and detailed argument for conceptualizing the USSR as a "state-capitalist" social-political order. In their well-informed and well-documented study of Soviet policies, they provide compelling evidence that the ruling administrative elite has in fact extracted surplus value from the workers and peasants in order to increase industrial production for its own sake, and that the Soviet planning system is so incomplete and inadequate that the USSR does have many characteristics of a capitalist system. While their analysis of the USSR in the pre-Gorbachev period is effective, they do seem a bit dismissive of the program of reform sponsored by the Gorbachev regime.

The ambitious scope of this study does, however, present some difficulties. In particular, the discussion of Trotskyism as a tendency in the Communist Party of the Soviet Union in the 1920s seems to be overly compressed. Students of the USSR would have gained from a more detailed analysis of Trotsky's views on the bu-

reaucratization of the Party, his conception of the peasantry, and his analysis of the Chinese revolution, which are all largely ignored in the standard treatments of the USSR. The discussion of the various Trotskyist parties is also overly compressed. As a result, it is often very difficult for the outsider to comprehend the significance of the unending ideological conflicts and disputes that helped to undermine and eventually destroy these organizations.

JONATHAN HARRIS

University of Pittsburgh
Pennsylvania

LARKIN, MAURICE. *France since the Popular Front: Government and People, 1936-1986.* Pp. xix, 435. New York: Oxford University Press, 1988. $64.00.

It is a historical truism of sorts that most major political changes occur in times of economic crisis. Invariably, new governments or administrations come into power advocating broad programs of social change. These programs often prove difficult or impossible to implement, chiefly due to the financial limitations imposed by the economic crisis that triggered the political change in the first place.

In a book that begins its examination of French history with the reformist attempts of Leon Blum's Popular Front in the mid-1930s and concludes with the Socialist regime of François Mitterrand in the mid-1980s, Maurice Larkin, Richard Pares Professor of History at the University of Edinburgh, repeatedly demonstrates the aptness of this sequence of events when applied to fifty years of French political, economic, and social history. Insightful and often witty in his commentary, Larkin approaches French history from a traditional institutional viewpoint and is unapologetic in stating bluntly that themes other than "the interrelation of people, government, and economy . . . receive sparser treatment."

This interrelationship is examined through a superimposed overlay that Larkin characterizes as "the four Cs" — class, constitution, clericalism, and colonialism — of which the primary and most constant is the issue of class. Despite the importance of the Popular Front, the Vichy regime, and the postwar recovery period, it is during the Fifth Republic under Charles de Gaulle that Larkin sees the most important changes occurring. The process of popularly electing a president from — ultimately — one of two candidates led to political coalitions resulting in a basic bipolarization of the political process. This bipolarization in turn spilled over into the parliamentary system, creating a kind of forced stability in governmental organization and structure that had been woefully lacking during the Fourth Republic.

Larkin is invariably positive in his evaluation of individuals. Even Pierre Laval receives a much milder judgment than most would accord to the man who exerted the real power within the Vichy regime. But overall, the thumbnail sketches of the major personalities of the period reflect one of Larkin's strongest talents; his brief commentaries on de Gaulle constitute the best I have seen.

This is not a book for beginners. Despite Larkin's skill as a writer and his ability to turn the occasional deft phrase, the volume, especially in the sections covering 1946-68, remains heavy reading. A multitude of informative tables and charts are included, most of which examine issues of economic growth both within France and in comparison with other European countries. A list of some eighty abbreviations provides an indispensable reference tool.

As is true of the writing of most British historians, there is an expectation of historical knowledge about Europe on the part of the reader that will make this book difficult to use in the American classroom. Though the impact of the European Coal and Steel Community and the European Economic Community is discussed at length, the basic concepts of each are never clearly presented. The same can be said for the Marshall Plan, and the Pinay loan of 1952 is described as both "famous" and "celebrated" without any real explanation of what it was. Nor will the average American reader receive enlightenment as to exactly what the

"highest average principle" as opposed to the "largest remainder principle" was, as applied to the apportionment of parliamentary seats in a proportional representation system.

Yet, despite its tendency toward factual overkill and too heavy a reliance on blow-by-blow chronological account, this volume for the most part fills successfully the need for a relatively brief, literate, and sophisticated overview of the French political, social, and economic experience during the past, turbulent, half century.

PAUL C. HELMREICH

Wheaton College
Norton
Massachusetts

PORTER, ROY. *Mind-Forg'd Manacles: A History of Madness in England from the Restoration to the Regency.* Pp. xii, 412. Cambridge, MA: Harvard University Press, 1987. No price.

Porter's scholarly book outlines and analyzes views of madness and the treatment of the mad in England from the end of the seventeenth century to the beginning of the nineteenth. In his work he does not eschew the complexities and contradictions in his subject matter. Instead he identifies the diversity of viewpoints and approaches to madness that coexisted in England at this time. He takes issue with the more polemical and unidimensional stance of Foucault in *Madness and Civilization.* Foucault wrote of the "great confinement" of 1660-1800 in Europe due, he claimed, to the rejection of the insane as subhumans because of their lack of rationality. Porter points out that, as far as incarceration was concerned, the nineteenth century was in fact the age of the "great confinement" and that in the seventeenth and eighteenth centuries humane and concerned responses to insanity were not uncommon. In literary circles madness even had a certain cachet, as when Drayton praised Kit Marlowe: "For that fine madness still he did retain, which rightly should possess a poet's brain."

Treatment of the mad ranged from the barbaric to the enlightened, and again these differing approaches coexisted in time. Porter's analysis points out that in the history of psychiatry there has been no smooth ride toward greater sophistication and understanding. Many of the seventeenth- and eighteenth-century writers he quotes could, by their subtlety and perspicacity, teach twentieth-century "practitioners in madness" a great deal. Of particular interest is Porter's analysis of the long history of somatic explanations of psychological disturbance and the tenacity with which experts and patients have always held on to such explanations. Porter makes a surprising and convincing case for his view that English psychiatry is founded on the "practical science" of madhouse keeping. He shows how physicians gradually took over the care of the mad from lay boarding house keepers and religious institutions, suggesting that "no diseases were so lucrative as those of the nervous kind."

This book is continuously fascinating. Porter's prose style is sparkling, and he fills the book with quotations and anecdotes. He gives a very rich picture of the "long eighteenth century" and the mentality of its people in many aspects other than those specifically related to madness. The issues this book raises are not by any means specific to England, nor are they specific to their historical period. The book challenges and highlights our contemporary views of madness, views that are still in flux and still plagued by dogma and conflict.

SHEILA GREENE

Trinity College
Dublin
Ireland

THOMPSON, F.M.L. *The Rise of a Respectable Society: A Social History of Victorian Britain, 1830-1900.* Pp. 382. Cambridge, MA: Harvard University Press, 1988. $30.00.

In this book, F.M.L. Thompson, who is director of the Institute of Historical Research at the University of London, has given us an overview of Victorian social history. While the contents will be familiar to specialists in this area, there is much that will interest the general reader for whom Thompson is writing.

Chapters deal with the economy, family life, homes and housing, work and play. Thompson concludes that the structure of society was more orderly in 1900 than it had been in the 1830s. This is a widely held point of view. He also contends that, despite differences in class, there was no real class conflict due to the opacity of the divisions within this multilayered society. This is a more controversial opinion, and, while I fully agree with Thompson, perhaps he might have noted more clearly that the issue is viewed differently by others.

In this book, intended to be read by laypeople, there is little information on topics dealing with intellectual history and high culture. It is a history of Victorian life at its most basic and does not treat great issues such as the question of science versus religion. The name of Charles Darwin does not appear in the index. Neither do the names of such eminent Victorians as George Eliot, John Henry Newman, Alfred Tennyson, or even — given the subject of the book — Thomas Carlyle. On the other hand, Gilbert and Sullivan and Sherlock Holmes are mentioned. This is not to criticize Thompson for failing to write the book he did not set out to write but to indicate that the theme of "respectable society" is looked at from a limited point of view. Victorian England was an age of moral and intellectual uncertainty as well as an age of great achievement, but I cannot find recorded here much about intellectual currents.

Within its limits, however, the book contains a good deal of information about Victorian society. People interested in history from below should find Thompson's effort worthwhile and interesting. The judgments are carefully thought out, fair, and generally convincing. The conclusion that the Victorian experience bequeathed structural, identity, and authority problems to the twentieth century is unremarkable but should be a reminder to some people that the death of the queen in 1901 did not ring down the curtain on the period to which Victoria gave her name. There is a firm foundation to the belief that Victorian Britain endured to 1914.

JOHN W. OSBORNE

Rutgers University
Newark
New Jersey

UNITED STATES

BAILEY, CHRISTOPHER J. *The Republican Party in the US Senate, 1974-1984: Party Change and Institutional Development.* Pp. vii, 166. Manchester: Manchester University Press, 1988. Distributed by St. Martin's Press, New York. No price.

KEPLEY, DAVID R. *The Collapse of the Middle Way: Senate Republicans and the Bipartisan Foreign Policy, 1948-1952.* Pp. xi, 197. Westport, CT: Greenwood Press, 1988, $37.95.

The Reagan era has engendered a welcome surge of scholarly interest in the Republican Party. While movements of the extreme Right have consistently attracted attention from historians and political scientists, the GOP has been largely ignored until fairly recently. The two works under review deal with Republicans in the U.S. Senate during different eras — the immediate postwar period and the 1980s — and thus provide a useful indication of continuity and change within the party.

David Kepley's book deals with Senate Republican divisions over foreign policy during the cold-war period. Kepley sees three distinct elements within the Senate GOP at this time: bipartisan internationalists, isolationists, and the China Lobby. Postwar bipartisanship was largely the creation of Senator Arthur Vandenberg, who chaired the Foreign Relations Committee during the Republican-controlled Eightieth Congress (1947-48) and mobilized most of the skeptical Senate GOP behind the Marshall Plan and the North Atlantic Treaty. Bipartisanship collapsed in 1949-51 due to the so-called fall of China, the Korean War, and McCarthyism. At this time the isolationists, led by Senator Robert Taft, and the China Lobby were allied in castigating the Truman-Acheson foreign policy. Since most of the China Lobby in the Senate was fundamentally internationalist, however, Eisenhower and Dulles were able to forge a new bipartisan consensus during the 1950s.

Kepley gives us a lucid and comprehensive account of these matters, but his study lacks any discussion of the wider political bases of these Republican factions. One would like, for example, to know more about why the China Lobby emerged when it did. It is also doubtful whether the label "China Lobby" is best suited to describe those Republicans — such as Senators Knowland and Nixon — who, although not traditional, eastern Atlanticists, were nevertheless converted by fear of communism into adherents of a global containment policy.

Christopher Bailey provides the first academic study of the Republicans in the Senate from 1981-84, when they took control of that body for the first time in a quarter century. Bailey discusses the rise of a new breed of Republican senator in the mid-1970s and, unlike Kepley, relates this to wider changes in the balance of forces within the GOP — specifically, the rise of the so-called New Right. Bailey notes how in the initial phase of the GOP Senate, due to the impact of the 1980 election victory and the adroit leadership of Howard Baker, the Republicans achieved a remarkable degree of unity and cohesion. As time passed, however, the Republicans began to revert toward the weak partisanship and anarchic behavior characteristic of their Democratic opponents in the 1970s.

It is a pity, however, that this study ends in 1984 rather than 1986, when Republican control of the Senate ended, since, among other things, Bailey thereby misses the opportunity to contrast the leadership of Robert Dole with that of Howard Baker. One also has the impression that Bailey overestimates the power and influence of the New Right senators within the Senate GOP and underestimates the influence of the moderate Republicans who actually chaired most of the major committees. After reading Bailey's account, one is left with the impression that at the end of the day the Republican Senate did not make that much difference. Institutional norms ultimately triumphed over partisanship.

It is to be hoped that these two fine works will encourage further research into various aspects of the Republican Party, which, after all, has been by far the most significant electoral vehicle of mainstream American conservatism since the New Deal.

NICOL C. RAE

Florida International University
Miami

CRONIN, THOMAS E. *Direct Democracy: The Politics of Initiative, Referendum, and Recall.* Pp. xii, 289. Cambridge, MA: Harvard University Press, 1989. $25.00.

Thomas Cronin informs the reader in the preface that he is in sympathy with populists but adds that "this is not an advocacy book." Nevertheless, Cronin's conclusions generally are supportive of the use of the three voter-participatory devices he examined.

The first three chapters provide a general review of the respective merits of direct rule by the voters versus representative government and includes a discussion of the views of Rousseau, Madison, Jefferson, and late-nineteenth-century populists.

Cronin next turns his attention to the major questions that have been raised relative to direct citizen lawmaking. Chapter 4 is devoted to the question of the competence of voters, and Cronin concludes they understand in general the questions they are called upon to decide and act in a competent manner. Cronin admits, however, that the initiative and the referendum require a degree of sophistication and may disenfranchise certain members of the electorate.

A major fear expressed by opponents of direct democracy is that the majority will trample upon the rights of the minorities. Acknowledging that minority rights have not been respected in some instances, Cronin reports that voters generally defeat propositions that would infringe upon minority rights and adds that legislative bodies have not always respected such rights.

Cronin's analysis of the recall leads him to conclude that the device "has not significantly improved direct communications between leaders and the led and has not ended corruption in politics." In addition, the recall has not produced more competent officials and probably has not strengthened representative government. With a relatively high voter signature requirement and other precautions, Cronin belies the recall as a useful device.

Although a supporter of the initiative and the referendum on the subnational level, Cronin strongly opposes their use on the national level. He stresses that "either process would involve making national laws based on general public opinion at a particular moment. Either process would reduce some aspect of political leadership and policymaking in a large and diverse nation to a Gallup-poll approach to public policy." His alternative is reforming the Congress to make it a more accountable and responsive body.

The two concluding chapters are largely a restatement of views presented in the earlier chapters. Relative to safeguards for the initiative and the referendum, Cronin advances suggestions that he admits are no more than a listing of ones that have already been adopted in various states.

Scholars will be disappointed by the book because it is not empirically based and does not examine the use of each type of initiative and referendum. The reader must turn to other sources of information to learn about experience with each type, as Cronin does not make distinctions between most of the types. Furthermore, the general nature of the discussion of the three participatory devices, while helpful, does not promote a full understanding of them. The reference to the endorsement of the indirect initiative by the National Municipal League should be to the National Civic League, which is the newer name for the National Municipal League.

The nature of the book apparently is attributable to its sponsorship by the Twentieth Century Fund, Incorporated, which supports the writing of books for a general audience. This book fulfills that goal admirably.

JOSEPH F. ZIMMERMAN

State University of New York
Albany

GODWIN, R. KENNETH. *One Billion Dollars of Influence.* Pp. v, 186. Chatham, NJ: Chatham House, 1988. Paperbound, $12.95.

EISMEIER, THEODORE J. and PHILIP H. POLLOCK III. *Business, Money, and the Rise of Corporate PACs in American Elections.* Pp. viii, 122. Westport, CT: Quorum Books, 1988. $35.00.

New technologies are often controversial with respect to their operation and influence, and this is especially true in politics. Godwin addresses these issues in the case of direct marketing, a relatively new instrument of political mobilization, while Eismeier and Pollock describe the activities and influence of corporate political action committees (PACs), whose numbers and contributions have soared since the mid-1970s.

Godwin's excellent analysis begins with historical and descriptive chapters on the strategies used both in direct mail and in direct marketing by television and telephone. This comparison of direct mail with electronic media reminds us that the techniques used in direct mail are not unique to it. Appeals to fear, for example, are often used to galvanize individuals about a political cause or to action; documenting that this technique is now used via the postal service does not hold one's attention for long.

Godwin, however, also examines the various consequences of direct marketing. The most original analysis and most compelling set of findings he provides concern direct marketing's influence on political participation. Godwin finds that recruitment appeals that rely on direct marketing widen the participation differential between low- and high-status individuals and also attract individuals with more extreme po-

litical views. The longer individuals with extreme positions remain as members, however, the more moderate their views become.

Godwin's assessment of direct marketing's influence on political parties and Congress relates the weakening of political parties and policy realignments in Congress to PACs. The assumption is that PACs would not be in business without direct marketing and that the reaction of parties and Congress to PAC behavior is in essence a response to direct marketing. Godwin's argument is not sufficiently persuasive, however, to reject the more reasonable and standard argument that PAC activity has caused these changes.

Eismeier and Pollock analyze corporate PAC spending in congressional elections during the 1980s, arguing that historical differences in regulation — traditional sector-specific regulation versus social regulation of the 1970s — cause corporate PACs to adopt one of three spending strategies: accommodationist, partisan, or adversarial. This argument has intuitive theoretical appeal and is supported by the authors' analysis.

Eismeier and Pollock find that a significant proportion of PAC contributions are made in state — in the PAC's home state — and that a significant number of corporate PACs do not have offices in Washington, D.C. In addition, in-state spending is typically more supportive of Republican incumbents and challengers than is out-state spending. Both of these factors suggest that PAC spending is localized, in that there is a trade-off between local and national strategies, namely, access to the local district's incumbent versus electing a Republican majority.

Eismeier and Pollock use their spending typology most effectively in examining how PAC spending is influenced by election-specific factors. Corporate PACs differ between themselves in terms of strategy, and these strategies change over time to accommodate short-term political forces. Thus, while corporate PACs were highly partisan in 1980 and 1982, by 1984 pragmatism had induced corporate PAC contributions to be more accommodationist, that is, more favorable toward Democrats.

Eismeier and Pollock address an enormously complex subject and succeed in convincing the reader that the world of corporate PACs is indeed a challenging one. The reader's task is equally challenging, however. The intellectual and analytical details included abound, to the extent that the reader is often lost as to their precise significance. Likewise, the data are presented poorly, with many confusing tables and limited documentation. Thus the value of Eismeier and Pollock's work is compromised by a lack of clarity in their argument and analysis.

A finding common to both books is that many fears about direct marketing and corporate PACs are unfounded. Neither direct marketing nor corporate PACs live up to their reputed effectiveness. Proposals to control such effects must recognize this, as Eismeier and Pollock suggest.

JAN E. LEIGHLEY

Texas A&M University
College Station

GRIFFITH, PADDY. *Battle Tactics of the Civil War.* Pp. 239. New Haven, CT: Yale University Press, 1989. $25.00.

Paddy Griffith's purpose is to examine lower-level tactics in order to correct misconceptions about the nature of the Civil War. This is not just a technical study of interest only to the military historian, however. Griffith challenges our whole conception of the Civil War. He argues that it was not unique in the sweep of Western military affairs; that it did not presage modern warfare; that the rifled musket — in general use for the first time in the Civil War — was not the primary reason for the huge casualties; that, in fact, the Civil War was largely a Napoleonic conflict instead of a dress rehearsal for World War I.

In much of this, Griffith is convincing. His underlying theme is American naiveté. The Civil War was so bloody because, like the French Revolutionary conflicts, it employed massed armies raised at large from the populace. This was the first time America had fought a war with such a military force, and thus American historians have latched onto the rifled musket to explain the bloodletting. While most Civil War historians have argued that Civil War battles were indecisive, thus prolonging the war and increasing its human cost, Griffith argues that, compared with European battle, nearly all the elements for decisive combat were present in the Civil War. The missing ingredients were the lack of a corps of fully trained generals who had the ability to exploit advantages and a reluctance among the democratic American people to accept the high casualty rates needed for this kind of warfare. While trying to accomplish their wartime goals with as little human loss as possible, the Americans lost chance after chance to bring the war to a quicker end.

In short, Americans tend to view the Civil War as unique because of our relative inexperience in fighting large-scale, sustained war. That is why Griffith's outsider perspective is so interesting and useful. He demands that we reconsider many hallowed themes of our interpretation of the meaning and conduct of the Civil War. In casting his net widely to cover nearly all aspects of the military side of the war, Griffith sometimes fails to fit all the various pieces neatly into his argument. For example, his contention that earthworks were important only for their psychological effect on the soldiers and offered little in the way of physical obstruction to enemy attackers or protection for the defenders does not ring true.

But, overall, one has to admit that many of Griffith's views make sense. It will take some time for historians to deal with them, and this short review is no place for a full examination. At the very least, this book is yet another sign that the study of Civil War military history is still conceptually evolving and thus remains healthy.

EARL J. HESS

University of Arkansas
Fayetteville

HAGERMAN, EDWARD. *The American Civil War and the Origins of Modern Warfare:*

Ideas, Organization, and Field Command. Pp. xviii, 366. Bloomington: Indiana University Press, 1988. $37.50.

Edward Hagerman is associate professor of history at York University in Toronto, Canada. His specialty is the American Civil War, a subject on which he has published numerous articles and has even written contributions to textbooks used at West Point and the Air War College. In this volume, as its title indicates, he tries to trace the influence of the War between the States on the evolution of modern warfare in general.

The book falls into six rather unequal parts. Part 1 deals with military doctrinal developments that took place from the fall of Napoleon to the beginning of the Civil War. Parts 2 and 3 deal with the organization of the Army of the Potomac and that of the Army of Northern Virginia, respectively, focusing — needless to say — on the emergence of professionalism. Part 4, in some ways the true heart of the book, describes the developing relationship between offensive maneuver on the one hand and stationary trench warfare on the other. Part 5 is a digression: it describes how the Army Corps of Engineers was swamped by the demands of the first large-scale modern war in history and had to be supplemented by volunteer units, a development that Hagerman sees as an "organizational irony." Finally, Part 6, called "New Thresholds of Modern Warfare," describes the campaigns that brought the Union troops to Richmond and to Savannah, putting particular emphasis on the relationship between maneuver, attrition, and exhaustion. The book, however, does not have a separate concluding chapter, and the subject of its last sentences is Confederate tactics in 1863.

This short summary cannot do justice to Hagerman's work, which bristles with original ideas. We learn that Frederick the Great, of whom Napoleon said that he had done things that he (Napoleon) had never dared to do, had relied on a strategy of "maximum result with minimum risk." Jomini, the French military commentator and strategist, is said to have learned the "entrenched defense" from Napoleon. The West Point graduates in command of the Union Army were fortunate to have studied with the great military theoretician Dennis Mahan, or else they might not have realized the advantage that cover can offer to troops fighting on the defense. Sherman's campaign in Georgia, in which he cut loose from his line of supply and fed his troops from the countryside, was a harbinger of logistic things to come. These ideas are nothing if not interesting and controversial, and surely military historians will have a field day taking them apart.

MARTIN VAN CREVELD
Hebrew University
Jerusalem
Israel

HENDRICKSON, DAVID C. *Reforming Defense: The State of American Civil-Military Relations.* Pp. xiii, 152. Baltimore, MD: Johns Hopkins University Press, 1988. $24.50.

Reforming Defense is a well-written treatise on contemporary American defense policy. Hendrickson presents three schools of reform-oriented criticism of defense policy and alternately explicates, ignores, challenges, and concurs with the particular observations of each. He consistently structures his analysis so that the classic tension between civilians and military professionals can shed light on the specific questions posed by the reformers. When all is said and done, however, Hendrickson has made it crystal clear that he believes that the critics will largely fail and that the failure is fortunate for America.

The three, interrelated schools of criticism are organizational, military, and administrative. The organizational reformers believe that the service orientation of defense decision making is inadequate. The military reformers believe that defense doctrine, weapons systems choices, operational concepts, and personnel policies are in error. The administrative reformers are concerned about mismanagement and inefficiency in defense.

Hendrickson sweeps through a lucid litany of tensions between the legislative and executive branches, and civilian and military leaders in government. He is unwilling to attribute the proliferation of ideas, policies, and costs of the past several decades to a lack of a single authority or other organizational defects such as interservice rivalries. He concludes that the Defense Reorganization Act of 1986, which attempts to enhance a non-service-based group of military experts under the direction of a strengthened chairman of the Joint Chiefs of Staff, is a sound reform and that a biennial budget process is the only remaining institutional reform needed.

The military reformers, who are largely civilians, criticize the military for its failure to study military history, for its rapid rotation of personnel, for underfunding of military readiness, and for an overemphasis on high-technology solutions. Hendrickson agrees. Military reformers are concerned that overall strategic doctrines regarding ground-force deployment in Europe, "force projection" with large aircraft carriers, and deep interdiction rather than close air support are misguided. Here, Hendrickson disagrees.

The basis for his acceptance or rejection of a specific criticism is not always obvious. Occasionally, it even appears to be whether or not the criticism is central to the role of the military or civilians. For example, since parts-procurement scandals fall into the domain of the civilians, criticisms and calls for change are well founded.

Hendrickson consistently believes that the relationship between the military and civilians is endlessly complex and can function well only if the informal quality of the relationship is correct. It "depends not so much on the formal institutional arrangements among civilian and military leaders as on the attitude each adopts toward the other."

Hendrickson seems to think that the civilian critics, the military reformers, have a bad attitude, that the military can and should resist civilian criticisms on most major policy fronts, and that it is, therefore, fortunate that Gary Hart was the "standard bearer of military reform . . . for his withdrawal from American political life leaves no obvious champion of reform ideas in the electoral arena."

ROMAN HEDGES

State University of New York
Albany

KUKLICK, BRUCE. *The Good Ruler: From Herbert Hoover to Richard Nixon.* Pp. 213. New Brunswick, NJ: Rutgers University Press, 1988. $17.95.

The Good Ruler by Bruce Kuklick posits that the success of American presidents should be gauged by the people's emotional response to them, not by the distinction or the fate of the policies they pursued. This would rescue discussion, the Andrew W. Mellon Professor of the Humanities at the University of Pennsylvania believes, from the subjective and conflicting assessments of scholars.

"Historians have faith in the electorate only when it shows the good sense to agree with them," declares Kuklick and wins our interest, if not complete conviction.

In brief essays on six presidents, he argues that the standing of each man reflects deep-seated personal truths that the public comprehended. Although careful to disavow an indiscriminate defense of numerical democracy, Kuklick clearly would like to demote scholars' proclivity to judge presidential achievement.

Despite the effectiveness and pithiness of this book, questions arise. One concerns the cohesive quality attributed to public opinion. For example, we are told that "the voters grasped the persona of the leader, irrespective of . . . 'manipulation' "; "commentators have neglected to see that Johnson's dilemma was. . . . [that] the president was vulgar . . . the public responded to his persona." Regarding the Eisenhower presidency, Kuklick writes that "the people wanted to feel at ease"; but who are "the people" who display such unity? They appear variously in these pages as those who are polled, display bumper stickers, write letters to the White House, or—most obviously—vote for presidents. Kuklick acknowledges only very indirectly that sizable numbers are excluded from all these collectives. Thus he notes when discussing civil rights legislation of the 1960s: "Extending the franchise enabled Negroes" — the use of the outdated term is not explained — "to help to choose the political leadership; . . . to participate." The implication of changes in the national electorate and exclusion from it are not discussed. To Kuklick the legislation is significant because it constitutes "the single exception to my view that analyzing achievement is subjective." That is, political leadership did make a difference in the demise of legal segregation and the denial of voting rights.

Differing interpretations by individual scholars may undermine credibility, but Kuklick's conclusion is curious. He accepts the common judgment on the impact of the civil rights laws because it is unanimous and hence does not "belie objectivity."

In part, Kuklick is speaking energetically to professional historians. In this vein, he returns repeatedly to the pastime of categorizing presidents, which he disparages. But the practice was tellingly dismissed thirty years ago by Bert Cochran, author of *Harry Truman;* it is not a new criticism. "By grading Presidents like term papers," Cochran wrote, "[we] sink into scholastic fatuity." What was at work was "a flatulent liberalism rotating around a core of romantic deification of the strong state."

The central contribution of *The Good Ruler* is that it encourages respect for the past. Kuklick summarizes:

Politics in this period is to be preeminently understood as an on-going communal emotional experience . . . the mass feelings that existed at any point in the past should be respected as facts (similar to our own present feelings) that fundamentally condition, and should condition past political behavior.

JANET CARTER

Bruner Foundation
New York City

LEVINE, RHONDA F. *Class Struggle and the New Deal: Industrial Labor, Capital, and the State.* Pp. xi, 233. Lawrence: University Press of Kansas, 1988. $25.00.

Rhonda F. Levine, a sociologist at Colgate University, has written a history book that challenges the whole galaxy of established New Deal scholars of the Left and the Right. Levine is a neo-Marxist scholar and she brings that perspective to the New Deal's overall ideology and results, with special reference to labor policy. Levine takes on "instrumentalist" Marxist theory and defends "structuralism," and, in particular, she embraces the scholarship of Nicos Poulantzas, a leading structuralist, who sees the state in a capitalist society as itself a fractured entity because of the conflict between capitalist groups. She intends her historical study of New Deal labor policy to be a case study that substantiates Poulantzas's more abstract thought. Levine develops what she calls "an alternate class-centered approach" as opposed to traditional pluralist or instrumentalist approaches to explain what happened to state labor policy in the New Deal era. She refutes the contention that the New Deal labor policy was reform capitalism; it was rather a "strategic compromise" between "monopoly capitalists" — big business — and the state to create the conditions for optimal capital accumulation. The debate between historians over revolution or evolution, over liberal change and/or conservative change becomes irrelevant. The New Deal, to Levine, was nothing but capitalist continuity brought about when organized labor struck an "informal bargain" with monopoly capitalism, a bargain that created the underlying economic structure of postwar America and that defeated the real possibility of working-class victory in the 1930s. The working class made progress, she agrees, but it was only to gain a new starting point for the class struggle as the "contradictions" in capitalism play out in contemporary America.

She puts flesh on this argument with two chapters that examine capitalist development and the state from 1890 to 1929 and the crisis generated by the Great Depression. Two chapters specifically treat the National Industrial Recovery Act as a state solution to the crisis.

One chapter narrates organized labor's growth in the 1930s, with special reference to the 1934 strikes. The two concluding topical chapters deal with organized labor's political efforts and, somewhat irrelevantly, the New Deal's government reorganization efforts of the late 1930s.

Levine has done extensive reading of basic sources and has used effectively some New Deal records. Most interesting and original are her surveys of Communist response to the New Deal and the response of other leftist groups. Nevertheless, in general, what she presents as narrative is often a standard survey. This book should be read for its tendentious argument and not for its contribution from new sources, as most history monographs are read.

JAMES A. HODGES

College of Wooster
Ohio

SOBEL, MECHAL. *The World They Made Together: Black and White Values in Eighteenth-Century Virginia.* Pp. xii, 364. Princeton, NJ: Princeton University Press, 1987. $25.00.

The recent flood of scholarship on the early years of the Chesapeake Bay region has turned attention away from the prominent few, such as Washington, toward the often faceless many, especially those hardest to learn about, including the slaves. Virtuoso techniques have made exciting reports on such unlikely topics as demographics, diseases, prices, land use, and broken bottles.

Just when the results seemed to be falling into a synthesis, Mechal Sobel's new book calls for a further expansion of vision. She says that the turn from white servant to black slave labor in eighteenth-century Virginia produced a fusion of African and English folkways. Previously, many scholars argued for a persistence of certain African traits while slaves acculturated to an English-derived society. Nobody claimed that the owners absorbed African ways on a significant scale.

Sobel makes a strong case. In contrast to many other scholars, she asserts that the various African societies from which slaves came had enough in common to make a basic set of African cultural norms. She also argues that white Virginians had traditions that were congruent with the Africans', traditions that often came from the pre-Reformation past and either persisted in spite of Protestant condemnation or were reinvigorated by contact with Africans. A striking example is in attitudes toward time. Sobel argues that seventeenth-century Virginian planters brought a clock-minded work ethic that their eighteenth-century successors could not impose on their slaves. The slaveowners also grew fond of considering their slaves as an extended family. The result was a violent mental discord that racked slaveowners, who sometimes shifted abruptly between pseudoparental solicitude and maniacal severity when slaves persisted in African work rhythms — until the owners adopted the African, or reverted to the pre-Reformation English, rhythms themselves. Sobel pursues the interaction through subjects like space and architecture, names and kinship, nature and the supernatural, and death and commemoration. The culmination comes in an interpretation of the religious revivals at the end of the eighteenth century that makes them a spiritual union of the African and European.

Sobel is remarkably persuasive, though she probably pushes the campaign too far at points; critics will debate where and how. Still, she has cast a new light on eighteenth-century Virginia — and, by extension, on all of the United States later. We will never see the picture the same way again.

SYDNEY V. JAMES

University of Iowa
Iowa City

VOGEL, DAVID. *Fluctuating Fortunes: The Political Power of Business in America.* Pp. xi, 337. New York: Basic Books, 1989. $20.95.

David Vogel attempts to go beyond the long-running debate on whether business is just another pluralist interest or whether it occupies a privileged position in our political system. This book argues that there is no need to choose between these two depictions of business power, for each perspective can be accurately applied to one or another of recent periods of American political history. He goes beyond the analysis of some other recent volumes on the power of business such as those written by Edsell and Ferguson and Rodgers on this topic, as he uses a longer-term perspective than just the last decade or two.

The central focus of *Fluctuating Fortunes* is that the power of business is not constant or stable but ebbs and flows with the economic cycles of the nation. During this century alone, Vogel sees three major sets of fluctuations in business's political power. Actually, Vogel wrestles with the much broader question of why the political fortunes of business seem to fluctuate from one political period to another. The answer, according to Vogel, is that the influence of business in American politics appears to be inversely related to the overall levels of economic prosperity in the nation. Business's political power is a function not of the business cycle but of the public's perception of the long-term strength of the American economy and its willingness or unwillingness to support the political agenda of business.

Fluctuating Fortunes focuses on the years after the Eisenhower administration and breaks down the 1960-88 political period into six subperiods that highlight the ebb and flow of the political influence of business. Vogel argues that business's power went from a secure base during the early 1960s into a period of significant decline between the mid-1960s and the mid-1970s. Business staged a comeback between the mid-1970s and the early 1980s and experienced slight erosion in the late 1980s. Vogel examines these periods by tracing business's political influence at the federal level on four sets of issues: the regulation of corporate social conduct — health, safety, and environment; tax policy; labor-management relations; and energy policy. During the period when the great effort was made to increase governmental intervention in the economy, 1969-72, the primary impetus

came from the Congress, not the White House. Vogel notes that all presidents during the post-Eisenhower period have been friends of business, but Congress after the 1964 elections came to be dominated by a new type of legislator responding to public-interest constituents and was more willing to consider regulatory legislation. Perhaps the most interesting chapter of the book examines the Reagan years and Vogel's conclusion that business suffered a decline in political influence during the 1980s. Vogel concludes that three long-term structural changes have occurred in American politics that have had an impact on the fortunes of business: the rise of public interest — and decline of organized labor — as the major opponent to business; the increase in the government's role as a controller of corporate social conduct; and a substantial increase in corporate America's lobbying activities.

Vogel has written a very interesting and extremely useful book. By giving a long-term perspective on the political fortunes of American business, he is able to offer his conclusions on the factors that appear to influence their ebb and flow. It seems likely that this book will set the framework for future discussions of business in politics and advocacy lobbying in contemporary American politics.

RONALD J. HREBENAR

University of Utah
Salt Lake City

WALTERS, RONALD W. *Black Presidential Politics in America: A Strategic Approach.* Pp. xvii, 255. Albany: New York State University Press, 1988. $44.50. Paperbound, $14.95.

Ronald Walters has been a central figure in the theory and praxis of black politics for the last two decades. In this study, Walters's major concern is how the minority black population in the United States can maximize its political power on the national stage. His main thesis is that a strategy of "dependent leverage" exercised within the confines of the Democratic

Party does not produce maximum dividends. The career of a few black politicians may or may not be advanced, but the collective interest of the black community remains benignly neglected. Walters advocates a politics of "independent leverage" that is far more commensurate with the material interest of the black community.

As was observed in the 1984 presidential campaign of Jesse Jackson, an autonomous political organization was able to bargain from a position of strength. Nonetheless, Walters points out that Jackson refrained from maximizing black political influence in the 1984 election when he arrived at a rapprochement with the Democratic Party's nominee, Walter Mondale, six weeks after the convention, even though the bargaining issues critical to uplifting the black community were not met.

Ronald Walters is persuasive in making the case that "independent leverage" politics is far more effective than a "dependent leverage" strategy. The problem with the theoretical construct is that the maximization of black political interest entails more than an autonomous black political apparatus that is uncompromising. There is a certain danger in devising a black political strategy in isolation from the state of the American economy and the internal dialectics of white civil society. In addition, minority politics invariably entails an unending quest for alliances.

The issues that Walters identifies as essential to the well-being of the black community are not exclusive to that community. Full employment, national health care, and affordable housing are issues of mass political significance. The majority of Americans, irrespective of color but respective of class, can find common ground on these democratic rights. What was historically significant about Jesse Jackson's presidential campaign in 1984 and 1988 was his ability to establish common ground on these critical issues. The articulation of these issues using a black-nationalist terminology helps to diminish their mass significance.

Walters has assembled an abundance of empirical data to support his thesis that an autonomous black political organization is indispensable to maximize black political influence on the national stage. This study constitutes a commendable addition to the growing body of literature on black politics in America.

BASIL WILSON

John Jay College
of Criminal Justice
New York City

SOCIOLOGY

BIRKEN, LAWRENCE. *Consuming Desire: Sexual Science and the Emergence of a Culture of Abundance, 1871-1914.* Pp. ix, 167. Ithaca, NY: Cornell University Press, 1989. $21.50.

This book finds the roots of the development of a "culture of abundance" in the functional interdependence between the models of human nature developed by neoclassical economists, Darwinian thought, and turn-of-the-century sexologists. The dissolution of gender differences, which presumably produced contemporary genderless consumers, parallels and reflects the dissolution of classical political economy. The old "productivist mentality" has been replaced by a "consumerist mentality" requiring consuming subjects unhampered by restrictive gender and age restrictions, whose sexuality is unconnected with reproduction. How did this happen? Despite Birken's occasional recognition of the connections between ideas and their concrete historical context, he does not succeed in making that connection clear to the reader. In this text, ideas succeed one another; "mentalities" rise and fall due, it appears, to a process of change from holism to individualism that originated in feudal times.

Throughout the book, Birken misses no opportunity to disparage Marx, reducing Marxism to "economic determinism." This standpoint, now fashionable and predictable, presupposes idealist methodological and theoretical assumptions, and Birken's work is no exception. His focus on changing cultural configurations precludes any in-depth examination of changes in the capitalist system establishing the material conditions for the development of consumerism — for example, crises of overproduction and underconsumption — and related ideologies. Reference to "the emergence of an industrialized culture that shifted the emphasis toward desire, in order to assure the absorption of a greatly increased production," however, betrays reliance on previously rejected patterns of determination. The arguments have some plausibility because it is the case that "by virtue of their empirical basis . . . ideas are really connected with one another" (Karl Marx and F. Engels, *The German Ideology*. [New York: International, 1947], p. 42).

The connection between polymorphous sexuality and consumption, a central issue in this work, was brilliantly analyzed, from a Marxist standpoint, by Reimut Reiche in *Sexuality and the Class Struggle*, a text remarkably absent from Birken's bibliography. For Reiche, production and consumption are very much part of most people's experience and cannot be reduced to their ideological construction. Consumption presupposes production and both are effective in shaping individuals' psychosexual development, imposing contradictory demands linked to the contradictory requirements of production — sexual repression — and consumption. Current ideological struggles around sexuality, which Birken interprets as expressions of right and left conservatism, are perhaps the expression of structural and psychological contradictions grounded in the qualitatively different ways in which men and women of different social classes, races, and ethnicities experience the demands of production and consumption.

Those interested in the sociology of knowledge will find this book useful as an exemplar of ideological analysis; idealists of all persuasions might find it more appealing.

M. E. GIMÉNEZ

University of Colorado
Boulder

BRUMBERG, JOAN JACOBS. *Fasting Girls: The Emergence of Anorexia Nervosa as a Mod-* *ern Disease*. Pp. 366. Cambridge, MA: Harvard University Press, 1988. $25.00.

An ongoing debate within the area of eating disorders is whether or not these disorders are more appropriately defined as medical problems or social problems. By asking what historical forces account for the prevalence of anorexia, Joan Jacobs Brumberg provides some insight into the matter.

The first chapter is an excellent overview of the anorexia nervosa literature. It includes a discussion of the demographic profile of bulimics, whether or not there is an epidemic, the influence of popular culture in its etiology, sources of information about the topic, theoretical models, and treatment strategies, among other subjects. The combination of the thorough review, a critical evaluation of the literature, and other insights make this chapter valuable reading for anyone even remotely interested in anorexia.

In the remaining chapters, Brumberg addresses whether or not anorexia nervosa is a recent disorder. She concludes that it is relatively new, but that pathological food-related behavior has existed since at least the medieval period. She convincingly demonstrates that food and food-refusing behavior is an important continuity over time in the female experience, although the reasons for and the interpretations of it have changed historically.

While placing all examples into the larger historical context, she provides well-researched case studies to illustrate how the motivation for self-starvation changed from drives for religious ideals to the current drive to be thin. For example, while both Catherine of Siena and Karen Carpenter refused food, she clearly demonstrates that it is as incorrect to call Catherine of Siena an anorexic as it is to call Karen Carpenter a saint. Her book is an important warning that focusing on only one factor in trying to explain food-refusing behavior is to oversimplify greatly the complexity of its etiology and its treatment. When reading this book, one realizes that this warning applies to many other problems that are individually experienced but have roots in the social milieu.

Certainly those who are just starting to become familiar with anorexia will find the book helpful, and those with more experience with the syndrome will benefit from putting it into a larger context. Her analysis is fascinating to a much wider audience, however, than just those concerned with eating disorders. Those interested in medical issues; historians; sociologists; and particularly anyone interested in women's struggles will find much in this book to learn and enjoy.

CAROL A. BAILEY

Virginia Polytechnic Institute
and State University
Blacksburg

DAVIS, DONALD FINLAY. *Conspicuous Production: Automobiles and Elites in Detroit, 1899-1933*. Pp. xiii, 282. Philadelphia: Temple University Press, 1988. $29.95.

This is a tale of men obsessed by cars and by the social status cars conferred. But this time our study of this pervasive cultural obsession focuses not on the consumers of the autos but rather on the producers of them. Donald Finlay Davis takes Thorstein Veblen's famous thesis about conspicuous consumption and applies it to the production end of things as well. Hence the title, and hence the thesis it represents. If Davis is correct, Detroit automakers of the first third of the twentieth century needed to manufacture expensive and impressive cars just as much as the American people generally needed to own them and to drive them. So compelling, in fact, was this psychological need that the great majority of all the would-be automobile producers soon went bankrupt in their attempt to make and market the ideal luxury car. Thus they tended to define themselves by the cars they made, and many paid a great price for so doing.

Since there were well over 200 Detroit automobile companies organized in these years, there is a plethora of detail to be dealt with here. Davis relegates a significant amount of this detail to his multitudinous notes and to his 28 tables. Together the notes and the tables take up almost 30 percent of the pages in the book. Even so, the reader at times becomes bogged down with all the detail still remaining in the text. There are frequently scores of names, numbers, and dates on a single page. The specifics threaten to overwhelm the narrative, and they also impede somewhat Davis's articulation of his own rather ingenious thesis.

There are, to be sure, at least some problems with the thesis itself. After all, the greatest Detroit automaker of them all, Henry Ford, manifestly does not fit the "conspicuous production" pattern. Davis's various attempts to make sense of Ford, especially against the backdrop of the Davis thesis, are not altogether persuasive. Moreover, the connection between "conspicuous production" on the one hand and, say, Detroit's banking debacle of 1933 on the other seems considerably less clear and causative to the reader than to the author. Finally, Davis may sometimes unduly minimize the old-fashioned profit motive. At least a few men doubtlessly dreamed of successfully making an expensive line of cars partly because of the greater margin of profit in such upscale autos—then and now. In a word, the Davis thesis, as imaginative as it is, seems somehow overargued. Nonetheless, there is a wealth of data in this study, and so it serves to further document the important role played by the automobile in American culture. Because of this, Davis's book deserves a place alongside the works of John B. Rae, Allan Nevins, and other able practitioners of the art and science of automobile history.

ROBERT P. HAY

Marquette University
Milwaukee
Wisconsin

QUADAGNO, JILL. *The Transformation of Old Age Security: Class and Politics in the American Welfare State*. Pp. xiii, 253. Chicago: University of Chicago Press, 1988. $27.50.

WACHTER, SUSAN M., ed. *Social Security and Private Pensions: Providing for Retirement in the Twenty-first Century.* Pp. xiv, 232. Lexington, MA: Lexington Books, 1988. No price.

Understanding the passage of the original Social Security measures in the United States may help to determine prospects for future retirement policies. In these complementary but contrasting works we find sociological collective and political economic decisionist assumptions. The Wachter collection draws on papers mostly by economists delivered at a conference at the National Press Club, Washington, D.C., on 24 April 1987. The topics are what is right with, what is wrong with, and what might be better in providing for retirement in the next century. Titles of the three parts clearly denote the coverage: "The Optimal Roles for Private and Public Retirement Insurance: Market Failure Rationales"; "Financial Status of the Elderly: Current and Twenty-first Century"; and "Planning for the Twenty-first Century: Policy Options."

In chapter 1, Jerry R. Green outlines the relations of market failure, Social Security, and demographics. In chapter 2, Alan S. Blinder answers the question, Why is the government in the pension business? Insightful comments are added by Andrew B. Abel and Robert D. Paul.

Thomas D. Hurd takes on, in the third chapter, the problem of forecasting the consumption and wealth of the elderly and finds prospects to be good. Next, Emily S. Andrews and Deborah J. Chollet consider future sources of retirement income as it affects the baby-boom generation and, again, find good prospects except for women retirees. Comments by Richard A. Ippolite appear unwarrantedly conservative, while Robert M. Ball follows Andrews and Chollet in anticipating an unexpected demand of private industry for public help in health care insurance, now surfacing in the national media.

Michael J. Boskin discusses future Social Security financing arrangements from the viewpoint of national savings. A comment by John B. Shoven elaborates on the huge success of the federal retirement system. In chapter 6, Mark V. Pauly notes the necessary distinction between acute-care insurance and chronic-care insur-

ance in discussing Medicare and health care costs of retirees. He urges shifting forward from the 1960s to the 1980s our principles of insurance coverage. Robert P. Inman comments on how Pauly's analysis fits within the wider agenda of income provisions for the elderly. In the following chapter, Michael J. Boskin, Laurence J. Kotlikoff, and John B. Shoven elaborate on the concept of personal security accounts as a proposed fundamental reform in Social Security, claiming that this type of account closes significant shortcomings in Social Security such as financial solvency, equity, efficiency, uncertainty, and lack of information. In her comment, Alicia H. Munnell puts fire to the suggestion by insinuating that nearly all should find the projected reforms misguided in the face of the huge, ongoing programs that affect nearly every American.

Lawrence H. Thompson, in chapter 8, tackles the problem of altering the public-private mix of retirement income by addressing a debate that has combined four concerns: "future cost of the system; impact on rate of investment; distribution of costs and benefits; and effect of system on retirement behavior." Michael J. Boskin comments on the thoughtful, provocative, yet concise analysis provided by this paper and concludes: "I agree with Thompson that it has been a source of tremendous achievements and that these achievements must be recognized and maintained in any sensible reform proposals."

Whatever policies the experts cook up between now and the twenty-first century, advocates will face the political realities of the time, as did the architects of the New Deal and Social Security in the 1930s. Concise theorizing about the welfare state leads Quadagno to an explanation of American "exceptionalism." She summarizes theories of welfare-state development and elaborates them at a more abstract level of analysis through the relation between welfare and organization of social production. The structure of the state as a separate force is viewed as having three tiers: an arena of political decision making; a matrix of social power; and changes within that power matrix. American exceptionalism is explained through historical analysis of three variables: weaknesses of the American labor movement; the power of private-sector initiatives; and the dualism of American economic development, north and south. The interplay of these variables produced welfare programs such that public policymaking has proceeded incrementally, a dual benefit structure exists, and the main function of most programs is to alleviate poverty rather than to institutionalize equality. The treatment of old-age benefits for Quadagno's individualizing comparison makes this clear.

PERRY H. HOWARD

Louisiana State University
Baton Rouge

SWAY, MARLENE. *Familiar Strangers: Gypsy Life in America.* Pp. xi, 155. Champaign: University of Illinois Press, 1988. $19.95.

Gypsies have for long captured the popular imagination. The cost has been that perhaps no other ethnic group in North America has been subject to so many stereotypes and so much misinformation. Marlene Sway's scholarly but highly readable study is a valuable contribution to an informed understanding of Gypsy life. Let me first commend her for her clarity of thought and lucid presentation of data. The book is divided into thematic chapters covering migration, religion, family, legal system, and economics. She presents the current state of academic knowledge on each of these areas as well as brings out the linkages between them. It is fascinating reading.

The Gypsies originated in India in the ninth century but have since become world wanderers. Sway gives a brief account of their migration patterns, which took them to Persia, Syria, Palestine, Egypt, and North Africa as well as to Europe and later to the New World. They have shown remarkable endurance; Sway estimates that there are 8 to 10 million Gypsies today in forty different countries, with about a million in North America. The Gypsies were able to survive hostile environments without being assimilated because of their religious ideology and tight social organization. The basis of Gypsy religion, as well as of family and kinship, is a series of intricate laws known as the *Marime* codes, which govern every aspect of their lives. These codes define all non-Gypsies as impure and require the social separateness of Gypsies. *Marime* rules have a logic and purpose strikingly similar to that of the pollution ideology of Hinduism, which governs caste codes. In an otherwise perceptive discussion, Sway, surprisingly, ignores this continuing relevance of the religious beliefs and categories that the early Gypsies took with them from India.

Sway argues convincingly that economic adaptability and the practice of economic territoriality are major factors in the survival of the Gypsies in North America. Also relevant is their own elaborate legal system that is able to enforce a high degree of conformity to group norms. This book gives a clear and scholarly account of how kinship, religion, law, and economic activity all reinforce Gypsy exclusiveness and overcome the lure of assimilation. *Familiar Strangers* also makes a significant theoretical contribution. It refutes the widely held view that middle-man minorities can persist over time only if the social system remains structurally unchanged. Sway shows that economic and other social changes have not affected the Gypsies as a middle-man minority; illiteracy and nomadism have saved them from the relentless pressure to assimilate.

This is a thoughtful and well-written book. It is recommended to anyone interested in Gypsy life as well as to students of ethnicity and minorities.

TISSA FERNANDO

University of British Columbia
Vancouver
Canada

TUCKER, SUSAN. *Telling Memories among Southern Women: Domestic Workers and Their Employers in the Segregated South.* Pp. xi, 279. Baton Rouge: Louisiana State University Press, 1988. $24.95.

Through *Telling Memories among Southern Women,* Susan Tucker seeks "to undo some of the silence" surrounding discussions of race and of relations between white women employers and black domestic workers. With the assistance of Mary Yelling, a black social worker, Tucker, who is a white librarian, interviewed 21 domestics and 21 employers. Transcribing, editing, and reediting each interview herself, Tucker created an innovative and provocative volume in which she organized the 42 brief narratives into five thematic sections and an epilogue. Introductions, headnotes, and a photographic essay provide interpretive cues and continuity. Tucker's own experiences growing up in the segregated South are woven through the analysis, adding both immediacy and ambiguity to her portraits.

The familiar themes explored—the transition from country to city and from live-in to day work; the role of domestics as mediators between the races; the sexual vulnerability of black women; the contradictions of race and class relations; the significance of "toting," uniforms, and naming practices to employers and employees; blacks' masking and whites' misunderstanding of domestics' feelings about their work and their employers—are more fully illuminated here than elsewhere and with a more acute sensitivity to their different meanings for blacks and whites.

Beginning each section with the words of black women, Tucker reverses the standard interpretive framework by making white women measure up to a black standard. In the section "Giving and Receiving," for example, Juliana Lincoln recalls one employer who "always asked about my children. In fact, she would always give me something. She *always* gave me something! So, see, they knew." Her recognition of white women's guilt about black women's forced neglect of their own children then shapes our reading of Frances Galvin's claim that "we all thought of giving to servants as sort of a mutual thing. They gave to us by working and not worrying about if they worked late or whatever, and we gave to them by helping out wherever we could, giving them things."

This is only one example of the complexities revealed through these parallel but interlocked narratives of gender, class, and race relations. Yet simple truths also appear. They help explain the deep personal and political transformations set in motion by the civil rights movement. Though not detailed here, the contributions of domestic workers to such early episodes as the Montgomery bus boycott further illustrate the practical and profound ways that relations between black domestics and white employers served as one of the crucial pivots around which Southern race relations developed.

NANCY A. HEWITT
University of South Florida
Tampa

ECONOMICS

DESAI, PADMA. *Perestroika in Perspective: The Design and Dilemmas of Soviet Reform.* Pp. viii, 138. Princeton, NJ: Princeton University Press, 1989. $14.95.

This book's special strength is that it neatly delineates the economic promise and perils of *perestroika.* Desai starts by recalling the status quo ante, showing how the overcentralized, bureaucratized Soviet political economy has led to an economic slowdown; how state planners use a production-financial-technological plan that has stifled industrial enterprise; how Soviet agriculture has been destroyed by collectivization; how the service sector has been all but ignored by the Soviet planners; and how the arrangements and formulas developed to promote foreign trade have been counterproductive, since they were not linked to any rational—that is, market—calculations of costs and benefits. She then goes on to analyze *perestroika* as a carefully calculated policy of Mikhail Gorbachev, developed to overcome the weaknesses of the Soviet economy while maintaining its socialist identity.

According to Desai, Gorbachev's restructuring does rationally address major problems of the Soviet economy. A new Law of State Enterprise is designed to increase financial responsibility, autonomy, and incentives for enterprise management. Workers on collective farms have been given a series of individual and group incentives to increase agricultural productivity through a surplus contract and leasing systems. Cooperatives, newly sanctioned by the state, are to develop a service industry, and new guidelines are evolving to facilitate foreign trade and investment rationally. Yet, in Desai's judgment, the reforms do not go far enough. Market rationality is limited by ideology and entrenched political interests, and substantive economic success is, therefore, unlikely. The economic reforms are limited by Soviet politics and culture.

While Desai is on firm ground in her economic analysis, her political and cultural analysis is not as convincing. Politics and culture are analyzed as "superstructure." The specific difficulties of nationalism are mentioned but its explosive potential is not recognized. The special role of an official truth, a persistent totalitarian culture, is not even considered. The discussion of the Soviet relationship with Eastern Europe is ill informed. The detailed strategies and accomplishments of opposition politics and culture are not appreciated. Desai soundly presents the formal changes in Soviet politics and culture without considering the political and cultural significance of unofficial social forces in the Soviet bloc. For this, the reader will have to go elsewhere.

Nonetheless, Desai does soundly deliver what her book's title promises. She puts the Soviet policy of economic restructuring—*perestroika*—in perspective. Her book outlines the fundamental contours and dilemmas of the Soviet economic reforms and thus provides a useful introduction for the nonexpert to the major changes occurring at present in Gorbachev's Soviet Union.

JEFFREY C. GOLDFARB

New School for Social Research
New York City

MITTELMAN, JAMES H. *Out from Underdevelopment: Prospects for the Third World.*

Pp. xviii, 204. New York: St. Martin's Press, 1988. $35.00. Paperbound, $12.95.

SINGER, MAX. *Passage to a Human World: The Dynamics of Creating Global Wealth.* Pp. xv, 390. New Brunswick, NJ: Transaction Books, 1988. $32.95. Paperbound, $16.95.

Starting around the middle of the fifteenth century, world commerce took off. Within the next century and a half, it would be fair to say, commercial life in Europe took hold and restructured a very large part of the creation of the wealth of a significant portion of the globe. It was this process—the growth of a world economy—that ripened into industrialization, while at the same time introducing a territorial division of the world into those nations that were rich as nations and those that were poor. I stress the categories of rich and poor nations because, and not coincidentally, within the former there were significant numbers of very poor people and within the latter a proportion of those who were, by any standard, rich.

There was nothing automatic about this development. Quite to the contrary, obstacles had to be overcome even if these might have appeared to contemporaries not so much as obstacles as merely the taken-for-granted state of the world that had to be dealt with in the pursuit of the holy grail of wealth. The Ottoman Empire certainly stood in the way, not to mention other entrenched and, for the time, equally advanced commercial systems. In overcoming these and other barriers to the accumulation of wealth, congeries of institutional arrangements arose, the totality of which eventually constituted a highly integrated and evolving social division of labor on a world scale.

Singular though this division of labor may be, it is a singularity of a multiplicity of labor forms and production processes all of which both create and express the highly uneven distribution of the product of that world economy.

This division of the world into rich and poor nations is the subject of the two books under review here, though that is all that they share. Let me begin with James Mittelman's *Out from Underdevelopment.* As the title suggests, Mittelman's question is simple: how do nations escape from the dynamic that has created and ensures their poverty? Mittelman identifies three strategies that nations have taken to overcome the barriers to national wealth: joining global capitalism, withdrawing altogether from the world system, and balancing the ties of dependency. For his first case, he uses Brazil as an example; in the second, China under Mao; and the third, Mozambique.

Mittelman spends more than a third of this slim volume in developing the theoretical framework he uses in his analysis of these three examples. After dismissing the ability of neoclassical economics to come to terms with the wealth of nations, he advocates a position he calls political economy and defines as "the laws that govern the production, distribution, and consumption of goods to satisfy human needs, as well as the state's capacity to organize and disorganize class forces, both within a social formation and at the global level."

He next turns to a critique of modernization and dependency theories. Though not particularly original, the criticism is useful for the noninitiated, because of both its accessibility and the use of examples from the real-life contemporary experiences of people living in poor nations.

In identifying those processes that may lead to wealth among poor countries, Mittelman opts for a version of Gunder-Frank's thesis of the development of underdevelopment. Though this part of the book offers no surprises, what is interesting is the use to which he puts his critique. Rather than depending on arid concepts, he considers the actual practices of international institutions as these were in fact shaped by the set of orthodox theories he criticizes. In short, what he is able to do is to demonstrate that ideas count and a lot.

This part of the book is interesting and worth considerably more space than Mittelman is willing to give it, at least in this volume. His real interest is the strategies employed by less developed countries in trying to find a way out from the dictates of a world economy that until now have been anything but favorable. This, then, is the final section of the book, and I will leave it to readers to decide if Mittelman has hit upon a solution or solutions that have until now eluded other commentators.

While I have very serious problems with the framework invoked by Mittelman—his treatment of wage labor as the sine qua non of world capitalism and of national economies as enjoying a more than relative autonomy vitiates precisely the theoretical framework he attempts to develop—at least there is an explicit framework within which readers can make judgments about the work as a totality. The same cannot be said for Max Singer's *Passage to a Human World.*

For Singer, the creation of a national wealth, along with national poverty — although the connection here is mine, not his — is axiomatic and need not be debated. It is worth quoting him at length:

About two centuries ago some societies began to learn how to increase the productivity of human work and thus to become wealthier and wealthier. Since then the first societies to learn have continued to apply what they had learned, and continued to learn more, so that their productivity has continued to grow and their wealth has continued to accumulate (p. 10).

So much for the complexity of history. So much for the major social institutions that cross national borders and ensure, at one pole, wealth and, at the other, poverty. So much for the possibility that both domination and exploitation played a role in ensuring that some areas of the world became wealthy at the expense of some others that became poor.

Singer's book is one of the most clear-cut examples of the problems of modernization theory that I have come across in many years, and because he is either unaware of the controversy or simply does not care, the book has the charms of being considerably less shrouded in academic mystique than other such endeavors.

Singer's central purpose is to establish that there is no natural limit to growth; there are enough products of the earth to sustain growth for generations to come. But his proof rests on rather shaky foundations. Consider, as just one example, his proof that there is no shortage of raw materials. Since a material is scarce if it costs a lot, says Singer, and since the price of raw materials is actually going down, not up, it is axiomatic that those materials are not scarce!

I, for one, believe, as does Singer—and this is probably the only thing we have in common—that scarcity is much less a question of natural limits than it is of the distribution of the world's wealth. The final chapters of the book are ingenious in their attempt to demonstrate how the world can meet projected population demands for hundreds of years to come. But the book, as a whole, is altogether offensive if in no other way than that its author treats as given that which is entirely open to serious question, not just by academics but by those who are suffering the most. Singer may be right in his prognostications, but not for the reasons he gives and therein lies the problem.

JOAN SMITH

State University of New York
Binghamton

VICKERS, JOHN and GEORGE YARROW. *Privatization: An Economic Analysis.* Pp. xii, 454. Cambridge: MIT Press, 1988. $39.95.

Privatization—transferring ownership from the government to the private sector—has altered values and economic life. As Madsen Pirie says, events have produced intellectual revolution, rather than ideas being the catalyst for change. This book tries to reverse this process and subject privatization to the criterion of efficiency. The book contains two parts: theoretical perspectives on ownership, competition, and regulation and their effect on efficiency; and an assessment of British privatization in the telecommunications, energy, transportation, and water industries.

To analyze the effects of ownership on efficiency, Vickers and Yarrow apply the principal-agent model to politicians or shareholders and to managers. They assume that politicians maximize social rather than personal welfare, but elsewhere the evidence indicates otherwise. For instance, they note that government provides little control to public corporations except for general objectives whose imprecision invites politicians and managers to pursue their personal welfare, though under the guise of social welfare. While Vickers and Yarrow mention property rights, they do not use them to analyze the efficiency consequences of a public or private corporation.

Instead, they believe that private ownership can produce greater efficiency than the government only in the presence of adequate competition. But what is adequate? For thirty years, government exacerbated rather than reduced inefficiencies. Buchanan and Tullock's theory of nonmarket failure—not mentioned—describes why public corporations behave less efficiently than private businesses in similar circumstances.

Vickers and Yarrow correctly argue that competition provides the incentives for firms to allocate resources efficiently. To facilitate competition the privatized firm should be divested into smaller units if it dominates the market. Otherwise, only price regulation will check monopoly power, and detailed regulation may reduce the efficiency from privatization. There is a trade-off between monopoly and efficiency, but we do not know the terms.

In part 2, Vickers and Yarrow note that the U.K. government verbally supported but did not increase competition by restructuring industries before privatization in the way Judge Green divested AT&T. Senior managers at British Airways, British Telephone, and British Gas fought divestitures. Managers at British Airways threatened to withdraw their cooperation if the government divested the airports from other functions. Rather than jeopardize privatization, the government capitulated. Why? Public choice suggests that politicians act self-interestedly.

Vickers and Yarrow correctly criticize the U.K. privatizations for wasting taxpayers' money by underpricing shares too much, selling shares too quickly, and spending too much on underwriting and advisory fees. Why did the government adopt these practices? Public-choice theory again suggests that politicians redistribute income to build support for their privatization policy and political party.

Where has the academic economists' sound advice been for the past ten years? This book fills a longtime void. Vickers and Yarrow claim that, in privatizing, too much attention has been paid to ownership and not enough to competition, but it is they who could have produced the ameliorating force. Belatedly this book introduces a note of caution and mitigation in the enthusiasm for privatization — not to dampen but simply to channel it.

DOUGLAS K. ADIE

Ohio University
Athens

OTHER BOOKS

ANSHEN, RUTH NANDA, ed. *Has Freedom a Future?* Pp. xxx, 153. New York: Praeger, 1988. Paperbound, $12.95.

AREND, ANTHONY CLARK. *Pursuing a Just and Durable Peace: John Foster Dulles and International Organization.* Pp. 256. Westport, CT: Greenwood Press, 1988. $39.95.

BARNETT, TONY. *Social and Economic Development: An Introduction.* Pp. viii, 232. New York: Guilford Press, 1989. Paperbound, $16.95.

BATES, ROBERT H., ed. *Toward a Political Economy of Development: A Rational Choice Perspective.* Pp. x, 393. Berkeley: University of California Press, 1988. Paperbound, $14.95.

BERGER, PETER L. and BOBBY GODSELL, eds. *A Future South Africa: Visions, Strategies, and Realities.* Pp. 344. Boulder, CO: Westview Press, 1988. $29.50.

BHATIA, B. M. *Indian Agriculture: A Policy Perspective.* Pp. 192. New Delhi: Sage India, 1988. $22.50.

BLAUNER, BOB. *Black Lives, White Lives: Three Decades of Race Relations in America.* Pp. 347. Berkeley: University of California Press, 1989. $25.00.

BLONDEL, JEAN and FERDINAND MILLER-ROMMEL, eds. *Cabinets in Western Europe.* Pp. xii, 262. New York: St. Martin's Press, 1988. $45.00.

BRODERICK, FRANCIS L. *Progressivism at Risk.* Pp. viii, 246. Westport, CT: Greenwood Press, 1989. $39.95.

BROWN, RICHARD HARVEY. *A Poetic for Sociology: Toward a Logic of Discovery for the Human Sciences.* Pp. xiii, 302. Chicago: University of Chicago Press, 1989. Paperbound, $14.95.

CHALIAND, GERARD. *Revolution in the Third World.* Revised ed. Translated by Diana Johnstone and Tony Berrett. Pp. xx, 296. New York: Penguin Books, 1989. Paperbound, $8.95.

CHEEK, TIMOTHY, ed. *Hu Yaobang: A Chinese Biography by Yang Zhongmei.* Pp. xxiv, 207. Armonk, NY: M. E. Sharpe, 1988. $29.95.

CHERRY, ROBERT. *Discrimination: Its Economic Impact on Blacks, Women, and Jews.* Pp. xii, 235. Lexington, MA: Lexington Books, 1989. No price.

CIMBALA, STEPHEN J. *Nuclear Strategizing: Deterrence and Reality.* Pp. x, 306. New York: Praeger, 1988. $39.95.

CLARKE, HAROLD D. et al., eds. *Economic Decline and Political Change: Canada, Great Britain, the United States.* Pp. xii, 290. Pittsburgh, PA: University of Pittsburgh Press, 1989. $39.95.

CLEMENCE, RICHARD V., ed. *Essays on Entrepreneurs, Innovations, Business Cycles, and Evolution of Capitalism.* Pp. xxxix, 341. New Brunswick, NJ: Transaction Books, 1989. Paperbound, $19.95.

COFFEY, JOSEPH I. and GIANNI BONVICINI, eds. *The Atlantic Alliance and the Middle East.* Pp. xii, 316. Pittsburgh, PA: University of Pittsburgh Press, 1989. $49.95.

COSTA, FRANK J. et al., eds. *Urbanization in Asia: Spatial Dimensions and Policy Issues.* Pp. ix, 412. Honolulu: University of Hawaii Press, 1989. $44.00.

COUGHLIN, RICHARD M., ed. *Reforming Welfare: Lessons, Limits, and Choices.* Pp. viii, 296. Albuquerque: University of New Mexico Press, 1989. Paperbound, $12.95.

CRANDALL, ROBERT W. and KENNETH FLAMM, eds. *Changing the Rules: Technological Change, International Competition, and Regulation in Communications.* Pp. 450. Washington, DC: Brookings Books, 1989. Paperbound, $12.95.

DAVID, CHARLES-PHILIPPE. *Debating Counterforce: A Conventional Approach in a Nuclear Age.* Pp. xvi, 260. Boulder, CO: Westview Press, 1987. Paperbound, $27.50.

DELETANT, DENNIS and HARRY HANAK, eds. *Historians as Nation-Builders: Central and South-East Europe.* Pp. xvi, 245. Portland, OR: ISBS, 1988. $59.95.

DICKE, DETLEV CHR. and ERNST-ULRICH PETERSMANN, eds. *Foreign Trade in the Present and a New International Economic Order.* Pp. xii, 427. Fribourg, Switzerland: University Press, 1988. Paperbound, $45.00.

DYE, THOMAS R. and HARMAN ZEIGLER. *American Politics in the Media Age.* 3d ed. Pp. xvii, 390. Pacific Grove, CA: Brooks/ Cole, 1989. Paperbound, $24.00.

FALCOFF, MARK, ARTURO VALENZUELA, and SUSAN KAUFMAN PURCELL. *Chile: Prospects for Democracy.* Pp. xiii, 80. New York: Council on Foreign Relations, 1988. Paperbound, $8.95.

FAN, DAVID P. *Predictions of Public Opinion from the Mass Media: Computer Content Analysis and Mathematical Modeling.* Pp. xviii, 202. Westport, CT: Greenwood Press, 1988. $42.95.

FINNIS, JOHN et al. *Nuclear Deterrence, Morality and Realism.* Pp. xv, 429. New York: Oxford University Press, 1987. $39.95.

FULLER, STEVE. *Philosophy of Science and Its Discontents.* Pp. x, 188. Boulder, CO: Westview Press, 1989. $32.95.

GERT, BERNARD. *Morality: A New Justification of the Moral Rules.* Pp. xxx, 317. New York: Oxford University Press, 1988. $34.00.

GOODHART, CHARLES. *The Evolution of Central Banks.* Pp. viii, 205. Cambridge: MIT Press, 1988. Paperbound, $11.95.

GREELEY, ANDREW M. *Religious Change in America.* Pp. vi, 137. Cambridge, MA: Harvard University Press, 1989. $25.00.

GRUZINSKI, SERGE. *Man-Gods in the Mexican Highlands: Indian Power and Colonial Society, 1520-1800.* Pp. 223. Stanford, CA: Stanford University Press, 1989. $32.50.

HAAS, MICHAEL. *The Pacific Way: Regional Cooperation in the South Pacific.* Pp. xxii, 183. Westport, CT: Greenwood Press, 1989. $42.95.

HAGLUND, DAVID G. and JOEL J. SOKOLSKY, eds. *The U.S.-Canada Security Relationship: The Politics, Strategy, and Technology of Defense.* Pp. 306. Boulder, CO: Westview Press, 1989. Paperbound, $29.50.

HAGSTROM, JERRY. *Beyond Reagan: The New Landscape of American Politics.* Pp. 322. New York: Penguin, 1989. Paperbound, $8.95.

HALL, KERMIT and JAMES W. ELY, Jr. *An Uncertain Tradition: Constitutionalism and the History of the South.* Pp. ix, 403. Athens: University of Georgia Press, 1989. Paperbound, $17.95.

HENDERSON, JAMES D. *Conservative Thought in Twentieth Century Latin America: The Ideas of Laureano Gomez.* Pp. xi, 217. Athens: Ohio University Press, Swallow Press, 1988. Paperbound, $11.00.

HILL, KIM QUAILE. *Democracies in Crisis: Public Policy Responses to the Great Depression.* Pp. xvi, 147. Boulder, CO: Westview Press, 1988. $35.95.

JERVIS, ROBERT, RICHARD NED LEBOW, and JANICE GROSS STEIN. *Psychology and Deterrence.* Pp. x, 270. Baltimore, MD: Johns Hopkins University Press, 1989. Paperbound, $12.95.

JOHNSON, PAUL. *Intellectuals.* Pp. x, 385. New York: Harper & Row, 1988. $22.50.

JOHNSON, ROBERT MATTHEWS. *The First Charity.* Pp. xviii, 234. Cabin John, MD: Seven Locks Press, 1988. Paperbound, $13.95.

JOSEPH, BENJAMIN M. *Besieged Bedfellows: Israel and the Land of Apartheid.* Pp. ix, 184. Westport, CT: Greenwood Press, 1988. $35.00.

KEELEY, MICHAEL. *A Social-Contract Theory of Organizations.* Pp. 288. Notre Dame, IN: Notre Dame Press, 1988. $32.95.

KERNS, VIRGINIA. *Women and the Ancestors: Black Carib Kinship and Ritual.* Pp. xv, 229. Champaign: University of Illinois Press, 1989. Paperbound, $14.95.

KHANDWALLA, PRADIP N., ed. *Social Development: A New Role for the Organizational Sciences.* Pp. 384. New Delhi: Sage Publications India, 1989. $27.50.

KIM, SAMUEL S., ed. *China and the World: New Directions in Chinese Foreign Relations.* 2d ed. Pp. xii, 339. Boulder, CO: Westview Press, 1989. $55.00. Paperbound, $17.95.

KOBURGER, CHARLES W., Jr. *The Cyrano Fleet: France and Its Navy, 1940-1942.* Pp. 151. New York: Praeger, 1989. $38.95.

LASKY, MELVIN J. *On the Barricades, and Off.* Pp. x, 480. New Brunswick, NJ: Transaction Books, 1989. Paperbound, $19.95.

LASSMAN, PETER and IRVING VELODY, eds., with HERMINIO MARTINS. *Max Weber's 'Science as a Vocation.'* Pp. xvii, 220. London: Unwin Hyman, 1989. No price.

LEE, PETER N. S. *Industrial Management and Economic Reform in China, 1949-1984.* Pp. x, 335. New York: Oxford University Press, 1988. $35.00.

LENG, SHAO-CHUAN, ed. *Changes in China: Party, State, and Society.* Pp. xvii, 368. Lanham, MD: University Press of America/White Burkett Miller Center of Public Affairs, 1989. Paperbound, $19.75.

LEVINE, MARC V. et al. *The State and Democracy: Revitalizing America's Government.* Pp. 211. New York: Routledge, Chapman & Hall, 1989. Paperbound, $17.95.

LICKLIDER, ROY. *Political Power and the Arab Oil Weapon: The Experience of Five Industrial Nations.* Pp. xv, 343. Berkeley: University of California Press, 1988. No price.

LIEBERTHAL, KENNETH G. and BRUCE J. DICKSON. *A Research Guide to Central Party and Government Meetings in China 1949-1986.* Pp. lvi, 339. Armonk, NY: M. E. Sharpe, 1989. $50.00.

LINNEMANN, HANS et al., eds. *Export-Oriented Industrialization in Developing Countries.* Pp. xii, 467. Athens: Ohio University Press, 1989. Paperbound, $25.95.

LOPES, CARLOS. *Guinea-Bissau: From Liberation Struggle to Independent Statehood.* Pp. viii, 194. Boulder, CO: Westview Press, 1987. $35.00.

LOWENTHAL, LEO. *Critical Theory and Frankfurt Theorists: Lectures—Correspondence—Conversations.* Pp. 262. New Brunswick, NJ: Transaction Books, 1989. $29.95.

MANDELBAUM, MICHAEL, ed. *Western Approaches to the Soviet Union.* Pp. x, 113. New York: Council on Foreign Relations, 1988. Paperbound, $10.95.

MARCUS, JUDITH and ZOLTAN TARR, eds. *Georg Lukacs: Theory, Culture, and Politics.* Pp. 224. New Brunswick, NJ: Transaction Books, 1989. $34.95.

MARGOLIS, MICHAEL and GARY A. MAUSER. *Manipulating Public Opinion: Essays on Public Opinion as a Dependent Variable.* Pp. 380. Pacific Grove, CA: Brooks/Cole, 1989. Paperbound, $23.75.

MARPLES, DAVID R. *The Social Impact of the Chernobyl Disaster.* Pp. xviii, 313. New York: St Martin's Press, 1988. $35.00. Paperbound, $14.95.

MAUTNER-MARKHOF, FRANCES, ed. *Processes of International Negotiations.* Pp. x, 541. Boulder, CO: Westview Press, 1989. Paperbound, $45.00.

McLENNAN, KENNETH and JACK A. MEYER, eds. *Care and Cost: Current Issues in Health Policy.* Pp. vii, 231. Boulder, CO: Westview Press, 1989. Paperbound, $24.50.

MITCHELL, CHRISTOPHER, ed. *Changing Perspectives in Latin American Studies: Insights from Six Disciplines.* Pp. ix, 238. Stanford, CA: Stanford University Press, 1988. $29.50.

MORGAN, GARETH. *Creative Organization Theory.* Pp. 369. Newbury Park, CA: Sage, 1989. Paperbound, no price.

MUNDAY, BRIAN. ed. *The Crisis in Welfare: An International Perspective on Social Services and Social Work.* Pp. 230. New York: St. Martin's Press, 1989. $35.00.

NAYAK, RADHAKANT. *Administrative Justice in India.* Pp. 248. New Delhi: Sage Publications India, 1989. No price.

PATTERSON, SAMUEL C., ROGER H. DAVIDSON, and RANDALL B. RIPLEY. *A More Perfect Union: Introduction to American Government.* 4th ed. Pp. xiv, 845. Pacific Grove, CA: Brooks/Cole, 1989. $36.50.

PELEG, ILAN and OFIRA SELIKTAR, eds. *The Emergence of a Binational Israel: The Second Republic in the Making.* Pp. x, 243. Boulder, CO: Westview Press, 1989. Paperbound, $29.50.

PERTIERRA, RAUL. *Religion, Politics, and Rationality in a Philippine Community.* Pp. 207. Honolulu: University of Hawaii Press, 1988. Paperbound, $16.00.

PFIFFNER, JAMES P. et al. *The Presidency in Transition.* Pp. xxxiv, 514. New York: Center for the Study of the Presidency, 1989. No price.

PIETERSE, JAN P. NEDERVEEN. *Empire and Emancipation: Power and Liberation on a World Scale.* Pp. xv, 421. New York: Praeger, 1989. $49.95.

PIKE, DOUGLAS. *Vietnam and the Soviet Union: Anatomy of an Alliance.* Pp. xvi, 271. Boulder, CO: Westview Press, 1987. $29.85.

PIPES, RICHARD. *Russia Observed: Collected Essays on Russian and Soviet History.* Pp. 240. Boulder, CO: Westview Press, 1989. $34.95.

POMPER, GERALD M. et al. *The Election of 1988: Notes and Interpretations.* Pp. 228. Chatham, NJ: Chatham House, 1989. Paperbound, $12.95.

REGULSKI, JERZY et al., eds. *Decentralization and Local Government: A Danish-Polish Comparative Study in Political Systems.* Pp. vii, 271. New Brunswick, NJ: Transaction Books, 1989. Paperbound, $29.95.

REJAI, MOSTAFA and KAY PHILLIPS. *Loyalists and Revolutionaries: Political Leaders Compared.* Pp. xxiv, 189. New York: Praeger, 1988. $35.95.

ROSS, LESTER. *Environmental Policy in China.* Pp. x, 240. Bloomington: Indiana University Press, 1988. $35.00.

SAFFELL, DAVID C. *Essentials of American Government: Change and Continuity.* Pp. ix, 194. Pacific Grove, CA: Brooks/Cole, 1989. Paperbound, $20.25.

SALIBI, KAMAL. *A House of Many Mansions: The History of Lebanon Reconsidered.* Pp. 247. Berkeley: University of California Press, 1989. $22.50.

SEELEY, JOHN R. et al. *Community Chest: A Case Study in Philanthropy.* Pp. 593. New Brunswick, NJ: Transaction Books, 1989. $49.95.

SENCHENKO, VLADIMIR IVANOVICH. *Soviet Ukraine: Socioeconomic Reference Book.* Translated by Alexander Khablenko. Pp. 206. Kiev: Politvidav Ukraini, 1986. Paperbound, $3.95.

SKEET, IAN. *OPEC: Twenty-five Years of Prices and Politics.* Pp. xi, 263. New York: Cambridge University Press, 1988. $29.95.

STERN, PAUL C. et al., eds. *Perspectives on Deterrence.* Pp. xiv, 343. New York: Oxford University Press, 1989. $42.00. Paperbound, $19.95.

STOCKWIN, J.A.A. et al. *Dynamic and Immobilist Politics in Japan.* Pp. xvi, 342. Honolulu: University of Hawaii Press, 1989. $36.00.

TAYLOR, JAY. *The Dragon and the Wild Goose: China and India.* Pp. xvii, 289. Westport, CT: Greenwood Press, 1987. $37.50.

TRATTNER, JOHN H. *A Survivor's Guide for Government Executives: How to Succeed in Washington.* Pp. ix, 96. Lanham, MD: University Press of America/Center for Excellence in Government, 1989. $24.75. Paperbound, $12.75.

TUMMALA, KRISHNA K., ed. *Equity in Public Employment across Nations.* Pp. xi, 245. Lanham, MD: University Press of America, 1989. Paperbound, $15.50.

UTLEY, ROBERT L., Jr., ed. *The Promise of American Politics: Principles and Practice after Two Hundred Years.* Pp. 309. Lanham, MD: University Press of America, Tocqueville Forum, 1989. Paperbound, no price.

WATSON, BRUCE W. and SUSAN M. WATSON, eds. *The Soviet Naval Threat to Europe: Military and Political Dimensions.* Pp. xvii, 383. Boulder, CO: Westview Press, 1989. Paperbound, $46.50.

WEBB, ALEX. *Under a Grudging Sun: Photographs from Haiti Libere 1986-1988.* Pp. 85. New York: Thames & Hudson, 1989. Paperbound, $19.95.

WEBKING, ROBERT H. *The American Revolution and the Politics of Liberty.* Pp. xii, 181. Baton Rouge: Louisiana State University Press, 1988. No price.

WEILER, PETER. *British Labour and the Cold War.* Pp. ix, 431. Stanford, CA: Stanford University Press, 1988. $42.50.

ZAGARRI, ROSEMARIE. *The Politics of Size: Representation in the United States, 1776-1850.* Pp. x, 165. Ithaca, NY: Cornell University Press, 1987. $27.95.

ZUCKERMAN, PETER A. *A New Covenant: Blueprint for Survival.* Pp. vii, 131. Washington, DC: American Peace Network, 1988. Paperbound, $7.50.

INDEX

STATEMENT OF OWNERSHIP, MANAGEMENT, AND CIRCULATION (See also attached P.S. Form 3526). 1A. TITLE: THE ANNALS OF THE AMERICAN ACADEMY OF POLITICAL AND SOCIAL SCIENCE. 1B. PUB. # 026060. 2. DATE OF FILING: October 1, 1989. 3. FREQUENCY OF ISSUE: Bimonthly. 3A. # ISSUES ANNUALLY: 6. 3B. ANNUAL SUB. PRICE: Paper-inst. $72.00; Cloth-inst. $89.00; Paper-indiv. $32.00; Cloth-indiv. $45.00. 4. PUB. ADDRESS: 2111 W. Hillcrest Dr., Newbury Park (Thousand Oaks), CA 91320. 5. HDQTRS. ADDRESS: 3937 Chestnut Street, Philadelphia, PA 19104. 6. PUBLISHER: Sara Miller McCune, 689 Kenwood Ct, Thousand Oaks, CA 91360. EDITOR: Richard Lambert, The American Academy of Political and Social Science, 3937 Chestnut St., Philadelphia, PA 19104. MNG'NG EDITOR: None. 7. OWNER: The American Academy of Political and Social Science, 3937 Chestnut Street, Philadelphia, PA 19104. 8. KNOWN BONDHOLDERS, ETC.: None. 9. NONPROFIT PURPOSE, FUNCTION, STATUS: Has not changed in preceding 12 months.

	Avg. No. Copies Each Issue During Preceding 12 Months	Act. No. of Copies of Single Issue Published Nearest to Filing Date
10. Extent & Nature of Circulation		
A. Total no. copies	6304	6638
B. Paid circulation		
1. Sales through dealers, etc.	441	642
2. Mail subscription	4870	4840
C. Total paid circulation	5311	5482
D. Free distribution/free copies	134	138
E. Total distribution	5445	5620
F. Copies not distributed		
1. Office use, etc.	859	1018
2. Return from news agents	0	0
G. Total	6304	6638

11. I certify that the statements made by me above are correct and complete. Stephen Horvath, Director, Sage Periodicals Press